The United States and the First
Hague Peace Conference

Published under the direction of the American Historical Association from the income of the Albert J. Beveridge Memorial Fund.

For their zeal and beneficence in creating this fund the Association is indebted to many citizens of Indiana who desired to honor in this way the memory of a statesman and historian.

The American delegates to the First Hague Peace Conference, in the usual order: Stanford Newel, Frederick W. Holls, Andrew D. White, Capt. Alfred T. Mahan, Seth Low, and Captain William R. Crozier. (*From Harper's Weekly,* XLIII [1899], 670)

The United States and the First Hague Peace Conference

By CALVIN DeARMOND DAVIS

PUBLISHED FOR THE

American Historical Association

CORNELL UNIVERSITY PRESS

ITHACA, NEW YORK

CORNELL UNIVERSITY PRESS

First published 1962

Library of Congress Catalog Card Number: 62-20971

PRINTED IN THE UNITED STATES OF AMERICA
BY VAIL-BALLOU PRESS, INC.

To My Mother and Father

Preface

THE present essay on the First Hague Peace Conference is an effort to examine in microcosm the two major themes of American foreign relations at the end of the nineteenth century. At that special moment in American history the nation was an aggressive power with imperial ambition. The Republic in 1898 waged war on Spain, a war of revenge for sinking the "Maine" and a war for the liberation of Cuba. Thereafter Americans sought colonial spoils and, generally, followed the national interest wherever it led. Yet even in those days of imperial struggle and intense nationalism the United States on occasion spoke out for peaceful settlement of international conflicts. This was the other side of the national policy. Both sides, both themes of our foreign relations, came to focus in the Hague Peace Conference of 1899.

I have based this study on as wide a range of historical materials as I could find. These include published records of the conference, published American, British, and German diplomatic papers, the minutes of the United States delegation at The Hague, and especially the unpublished archives of the Department of State and the unpublished personal papers of the

American delegates and of other American statesmen at the turn of the century.

I should like to record my debt to archivists and librarians at the National Archives, the Library of Congress, the Swarthmore College Peace Collection, and the libraries of Columbia, Cornell, and Duke universities and the University of Rochester.

Grants from the Graduate Research Council of Indiana University and the Social Science Foundation Fund of the University of Denver made possible the completion of this study. I am grateful for this help.

I would like to express my appreciation also to Professor Robert Quirk of Indiana University and to Professors Raymond G. Carey and George Barany of the University of Denver, who read and criticized portions of the manuscript, often saving me from error. This essay was originally a doctoral dissertation written under the direction of Professor Robert H. Ferrell at Indiana University. Without the careful criticism and inspiring guidance of this accomplished scholar, this work could not have been completed. It is not possible to express adequately my gratitude for his help.

For permission to quote from copyrighted material I am indebted to the following: Curtis Brown, Ltd., for E. J. Dillon, *The Eclipse of Russia*, published in 1918 by George H. Doran Company, copyright 1918 by E. J. Dillon, copyright renewed 1946 by Kathleen Dillon, by permission of the author's estate; Carnegie Endowment for International Peace for James Brown Scott, ed., *The Proceedings of the Hague Peace Conferences: The Conference of 1899;* The Johns Hopkins Press for James Brown Scott, *The Hague Peace Conferences of 1899 and 1907;* the Controller of Her Britannic Majesty's Stationery Office for G. P. Gooch and Harold Temperley, eds., *British Documents on the Origins of the War, 1898–1914;* Ginn and Company for *Memoirs of Bertha von Suttner: The Records of an Eventful Life;* Houghton Mifflin Company for Allan Nevins, ed., *Letters of Grover Cleveland, 1850–1908;* the David McKay Company,

Inc., for Edward J. Bing, ed., *The Secret Letters of the Last Tsar: Being the Confidential Correspondence between Nicholas II and His Mother, Dowager Empress Maria Feodorovna*, first published by Longmans, Green and Company; and Charles Scribner's Sons for Royal Cortissoz, *The Life of Whitelaw Reid*.

CALVIN DEARMOND DAVIS

Denver, Colorado
April 1962

Contents

The United States and the First
Hague Peace Conference

I

A Duality in
American Foreign Policy

THE closing decades of the nineteenth century saw a strange duality in international affairs, for the great powers of the world prepared for war at the same time that they talked ardently about peace. In the last years of the century, tension grew markedly among the powers. Industrial and commercial rivalry and competition to secure colonies in the backward regions of the earth generally characterized relations among the states of the time. Governments increased their military forces and improved their training and equipment. Statesmen formed alliances while the military leaders prepared for war. Rumors of impending conflict abounded. Yet simultaneously many leaders discussed plans for preserving peace. There were peace societies in America, Britain, and in western and central Europe; lawyers and pacifists advocated arbitration as a substitute for war; and even among the statesmen who were energetically preparing their nations for war, there were many who often declared publicly and believed privately in pacific solutions of international disputes.

It was during those years of tension and foreboding prior to the First World War that the United States began to assume the position of a great power, and American statesmen differed little in their hopes and fears from the leaders of Europe. There was, of course, a strong feeling of isolation among the makers of American policy. Ever protesting loyalty to President Washington's injunction about avoiding entangling alliances and abstaining from participation in the strife of the European political system, American leaders found guidance in Monroe's famous message of December 2, 1823. Quoting that great doctrine as though it were Holy Writ, they asserted American claims to leadership in the Western Hemisphere and warned European powers to refrain from extension of their power and territory in the New World. New in its position as a leader among nations, the United States had no interest in alliances with other powers. Unlike the powers of the European continent or the new great power of Asia, Japan, America made little effort to build a strong army. Like those powers and like the ancient mistress of the seas, Great Britain, she did, however, concern herself with building a navy. And like the other great powers, she joined in the competition for colonial empires. Even so, as she entered into the duties attendant upon a nation with naval and colonial interests, she announced her desire for world peace. As the nineteenth century closed, the American Republic could claim success both as a warlike, imperial nation and as a leader in the advance of pacific means for deciding international difficulties. In the brief war with Spain in 1898 the United States gained satisfaction for the ambitions of certain Americans who desired those visible appurtenances of world power—colonies. By conspicuous participation in the First Hague Peace Conference of 1899, she claimed leadership as an advocate of international peace.

I

What, first of all, was the American military posture in the last decades of the nineteenth century? In what ways had the American military establishment developed as, coincidentally, people in the United States wished and worked for international peace?

The Civil War had proved disappointing to those Americans who advocated a new American behavior as a great power. That the United States could expect to be considered a world power had been obvious as early as that war, for the great conflict had demonstrated the enormous military and industrial strength which the Republic could, if necessary, call forth. At the close of the Civil War—the mightiest military struggle of the century between the Napoleonic Wars and the First World War—the United States had the world's strongest army and possibly its strongest fleet. She did not long maintain this military power and displayed little interest in assuming a position of world leadership. Rapidly the nation disbanded her military power; most soldiers quickly returned to civil life; few were again to wear a uniform save that of a veteran's organization. The Union army had about a million men in its ranks on May 1, 1865; eight months later 800,000 had been discharged. The need for soldiers to occupy the South, and the slight possibilities of war against the French in Mexico or of armed punishment of the English for permitting the Confederates to build warships in British shipyards, compelled the federal government to maintain an army of moderate size for several years, but as Reconstruction progressed and the danger of conflicts with Britain and France disappeared, people felt that the army could perform its duties with a minimum of troops. Congress in 1869 reduced it to 45,000 effectives, despite protests of Westerners anxious for more aid against Indian outbreaks. Congress in 1870 set the army's authorized strength at 30,000. Four years later the army was down to 25,000 men.[1]

For years thereafter the United States army remained a pathetically weak military organization. From 1874 to 1898 it seldom consisted of more than 25,000 men. With this tiny force it

[1] C. Joseph Bernardo and Eugene H. Bacon, *American Military Policy: Its Development since 1775* (Harrisburg, Pa., 1955), pp. 235–239.

subdued the Plains Indians and occasionally intervened in industrial disturbances. The Spanish-American War demanded rapid expansion, and around the small regular army there hastily assembled a volunteer force of approximately 250,000; but the army handled its task only with tremendous difficulty.[2] Its permanent staff labored valiantly, but was ill prepared to meet problems with the speed the short little war demanded. There was bungling, inefficiency, and inconvenience. After the United States won, even those Americans most elated by success realized that the army had mismanaged and that so great a victory could not have come if the enemy had been a great power instead of Spain. Still, few leaders after the war contemplated an army comparable to those of European powers. President William McKinley in his annual message of December 3, 1900, reported the army's strength as 100,000 and promised that according to an act of Congress of March 2, 1899, the army by June 30, 1901, would go back down to 2,447 officers and 29,025 men.[3]

Development of the army during the late nineteenth century thus gave little evidence that the United States wished to compete in armament races with other great powers, and it was only in the growth of the United States navy that the new national spirit of America appeared clearly. Many Americans backed an ambitious naval building program. By the close of the century the United States ranked fourth among naval powers and had fought a war in which her navy's role had proved decisive.

The United States reached her rank on the ocean during a period of only seventeen years, and this period of naval growth followed an era when the navy had almost disappeared. During the fifteen years following the Civil War the American navy was more neglected even than the army. By 1866 the total number

[2] *Ibid.*, p. 282.

[3] James D. Richardson, ed., *A Compilation of the Messages and Papers of the Presidents* (Washington, 1912), IX, 6449. Hereafter cited as Richardson, *Messages and Papers*.

of seamen was only 13,600, and in 1869 the navy's total enlisted personnel was fixed at 8,500.[4] The powerful fleet of 1865 almost literally disintegrated. The finest armored ships were sold abroad. Smoothbore guns rather than modern rifles were used on most vessels. Foreign naval officers visiting American warships eyed the equipment and construction of those ships as though looking upon relics in a museum.

Reasons for this neglect are not hard to find. Many Americans in 1865 believed that the nation had fought its last great war. And for a time the country's attention went to Reconstruction, settlement of the Great Plains, and problems accompanying industrialization. The Latin-American states, weak and divided, could threaten the nation in no warlike way. Canada appeared an excellent hostage, ensuring reasonably good British behavior. Should a European force approach American shores, its heavy iron ships could enter harbors only with difficulty, and, therefore, a few wooden ships and iron monitors seemed adequate defense.[5] As for the old argument that a battle fleet would protect commerce, most American maritime commerce had gone under foreign flags because of depredations of Confederate commerce raiders during the Civil War.

After ignoring the navy for years, politicians finally turned to naval matters. Reconstruction receded into the background, settlement of the Great Plains progressed, and some Americans began to observe with more attention the other nations of the world. Animosities among European states aroused some slight apprehension. Many Americans, conscious of their nation's industrial growth and her tremendous resources, envied the glory gained in colonial adventures by other powers. Was it not time to rebuild American mercantile interests on the seas and for the Republic to make her voice heard in the affairs of the world? But how could the United States pursue her destiny without

[4] Bernardo and Bacon, pp. 257–258, 270.
[5] George T. Davis, *A Navy Second to None: The Development of Modern American Naval Policy* (New York, 1940), pp. 14–15.

a fleet? She could not. Late in the administration of President Rutherford B. Hayes, leaders of the Democratic majority in Congress began investigating the navy.

Congressional leaders became increasingly aware of the nation's weakness on the seas, but they took no serious steps toward reform until 1881. Americans, as mentioned, were becoming increasingly interested in the imperial struggles of the powers in various regions of the world. There were rumors that several European nations were considering joint control of a Panamanian canal being built by the French Panama Canal Company. President James A. Garfield's secretary of state, James G. Blaine, loudly opposed European control of such a canal and laid plans for stronger American leadership in the Western Hemisphere. It was clear that naval building was imperative. The Treasury, usually burdened with an annual surplus of more than $100,000,000, could easily finance such a building program. Garfield's secretary of the navy, William H. Hunt, studied naval reform, appointed a board of naval officers to plan for reconstruction of the navy, and sent its recommendations to Congress.

Hunt resigned after the death of Garfield, but President Chester A. Arthur's naval secretary, William E. Chandler, continued the work. Congress responded to executive leadership by first, in 1882, forbidding repair of wooden warships if the cost of repair should be greater than 30 per cent of a new ship of the same size and class. In 1882 it decreed a lower limit of 20 per cent. Then in the following year Congress authorized four small unarmored steel ships. These ships, powered by sails as well as steam, were evidence of the new interest of the United States in sea power.[6] From 1882 rebuilding went forward in earnest. Although many naval and political leaders desired a navy capable of only coastal defense, the nation had gained rank among the world's naval powers by the middle years of the 1890's.

[6] For the rebuilding of the navy, see Harold and Margaret Sprout, *The Rise of American Naval Power, 1776–1918* (Princeton, 1939), pp. 181–201.

There were other signs of revival of interest in naval power in America. Accompanying the rebuilding of the fleet came study of tactics and strategy by the officers and men who were to sail the new ships. The Navy Department established a war college on Coaster's Harbor Island at Newport, Rhode Island, in 1884. There, during the first years of the new navy, the greatest of all American philosophers of sea power, Captain Alfred Thayer Mahan, explained his theories concerning the role of sea power in determining the fate of nations. Mahan accepted a lectureship in naval history and tactics at the War College, and undertook intensive preparations for his assignment. Reading the history of naval warfare in ancient times and of the wars of the seventeenth and eighteenth centuries, he developed a set of lectures which, he believed, would imbue his students with a conviction of the importance of the navy. By the time he took up his lectureship in 1886 he found himself not only a teacher but also the president of the new school.[7]

Mahan occupied the presidency of the Naval College for only three years, but he made a lasting impression on his students. Carefully he explained how an adequate navy, although so small against the vastness of the ocean, could control the sea. Since a navy commanded the surest and quickest routes for transport of men and supplies, it was essential that it guard those routes. But the role of a mere guardian was not enough for a navy, according to Mahan. Destroying the battle fleets of its enemies, it could make certain its authority over the best transportation routes. It followed, then, that a fleet like that being built by the United States, although of some protection for the coasts, was woefully inadequate for major duties in time of war. It was necessary that an American navy meet and destroy the capital ships of its enemies. Mahan recognized that the steam-driven steel ships being built had been largely untested in combat, but from his studies of warfare in the days of sail- and oar-driven ships of

[7] W. D. Puleston, *Mahan: The Life and Work of Captain Alfred Thayer Mahan, U.S.N.* (New Haven, 1939), pp. 74–81.

ancient times and of sailing ships of the recent past he demonstrated that modern technology had left unchanged many of the
principles which for centuries had governed naval warfare.

As everyone knows, Mahan's ideas were highly influential in
important circles outside his naval world. Revising his lectures,
he published them in 1890 under the title, *The Influence of Sea
Power upon History, 1660–1783*. Few of his ideas were really
new, but the clarity and conviction with which he expressed
himself, together with the timeliness of his views, won quick
recognition. Europeans liked his opinions. British naval authorities made a hero of the sailor-writer. Germany's Emperor William II placed *The Influence of Sea Power* in his naval libraries.
Americans were impressed. Henry Cabot Lodge, then at the
beginning of his long Congressional career, praised Mahan. The
young Theodore Roosevelt, already an advocate of an ambitious
foreign policy and a strong navy, became one of Mahan's
friends.[8]

Although Congress while appropriating money to expand the
fleet had spoken of the new ships as designed for defense, a
navy for offensive operations was in fact built. Most Americans
willingly backed this expansion of their armed might on the
oceans; they thought of the fleet as a defensive arm. The loudest
of the backers of the navy frequently advocated its use in war
whenever an acrimonious dispute arose with another nation.
Roosevelt and Lodge were among the most aggressive of the
militants, and through them and their followers America asked
for a part in the imperial struggles which marked the close of
the nineteenth century.

2

While the advocates of a strong navy and an ambitious foreign
policy had some successes, advocates of peace were also heard.
The Quakers, long a vocal group opposed to war, were in the
van of movements to end war. Together with other peace ad-

[8] *Ibid.*, pp. 122–123, 134.

vocates they were in the organized peace movement which had appeared in the United States following the end of the Napoleonic Wars in 1815. Of pre–Civil War peace societies, the American Peace Society, organized in 1828, was most influential. It spread its gospel through its journal, the *Advocate of Peace*, and also through lectures. The society's leaders called upon the government to urge other nations to adopt arbitration as a substitute for war. One of its most distinguished leaders, William Ladd, had published in 1840 an ambitious proposal for a court of the nations. In its campaigns the society enlisted several prominent men—Charles Sumner early in his public career won its acclaim for brilliant advocacy of peace.[9] The society worked with peace societies in other lands, especially with its British counterpart, the London Peace Society, organized in 1815. The British organization probably included more Quakers than did the American Peace Society. The London society also championed other reforms, but the American group paid scant attention to reforms other than abolition of war.[10]

As the dispute over extension of slavery became acute during the 1850's, the American peace movement lost some of its zeal, and the Civil War threatened to destroy the American Peace Society altogether. Many members forgot their interest in peace to support the Union war effort. The editor of the *Advocate of Peace*, George C. Beckwith, urged punitive measures against the South and proposed execution of some Confederate leaders. This stand did not at all meet approval of the London Peace Society, and to many of its members the American organization's policy appeared contradictory. The close of the war seemed to be bringing the Peace Society's demise.[11]

Within a few years the society recovered strength. Again the

[9] Merle Curti, *The American Peace Crusade, 1815–1860* (Durham, N.C., 1929), pp. 58–60; Merle Curti, *Peace or War: The American Struggle 1636–1936* (New York, 1936), pp. 40–43.

[10] Christina Phelps, *The Anglo-American Peace Movement in the Mid-Nineteenth Century* (New York, 1930), pp. 45–46.

[11] Curti, *Peace or War*, pp. 50–73, 83.

Advocate of Peace advocated peace. The society in 1872 secured 12,000 signatures to a petition urging Congress to make further reductions in the army and to insert arbitration clauses in all future treaties negotiated by the United States. On that occasion the society suggested that Congress take initiative in calling upon the nations to create an international court and a congress of nations. By the end of the century the society was led by men as forceful as William Ladd of the pre–Civil War period. Robert Treat Paine of Boston, a wealthy philanthropist, great-grandson of the Robert Treat Paine who signed the Declaration of Independence, became the society's president in 1891 and served in that capacity until his death in 1910. Dr. Benjamin Trueblood, a noted Quaker scholar, was secretary from 1892 until his death in 1916; as editor of the *Advocate of Peace*, Trueblood was one of the country's leading exponents of arbitration.[12]

The post–Civil War peace movement did not have to rely exclusively on the American Peace Society for leadership, for soon after the war a group of some thirty peace lovers, displeased with the Peace Society's support of the Northern war effort, formed the Universal Peace Union. To head their organization they chose Alfred Love, a young Philadelphia wool merchant who during the war had been a conscientious objector. Love served as the Union's president until his death in 1913. Throughout his long career as a peace leader this quiet, gentle man commanded support of many of the nation's sternest opponents of war. There was, however, little that was quiet and gentle about the tactics of the Universal Peace Union. Twelve years after its founding the Union had about ten thousand members but was rarely able to spend more than a thousand dollars a year. The Union was the most flamboyant of all American peace organizations. Peace bells, eye-catching slogans, noisy meetings marked its career. At Mystic, Connecticut, the Union held annual conferences which demanded abolition of war with all the enthusiasm of a frontier revival. In its journal, *The Peace-*

[12] *Ibid.*, pp. 75–76, 123.

maker, it published a stream of demands for ending war. From headquarters in Philadelphia's Independence Hall, the Union kept an eye on the nation's leaders. Alfred Love frequently went to Washington to lobby in the halls of the Capitol.[13]

What was the program of the Universal Peace Union? The Union demanded disarmament of all nations and opposed efforts to strengthen the army and navy. It was against military training in schools and colleges. It campaigned for a constitutional amendment abolishing the power of Congress to declare war. The Union placed its greatest hopes for early success in permanent treaties of arbitration. Mrs. Belva Lockwood, a Union leader, thus expressed the organization's aim: "Our great *but* [aim] to-day is, first, permanent treaties of arbitration between the United States and the great Christian nations of the world; a permanent International Arbitration Court, and gradual disarmament." [14]

There were ancillary concerns. The Universal Peace Union was concerned about industrial strife. Alfred Love in 1884 arbitrated a strike of 30,000 Philadelphia shoe workers.[15] Belva Lockwood was as ardent a worker for woman suffrage as for peace; the National Equal Rights Party of the Pacific Coast nominated her for president of the United States in 1884 and again in 1888. She was as active in the legal profession as in reform and peace activities. Admitted to the bar of the District of Columbia in 1873, she became the first woman lawyer to practice before the Supreme Court. She gained prominence in the peace movement when she became a member of the International Peace Bureau of Berne and secretary of that organization's American branch.

In enumerating peace organizations and activities one must mention the Woman's Christian Temperance Union. Organized

[13] *Ibid.,* pp. 76–80, 143.
[14] "The Growth of Peace Principles; and the Methods of Propagating Them," *American Magazine of Civics,* VI (1895), 515.
[15] Curti, *Peace or War,* p. 78.

in the United States in 1874, it included among its many activities the struggle against war. Under the leadership of Frances Willard this organization assumed forty-one lines of work. Each was directed by a department of the parent organization, and for many years a Maine lady, Mrs. Hannah J. Bailey, directed the department furthering international arbitration. In 1895 she explained her organization's interest in arbitration:

The Woman's Christian Temperance Union is, itself, organized mother-love, and, as a part of the duty of a mother is to make peace in her family when contentions exist, or, better still, to prevent them by timely care, it is fitting that the W.C.T.U. have a department of Peace and Arbitration. The work of peace is especially adapted to women. They are expected to be in sympathy with every peace measure. When women shall have a direct voice in politics, and in determining the continuance of carnal warfare, doubtless the former will become more purified and the latter be abolished altogether.[16]

Pursuing this goal, the WCTU distributed millions of pages of antiwar literature, and the Peace and Arbitration Department's publications, *Pacific Banner* and *The Acorn,* found their way into thousands of homes. Mrs. Bailey hoped that through education her department might subdue combative instincts in human beings before children could attain adulthood. Among children she organized peace bands and sought to counteract militaristic teachings in schools and Sunday schools. The play of youngsters, in which they sometimes pretended to wage war, brought Mrs. Bailey's sharp disapproval.[17]

Quakers occupied high position and held much power in the American Peace Society, the Universal Peace Union, the Woman's Christian Temperance Union, and many less prominent

[16] *Report of the First Annual Meeting of the Lake Mohonk Conference on International Arbitration, 1895* (Lake Mohonk, 1895), p. 67. Reports of these conferences are hereafter cited as *Mohonk Conference,* with the year of the conference added.

[17] *Ibid.,* pp. 68–69.

antiwar groups. That sect nonetheless felt need of a peace organization of its own, and at the suggestion of the Yearly Meeting of Ohio Friends, Quakers from all parts of the country gathered in Baltimore in 1866 to plan a peace association. In the following year there appeared the Peace Association of Friends. This organization acquired an influential position in the antiwar movement. Its publication, the *Christian Arbitrator and Messenger of Peace,* circulated widely. William G. Hubbard, president of the Association, could report in 1895 an annual distribution of four to six thousand copies of the *Christian Arbitrator,* and many of these copies went to ministers. By the last decade of the century the Peace Association circulated its literature in every state and territory. From coast to coast, speakers spread the gospel of peace and arbitration. The association's representatives addressed students in colleges, high schools, and academies. Every expression of sympathy and gratitude increased the Friends' conviction that their conflict against war was attaining success.[18]

Government officials and important lawyers in the United States also championed the cause of peace. These individuals rarely dared to dream of abolition of war, but they believed that arbitration could reduce conflicts and help solve diplomatic controversies. The decision of the Alabama Claims dispute with Great Britain by a court of arbitration at Geneva in 1871 won praise by men high in public life in the United States and Great Britain. For years arbitration advocates pointed to the Geneva arbitration as beginning a new era in international relations. President Ulysses S. Grant was tremendously proud that this event happened during his administration. He too became something of an arbitration enthusiast whenever the idea was mentioned. As a former president he declared in an address before a Philadelphia group after his voyage around the world:

Though I have been trained as a soldier, and have participated in many battles, there never was a time when, in my opinion, some

[18] *Ibid.,* pp. 65–66.

way could not have been found of preventing the drawing of the sword. I look forward to an epoch when a court recognized by all nations will settle international differences instead of keeping large standing armies, as they do in Europe.[19]

Then there were the international lawyers. During the period from the Civil War to the Spanish-American War the United States produced scholars whose achievements in international law brought acclaim both in America and Europe. American lawyers traveled in Europe and met men of similar interests. David Dudley Field of New York, brother of Supreme Court Justice Stephen J. Field, was one of the first American international lawyers to win recognition abroad. Field in 1872 produced a draft for a code of international law in which he proposed simultaneous reduction of armaments, development of peace machinery for a commonwealth of nations, and the sending of disputes which diplomacy could not settle to high commissions; according to Field's plan, disputes were to go to arbitration tribunals if the commissions failed.[20] Scholars in international law studied ancient and medieval history to find precedents for arbitration. They studied the ancient Greek states and medieval arbitration by the popes. Yale's Theodore Woolsey trained many young men in international law. John Bassett Moore at Columbia became the country's leading scholar in the field. Often he went to Washington to advise the State Department, and frequently he held important positions in the department. Congress in 1893 appropriated funds to finance an exhaustive study of arbitration, and Moore was the logical choice to compile this ambitious study. His monumental six-volume *History and Digest of the International Arbitrations to Which the United States Has Been a Party* was a testimony to his prodigious labor and scholarship for world peace.

[19] Quoted in David Dudley Field, Andrew Carnegie, Dorman B. Eaton, Morris K. Jesup, and Abram S. Hewitt, *Memorial to Congress, 1888* (pamphlet in the Swarthmore Peace Collection, Swarthmore College Library), p. 7.

[20] Curti, *Peace or War*, p. 97.

Such was the view of peace workers—scholars, devotees, certain government officials. Somewhat different, as we have seen, were the views of the new advocates of national preparedness—the disciples or supporters of such individuals as Captain Mahan. At times the late-nineteenth-century arbitration movement encountered the strong sentiment favoring a navy and an aggressive foreign policy. At the turn of the century, however, both groups found occasion for believing they had triumphed.

II

Anglo-American Arbitrations

FROM the close of the Civil War to the end of the century, international arbitration won its greatest victories and endured its most disappointing defeats in the relations between the United States and Great Britain. In no other countries were arbitration advocates more confident that the advance of international judicial methods could reduce armed conflict. During the thirty years preceding the First Hague Peace Conference, American and British friends of international arbitration saw their governments adopt some arbitral methods for settling international disputes, and such occasions became victories in the struggle to maintain peace. There also were defeats for arbitration, and peace leaders then tried to learn the cause of failure so as to work better in the future. From experience there grew a large body of knowledge in the theory and practice of international law. When the First Hague Peace Conference met in 1899, among its members were statesmen and lawyers with considerable practice in adjusting disputes between nations.

The Anglo-American arbitration at Geneva in 1871 had caught the imagination of advocates of judicial methods for settling international disputes. Although the Geneva settlement came through diplomacy as much as arbitration, its results

England was difficult enough without campaigning at the same time for a treaty with France.[4]

In America business and civic leaders joined the move for an arbitration treaty with England. The mayor of New York appointed a committee of David Dudley Field, Andrew Carnegie, Dorman B. Eaton, Morris K. Jesup, and Abram S. Hewitt to draw up a petition to Congress. These men produced a remarkable document, intelligent and persuasive, which called upon Congress for a joint resolution favoring a treaty with Britain. Anticipating objection of a kind which was to hinder American participation in world affairs for decades to come, the petition stated:

We know that it is one of the traditions of our Republic to avoid entangling alliances, and we do not wish to break the tradition. The treaty which we advocate creates no entanglement and no alliance. It would not bind us to help our kinsmen beyond the sea, any more than it would bind them to help us. On the contrary it would bind them to let us alone, if we let them alone. The tradition has not prevented our entering into many treaties; the statute books are full of them. There are treaties of amity and commerce with every civilized country on the face of the earth, filled with minute regulations for the conduct of Government and people, and we are at this moment engaged in daily transactions, numberless in fact, under a postal convention, concluded at Berne in 1874, by which we have bound ourselves to twenty other sovereign states.[5]

The work of arbitration advocates aroused considerable interest in Congress, and in June 1888 the Senate Foreign Relations Committee reported a resolution calling upon the president to negotiate arbitration treaties with any government with which the United States had diplomatic relations, "from time to time as fit occasions may arise." Neither the Senate nor the House

---

[4] A. C. F. Beales, *The History of Peace: A Short Account of the Organized Movements for International Peace* (London, 1931), pp. 189–190.

[5] David Dudley Field *et al.*, *Memorial to Congress, 1888*, pp. 9–10.

acted upon the resolution that session, but in January 1890 Senator John Sherman of Ohio reintroduced it. This time the measure passed both houses—the Senate on February 14, 1890, and the House on April 3.[6]

Thereafter matters moved slowly. The State Department did little to further the Congressional proposal other than communicate the resolution to other governments. Although peace leaders may have expected prompt response from Great Britain, three years passed before the House of Commons passed a resolution acknowledging that of Congress.

At this moment there came a new American move in interest of arbitration—the First International American Conference. From October 2, 1889, to April 19 of the following year, President Benjamin Harrison was host to this large group. The conference considered projects for hemispheric prosperity and unity, and its most important deliberations seemed those relating to arbitration. A convention was drawn up by which the American states were to arbitrate all disputes which diplomacy could not settle, save questions of independence. It appeared that the American nations were taking a long step toward abolition of war and establishment of a reign of law in the Western Hemisphere. Closing the conference, Secretary of State James G. Blaine exultantly declared:

If, in this closing hour, the Conference had but one deed to celebrate, we should dare call the world's attention to the deliberate, confident, solemn dedication of two great continents to peace, and to the prosperity which has peace for its foundation. We hold up this new *Magna Charta*, which abolishes war and substitutes arbitration between the American Republics, as the first and great fruit of the International American Conference.[7]

Blaine's joy was premature; the convention was not ratified. It

[6] *Congressional Record*, XIX, pt. 6 (1888), p. 5239; XXI, pt. 1, p. 581; pt. 2, p. 1325; pt. 3, p. 2986.
[7] James W. Gantenbein, ed., *The Evolution of Our Latin-American Policy: A Documentary Record* (New York, 1950), p. 58.

became another instance in which arbitration seemed on the verge of spectacular triumph, only to be defeated badly. Yet that ill-fated treaty was to play a part in negotiation for an Anglo-American arbitration agreement, for it expressed hope that European powers and the American nations would settle disputes by arbitration. The State Department, acting upon request of the conference, communicated this wish to European foreign offices.

Randal Cremer decided that the House of Commons should pass a resolution in response to the general Congressional resolution of 1890 and the sentiment of the International American Conference. Introducing a motion to this effect on June 16, 1893, he received support not only of Prime Minister Gladstone but of the opposition. Practically all speakers seemed anxious to champion arbitration. After several minutes of friendly debate, the House of Commons resolved unanimously that Her Majesty's government should cooperate with the United States in an arbitration agreement.[8]

The laudatory speeches accompanying the House of Commons resolution reflected growth of peace and arbitration sentiment during the years since Cremer's 1887 mission to Washington. The International American Conference had been only one event which gave world-wide publicity to principles of the peace movement. Parliamentarians and pacifists had formed international organizations to promote peace ideas. Peace books and journals had appeared. Forceful leaders had come to prominence in the peace movement. In fact, developments in that movement between 1887 and 1893 were so important that any study of factors which later determined the course of the First Hague Peace Conference would be incomplete without discussion of them.

A year to the day after his interview with President Cleveland, Randal Cremer, on October 31, 1888, led a delegation

[8] *Parliamentary Debates*, 4 ser., XIII, June 2 to June 23, 1893 (London, 1893), cols. 1239–1273.

from the House of Commons to Paris, where they joined a group of French deputies under Frédéric Passy in an appeal to Britain, America, and France to negotiate arbitration treaties. This meeting had a more important result than the appeal to these powers, for it invited members of parliaments of other nations to meet in Paris on June 29, 1889, to consider maintaining peace. Almost one hundred legislators from Britain, France, Belgium, Hungary, Italy, Norway, and the United States met in Paris to found the Interparliamentary Union, an organization which became, almost from the day of its creation, one of the most respected groups devoted to world peace.[9] In their national legislatures its members championed arbitration and world organization. In annual conference the Union set forth careful schemes for improving arbitration and establishing a world court. A committee at the Brussels conference of the Union in 1895 presented a plan for a permanent international court, which four years later influenced the Hague Peace Conference.[10]

Founding the Interparliamentary Union was one of two major events in peace-movement history occurring in Paris in June 1889. On June 27, two days before the first meeting of the Interparliamentary Union, European and American peace leaders had concluded a four-day Universal Peace Congress—the first of conferences which met annually from 1889 to 1913, excepting 1898 and 1899. From 1843 to 1853 pacifists had held large international congresses; and in 1867 at Geneva, at Paris in 1878, and in Brussels in 1882 they had attempted to repeat their earlier successes. The conferences which began in 1889 surpassed in attendance all earlier international pacifist meetings. So en-

[9] Representative Justin R. Whiting of Michigan was the only American at this conference. Few American lawmakers became members of the Union before it held its annual conference in St. Louis in 1904 (H. Davis, p. 16).

[10] Merze Tate, *The Disarmament Illusion: The Movement for a Limitation of Armaments to 1907* (New York, 1942), p. 89; James L. Tryon, *The Interparliamentary Union and Its Work* (Boston, 1910), p. 4.

thusiastic was the response to the conferences of 1889 and 1890 that pacifist leaders found necessary a permanent organization to arrange future meetings. The International Peace Bureau, established at Berne in 1891, became a coordinating agency for peace work around the world.[11]

Associations of lawmakers and conventions of talkative peace workers could reach directly only a few people, but that *annus mirabilis* of the peace movement, 1889, also produced a most effective appeal to the world's reading public. The Austrian Baroness Bertha von Suttner in 1889 published a novel, *Die Waffen Nieder* ("Lay Down Your Arms"), which attacked war in highly emotional fashion. With justice the book has been called the *Uncle Tom's Cabin* of the peace movement.[12] Like *Pilgrim's Progress* and *Gulliver's Travels*, it was translated into almost all written languages. Fame surrounded the Baroness von Suttner; establishing a journal called *Die Waffen Nieder* after her novel, she became one of the recognized peace leaders of central Europe.[13] The reception accorded her writings was proof of the popular appeal of the late-nineteenth-century peace movement.

2

Advocates of peace were almost as conspicuous in the United States from 1887 to 1893 as in Europe. It was during those years that Robert Treat Paine and Benjamin Trueblood began their leadership of the American Peace Society. It was in 1887 that the WCTU established its peace and arbitration department under Hannah J. Bailey.

Arbitration had powerful political friends in America. From

[11] Devere Allen, *The Fight for Peace* (New York, 1930), pp. 473, 480–482; Tate, *Disarmament Illusion*, pp. 69–84.

[12] Allen, p. 286.

[13] Alfred Nobel helped finance Bertha von Suttner's journal. Her influence is believed to have been a factor in Nobel's decision to provide for a peace prize in his will. She won the prize in 1906 (Tate, *Disarmament Illusion*, pp. 53–54).

such men as Thomas F. Bayard, the American ambassador to Great Britain, and also the powerful Senator Sherman, the American Peace Society secured much sympathy.[14] At the opening of Congress in December 1894 Robert Treat Paine and Benjamin Trueblood interviewed members of the foreign relations committees of the House and Senate in support of their long-desired treaty. They learned that Representative William Everett of Massachusetts had failed, despite strong effort, to get a resolution reported by the House committee. Members of the Senate committee were no more encouraging and pointed out that after all it was the president's duty to negotiate treaties. They thought it unwise for the Senate to pass more resolutions calling for an Anglo-American arbitration treaty. Paine and Trueblood had some success with Secretary of State Walter Q. Gresham. The secretary was so occupied with other matters that he could not undertake negotiations, yet he convinced his visitors that he was anxious to do so.[15] Gresham did hope to begin negotiations. In a letter of December 31, 1894, he implied that he expected a treaty to be ready for ratification within six months.[16]

Early in 1895 there came a beginning of action. Congressman William J. Coombs of New York on January 19 introduced a resolution calling for a treaty. This measure brought a flurry of pacifist activity; over six thousand persons, from Maine to California, signed a petition urging action.[17] The resolution did not pass, but the prayers of the pacifists were not going unheard. During the spring of 1895, Secretary Gresham and Sir Julian Pauncefote, the British ambassador, had several conversations in which they explored the possible principles on which to base a

[14] Sherman to Trueblood, Jan. 19, 1894, and Bayard to Trueblood, May 28, 1894 (Benjamin Trueblood Correspondence in the American Peace Society Papers, deposited in the Swarthmore Peace Collection).

[15] Robert Treat Paine, address, in *Mohonk Conference, 1895*, pp. 35–36.

[16] Letter cited in *The Nation*, LXII (Feb. 13, 1896), 133.

[17] *Congressional Record*, XXVII, pt. 2 (1895), pp. 1154–1155; Belva Lockwood, *American Magazine of Civics*, VI (1895), 509.

treaty. All seemed to be going well when, in April, Secretary Gresham fell ill. He died on May 28.

There was only a short pause in the progress of the peace movement. Gresham's demise did not halt the movement, for only a week after his death some fifty of the country's arbitration exponents met at a summer hotel on Lake Mohonk in the Catskill Mountains of New York. They had come at the invitation of the hotel's owner, a former Quaker schoolmaster, Albert K. Smiley, a man whose soul was full of benevolence—his whisker-fringed face radiated that fine quality. He had money and accommodations to make possible the company of others who shared his views. At his hotel in former years he had called conferences to discuss helping Indians and Negroes. In 1895 he decided to aid mankind by study of arbitration. The conference at Lake Mohonk that summer proved the first of twenty-two meetings on peace and arbitration.

The list of guests at the First Lake Mohonk Conference on International Arbitration read like a pacifist *Who's Who*. Paine and Trueblood represented the American Peace Society. Mrs. Bailey stood for the WCTU's interest in peace. William G. Hubbard, president of the Peace Association of Friends, spoke for his organization. The famed preachers, Edward Everett Hale and George Dana Boardman, were there. For a week these individuals discussed ways to end war. They saw a warless world through an idealistic haze which obscured the harshness in human nature. In their conclusions were paragraphs on arbitration treaties and international courts—but no word of regret for Secretary Gresham. They gave attention to a treaty with Britain and adopted a resolution that England and America act at once.[18]

While the Mohonk arbitration advocates were at work, Cleveland grieved over Gresham, and at last considered appointment of a new secretary. He announced on June 10 that

[18] *Mohonk Conference, 1895*, pp. 81–82.

Attorney General Richard Olney would head the State Department. Peace leaders hoped that the sharp-spoken Olney would take interest in arbitration. These hopes were to be realized, but for the moment the new secretary coupled arbitration with war-like gestures in such fashion as to shake faith of peace workers everywhere.

It is a well-known story, which need not be told here, how Olney in 1895 at request of Cleveland sent to Britain a note which the president described privately as a "21-inch gun"—advising the British to arbitrate their dispute over jungle territory with Venezuela. When Olney's note evoked a belated refusal from London, there was talk of war. Cleveland in December 1895 angrily submitted the matter to Congress, closing his message with stirring appeal to the national honor, announcing:

I am, nevertheless, firm in my conviction that while it is a grievous thing to contemplate the two great English-speaking peoples of the world as being otherwise than friendly competitors in the onward march of civilization and strenuous and worthy rivals in all the arts of peace, there is no calamity which a great nation can invite which equals that which follows a supine submission to wrong and injustice and the consequent loss of national self-respect and honor, beneath which are shielded and defended a people's safety and greatness.[19]

The arbitration movement, recently so hopeful, seemed to wither overnight. Rarely has a presidential message received such approval. Governor William McKinley of Ohio announced that the people of his state would back the president's policy. Theodore Roosevelt said the president's last paragraph should be taught in all the country's schools.[20] Senator Lodge, sojourning in London, demanded immediate declaration of war. Ex-President Harrison announced willingness to fight by the side of

[19] Richardson, *Messages and Papers*, VIII, 6090.
[20] Charles Callon Tansill, *The Foreign Policy of Thomas F. Bayard, 1885–1897* (New York, 1940), p. 726.

former rebels against the "ancient enemy." [21] In Congress the message was acclaimed as no other communication from President Cleveland had been. A bill passed the House and the Senate —the House unanimously—for $100,000 to defray expenses of a boundary commission.

Cleveland and Olney were in truth somewhat alarmed by this reaction. They were pleased to have their policy approved—but the calls for war were something else. Soon, luckily, they learned that the nation was not as much in favor of a strong policy as had at first seemed the case. Businessmen decried thought of war; a near panic on the New York stock exchange on the Friday following the message seemed to come from fear of conflict. The New York *Evening Post* and *The Nation*, both of which had long supported Cleveland, denounced the administration. Joseph Pulitzer, himself later a jingo, called Cleveland's policy "jingo bugaboo." [22] Most of the nation's authorities on international law condemned the administration's view that the Monroe Doctrine implied arbitration.[23]

Fortunately nothing came of this grand contretemps. Few Englishmen demanded war. Leaders of both church and state urged settlement. The Salisbury cabinet desired such a solution. A German war scare distracted attention: Germany's Emperor William II on January 2, 1896, sent his famous telegram congratulating President Kruger of the Transvaal for having defeated and captured the filibustering Jameson raiders; the telegram implied that Kruger's Boers had defeated a force which was acting with the blessings of British officials. Englishmen raged at Germany; war preparations began. How could anyone in the island realm contemplate war with America at such a

[21] Quoted in Matilda Gresham, *Life of Walter Quintin Gresham, 1832–1895* (Chicago, 1919), II, 796.

[22] Quoted in A. L. Kennedy, *Salisbury, 1830–1903* (London, 1953), p. 261.

[23] Tansill, *Foreign Policy of Thomas F. Bayard*, p. 727; Allan Nevins, *Grover Cleveland: A Study in Courage* (New York, 1932), pp. 642–643.

moment? Soon the British ambassador to Washington, Sir Julian Pauncefote, and the Venezuelan minister, Don José Andrade, began negotiations for a treaty by which their governments were to submit the boundary dispute to arbitration, and Britain and America were again friends.[24]

Long before the signing of the Pauncefote-Andrade treaty in February 1897, Olney and Pauncefote were negotiating an Anglo-American treaty. After the emotions of Cleveland's message of December 17, American and British statesmen shuddered at the absurdity of the crisis and the threat of war. They turned to an arbitration treaty.

It met wide approval. English peace organizations found a powerful ally in the flamboyant and outspoken W. T. Stead, editor of the *Review of Reviews,* who filled his journal with demands for the treaty. To reach as many people as possible, he published a penny pamphlet, *Always Arbitrate before You Fight: An Appeal to All English-speaking Folk.* As if to flatter the American Republic he declared: "Arbitration is regarded in America as an American principle as national as the Monroe Doctrine."[25] In the United States many persons agreed. Throughout the nation civic and religious leaders marked Washington's birthday in 1896 by public meetings for an arbitration treaty, and in April former cabinet officers, university presidents, clergymen, Civil War generals, and peace leaders held a national conference in Washington to urge action by the president.

[24] The negotiations between Pauncefote and Andrade proceeded slowly. In fact they did not conclude their treaty until February, after the signing of the Anglo-American arbitration treaty. The Pauncefote-Andrade treaty, however, did prepare the way for a peaceful settlement of the boundary dispute. An arbitral tribunal tried the case in Paris under the terms of the treaty, handing down a decision largely favorable to Great Britain on October 3, 1899. For some controversial aspects of that decision, see Clifton J. Child, "The Venezuela-British Guiana Boundary Arbitration of 1899," *American Journal of International Law,* XLIV (1950), 682–693.

[25] W. T. Stead, *Always Arbitrate before You Fight: An Appeal to All English-speaking Folk* (London, 1896), p. 46.

They presented a resolution to President Cleveland. The chief executive and Secretary Olney assured the conference that they were negotiating the treaty with Britain.[26]

Meanwhile bar associations studied application of legal principles to international controversies. No organization of lawyers exceeded the New York Bar Association in efforts to advance arbitration. Meeting in Albany in January 1896, it appointed a committee to devise a plan for a permanent Anglo-American tribunal. The committee soon concluded that to establish a court for only two nations would be impractical if not impossible and decided to plan a tribunal named "The International Court of Arbitration," open to all nations. It completed its work after weeks of study, and on April 16 the Bar Association approved the plan. A delegation went to President Cleveland who was impressed; he told his callers that "there is one fact about the matter: you have a *plan;* nobody else has given us a plan." [27] Cleveland had at last become an exponent of arbitration; the furor over his Venezuelan message had turned him into a supporter of ideas for peace.

Secretary Olney had need for plans like that of the New York State Bar Association, for he too had become a champion of arbitration. Hardly had the Venezuelan smoke cleared when he turned to the projected treaty of arbitration, unfinished at Gresham's death. The secretary did not wish to press the matter; perhaps he feared that if he did so Lord Salisbury would think he was admitting the unwisdom of his Venezuelan policy. But he found a way to send hints to London. He secured assistance from Henry Norman, the London *Daily Chronicle's*

---

[26] *The American Conference on International Arbitration Held in Washington, D.C., April 22 and 23, 1896* (New York, 1896), p. 149; For the conference John Bassett Moore prepared a short history of arbitration, "Historical Notes on International Arbitration," which was published in the report, pp. 170–218. This work has since been republished in *The Collected Papers of John Bassett Moore* (New Haven, 1944), II, 27–70.

[27] W. Martin Jones, address, in *Mohonk Conference, 1897*, p. 69.

Washington correspondent, and Norman published articles on arbitration in the *Chronicle* designed to sound English opinion. The journalist did not limit himself to the articles; realizing that no treaty could be ratified without consent of the Senate, he asked members of the Senate Foreign Relations Committee to state their opinions; most senators seemed cordial.

Washington's new attitude aroused keen interest in London. Would this not be a good time to put relations with the United States on an amicable, long-term footing? Salisbury resolved to try; on March 5, 1896, he proposed that the two governments negotiate the treaty of arbitration. The prime minister saw no far-reaching treaty. He wished no agreement which would send cases involving national honor or territorial claims to an arbitral tribunal; he did not wish the two powers to obligate themselves to accept arbitral decisions.

Cleveland and Olney thought his proposals too conservative, for now they were as firm in devotion to arbitration as a few months before they had been to the Monroe Doctrine. Cleveland wrote the following comment on one of Salisbury's notes: "Without arbitration, diplomacy. If that fails war and sacrifice of life and retrogression in civilization." [28]

Olney and Pauncefote labored on the treaty. Pauncefote was as warmly in favor of arbitration as Olney, but the two were unable to reconcile their governments' views. Olney became so exasperated with the British position in June 1896 that he permitted his irritation to become known; for a time it seemed that the negotiations would collapse, leaving Anglo-American relations injured rather than helped. Both governments in July 1896 openly sought popular support by publishing their correspondence. The American position won greater favor on both sides of the Atlantic; faced with dissatisfaction at home, Lord

[28] Quoted in Nelson M. Blake, "The Olney-Pauncefote Treaty of 1897," *American Historical Review*, L (1945), 231. Blake's article is the best account of the negotiations and the defeat of the treaty.

Salisbury capitulated. Returning to Washington that autumn from vacation in England, Pauncefote had instructions to negotiate along lines desired by the secretary of state. Olney and Pauncefote signed the treaty on January 11, 1897.[29]

Workers for arbitration were elated, for although the treaty was to run only for five years it promised to make real many of their dreams. It could settle practically all territorial and pecuniary disputes. Nowhere could one find exception for cases involving "national honor." Even more important were rules for setting up the tribunals. True, these special tribunals were far from being the permanent world court recommended by the New York Bar Association, but if they proved successful, could they not lead to such a tribunal?

Cleveland, anxious for ratification before the end of his term, sent the treaty to the Senate the day it was signed. He told the senators that the "examples set and the lesson furnished by the successful operation of this treaty are sure to be felt and taken to heart sooner or later by other nations, and will thus mark the beginning of a new epoch in civilization." [30]

British statesmen were pleased. Parliament opened a week or so later, and Queen Victoria's speech from the throne announced the news in glowing terms. No other part of the speech aroused so much satisfaction. Sir William Harcourt, leader of Her Majesty's opposition, outdid the government in praise of the treaty.[31] Most English statesmen saw a large advance in international law. Privately some of them were not so pleased by the improvement in international law as by the thought that they could expect fewer annoyances from Americans; even Sir Julian Pauncefote, sincere in his devotion to arbitration, wrote that "the great Arbitration Treaty will take the wind out of the

[29] *Ibid.,* pp. 231–234.
[30] Richardson, *Messages and Papers,* VIII, 6179.
[31] *Parliamentary Debates,* 4th ser., XLV, Jan. 19 to Feb. 8, 1897 (London, 1897), cols. 3, 49–51.

sails of the Jingoes as regards Great Britain & the Eagle will have to screech at the other Powers, & let the British Lion nurse his tail." [32]

But American senators enjoyed twisting the lion's tail too much to consent to a treaty which would deprive them of that interesting sport. The more that senators studied the treaty the more they found wrong with it; behind every phrase were dangers. To senators with ultrarepublican sensibilities one clause was offensive: it provided for the naming of umpires to the tribunals by the king of Sweden and Norway in event Britain and the United States failed to agree upon appointments. Some senators feared the treaty would hinder the government in its efforts to secure England's renunciation of her rights in a future Isthmian canal. Several feared the agreement would endanger traditional principles of American foreign policy.

Fearing the worst, friends of the treaty sought to bring pressure on the Senate, and William E. Dodge of New York, head of the National Arbitration Committee, appealed to fifty thousand ministers and three thousand other persons for help. There were meetings on behalf of the treaty in many parts of the country. Legislatures of six states—Massachusetts, Connecticut, Delaware, South Carolina, Alabama, Minnesota—urged ratification. Frederic R. Coudert and former Senator George F. Edmunds, noted international lawyers, worked for the treaty. In New York the *World* and the *Times* threw their energies into the fight.

But the treaty had enemies. Irish-Americans found nothing good in the prospect of a friendly agreement with England. In the Middle West the Chicago *Tribune* lost no opportunity to denounce the work of Olney and Pauncefote. In New York the *Journal* and the *Sun* refuted the arguments of the *Times*.[33]

[32] Pauncefote to Salisbury, Jan. 1, 1897, Salisbury Papers, quoted in Charles S. Campbell, Jr., *Anglo-American Understanding, 1898–1903* (Baltimore, 1957), p. 6.

[33] Blake, pp. 234–238.

Even some individuals who favored ratification could see little value in the treaty. Speaking before a New York yacht club, the rising young politician Theodore Roosevelt said:

Arbitration and peace are both great things, and the recent arbitration treaty may be a wise measure, but almost concurrently with the news of its successful consummation came word that England was about to build ten new warships. That is the kind of arbitration treaties we want—backed up by ten new warships of the newest type and carrying the best guns American ingenuity can devise—because no amount of international law or arbitration treaties is going to save the Nation when the call to arms is sounded.[34]

Leaving the White House on March 4, 1897, Cleveland had only few regrets, but one was that his treaty had gone unratified. Still, listening to his successor's inaugural, he heard heartening words. William McKinley, speaking of the treaty, said:

Since it presents to the world the glorious example of reason and peace, not passion and war, controlling the relations between two of the greatest nations in the world, an example certain to be followed by others, I respectfully urge the early action of the Senate thereon, not merely as a matter of policy, but as a duty to mankind. The importance and moral influence of the ratification of such a treaty can hardly be overestimated in the cause of advancing civilization.[35]

The Senate in special session again debated ratification. By late March it appeared that the treaty could pass only with such amendments as: (1) elimination of the clause pertaining to the king of Sweden and Norway; (2) consent of the Senate by a two-thirds majority before any dispute could go to arbitration; (3) Senate approval of appointments to tribunals of arbitration. The chairman of the Senate Foreign Relations Committee, Cushman K. Davis, together with Senator Lodge, was happy at the prospect of ratification on these terms. It is not unlikely they

---

[34] Quoted in New York *Times*, Feb. 10, 1897.
[35] Richardson, *Messages and Papers*, VIII, 6242.

expected the Senate to gain greater power over relations with Britain than it had enjoyed before. But a die-hard group led by Senator John T. Morgan of Alabama determined that even the weakened treaty should be defeated. On May 5, 1895, the Senate voted and the irreconcilables won; the treaty was defeated by three votes.[36]

The treaty had failed. "The Lord rebuke thee, O Senate," wrote Benjamin Trueblood.[37] Scathingly the New York *Times* fixed blame:

We judge that the arbitration treaty was beaten because England is a gold standard country and because it was negotiated by GROVER CLEVELAND and RICHARD OLNEY. With very few exceptions the twenty-six Senators who voted against ratification are free silver men. Many of them are rabid enemies of CLEVELAND.[38]

The *Times* may have been correct in attributing defeat to silverites. Many senators were also moved by anti-English bias, and by reluctance to approve a measure which could involve departure from the Republic's traditions of isolation. Senator Davis, who had done his best to amend the life out of the treaty, attributed defeat to disapproval of Britain's attitude toward Greek efforts to free Crete from Turkey and to her "evident designs on the Transvaal." [39]

Bravely the friends of peace and arbitration picked up the

[36] Blake, pp. 236–237, 240. A few months after the treaty's defeat, Senator Davis publicly defended the Foreign Relations Committee's amendments as necessary to protect the Monroe Doctrine and the sovereignty of the United States, and he expressed hope for conclusion of a new treaty incorporating the committee's recommendations. For his opinions see Cushman K. Davis, *Lectures on International Law before the Faculty and Students of the University of Minnesota, October, 1897* (St. Paul, 1897), pp. 50–64.

[37] *Advocate of Peace*, LIX (1897), 125.

[38] New York *Times*, May 7, 1897.

[39] *Ibid.*, May 6. For a discussion of the treaty's defeat, see W. Stull Holt, *Treaties Defeated by the Senate: A Study of the Struggle between President and Senate over the Conduct of Foreign Relations* (Baltimore, 1933), pp. 154–162

pieces of their effort. They sought to campaign for a new treaty. The Third Lake Mohonk Arbitration Conference in June 1897 called upon President McKinley to reopen negotiations with Britain.[40] The president made a gesture and in his first annual message in December 1897 declared that the

best sentiment of the civilized world is moving toward the settlement of differences between nations without resorting to the horrors of war. Treaties embodying these humane principles on broad lines, without in any way imperiling our interests or our honor, shall have my constant encouragement.[41]

But international arbitration was no longer a primary concern of the McKinley administration—if it had ever been. Tension was increasing between the United States and Spain. War—with someone—was proving almost impossible to prevent. American anger over Spanish misrule in Cuba had been growing for years, and so had the desire for military glory and empire in some groups in the United States. When the "Maine" exploded in Havana harbor on February 15, 1898, Americans found excuse for war. Spain agreed to practically all American demands and on March 30 offered to arbitrate all disputes arising from the "Maine" disaster. The powers of Europe urged peace on McKinley. But the president sent a war message to Congress on April 11. Again the Republic which wished to appear a champion of peace through arbitration scorned the methods she advocated, this time by beginning an unnecessary war.

[40] A platform adopted by the Mohonk Conference declared that defeat of the treaty was only temporary (*Mohonk Conference, 1897*, pp. 130–131).
[41] Richardson, *Messages and Papers*, VIII, 6267.

III

The Czar's Rescript

AUGUST of 1898 was a glorious month for the administration of President William McKinley. Spain, exhausted after a struggle lasting barely a hundred days, sued for peace. At the White House on August 12, Secretary of State William R. Day and the French ambassador, Jules Cambon, who was acting for Spain, signed a protocol ending hostilities. Spain recognized Cuban independence and agreed to cede Puerto Rico and an island in the Ladrones to the United States. Details of the peace settlement were to be worked out at a conference in Paris later in the year. To those Americans who had desired the war it seemed that their wishes had been realized beyond expectation. Their country had freed Caribbean peoples from an oppressive foreign rule and had, at the same time, won recognition as a world power. Since April 1898 the United States had attracted more world attention than any other power. It was true that many of the nations disapproved of the war with Spain, but that was of no great concern to American advocates of the war. It had been exhilarating to win battles against the forces of a European power—even one in decline.

In the days following signature of the protocol, foreign observers followed events in Washington with care. Would the

United States take the Philippines and become one of the imperial powers? Would America enter the intrigues of Europe, making alliances and building large armies? The future role of the United States in international affairs seemed a great question in August 1898.

Late in that month such matters became less interesting than a sudden dramatic move by the Russian government. The ambassadors and ministers accredited to the Romanov court expected nothing unusual on August 24 at the weekly reception of Czar Nicholas II's foreign minister, Count Michael Muraviev.[1] As soon as they entered the reception room, they perceived that this meeting was not the usual affair. The count was standing near a table on which were piled copies of an official document. To each diplomat Muraviev gave a copy. Reading hastily, the diplomats saw that they had received information requiring consultation with their governments. Many were shocked; almost all were surprised. The czar of Russia had proposed an international conference to consider ways for ending competition in armaments.[2]

Said the rescript:

This conference should be, by the help of God, a happy presage for the century which is about to open. It would converge in one powerful focus the efforts of all States which are sincerely seeking to make the great idea of universal peace triumph over the elements of trouble and discord.[3]

The foreign minister could give little further information about his sovereign's wishes, for he was to leave within a few minutes for Moscow to attend the czar at the dedication of a statue of Alexander II. The American ambassador at St. Peters-

---

[1] All dates are rendered New Style.

[2] W. T. Stead described the announcement of the rescript in *The United States of Europe on the Eve of the Parliament of Peace* (London, 1899), p. 118.

[3] From a translation of the rescript in James Brown Scott, *The Hague Peace Conferences of 1899 and 1907* (Baltimore, 1909), II, 1–2.

burg, Ethan A. Hitchcock, was as surprised as any of his colleagues, but the rescript pleased him. He congratulated Muraviev, and assured him that his government would give the invitation full approval.[4]

I

The Russian foreign ministry did not give the rescript to the press until August 28, so that it could appear on the day of unveiling of the Kremlin statue of Alexander II.[5] Nicholas II perhaps hoped for a favorable comparison with his grandfather, the "czar liberator." But the peace rescript, as it came to be called, aroused the suspicion of foreign governments. Why should the lord of the world's largest army wish to limit armaments? Was he sincere? Could he be masking some aggressive intent?

In Washington the rescript was discussed at the Navy and War Departments. The head of the naval strategy board, Captain Mahan, thought that the quick American victory over Spain accounted for the czar's invitation. Russia, Mahan believed, feared *rapprochement* of England and America and appearance of the United States in the Far East.[6] Many colleagues shared his views, yet other high officials were convinced that the czar was not concerned with American armaments, insignificant when compared with Europe.[7]

From the State Department there were few comments. Secretary Day, soon to resign his office to head the peace commission in Paris, was absent when the rescript of August 24 arrived. Nor were there any reported reactions from the White House, for McKinley was traveling in Pennsylvania and Ohio.[8]

Upon return from Moscow to St. Petersburg, Muraviev gave

[4] Ethan A. Hitchcock to William R. Day, Aug. 25, 1898, in *Papers Relating to the Foreign Relations of the United States, 1898* (Washington, 1901), pp. 540–541. Hereafter cited as *FR, 1898*.

[5] New York *Times*, Aug. 29, 1898.

[6] Alfred Thayer Mahan to Samuel A'Court Ashe, Sept. 23, 1899, Samuel A'Court Ashe Papers, deposited in the Duke University Library.

[7] New York *Times*, Aug. 30 and 31, 1898.   [8] *Ibid.*, Aug. 30.

the diplomatic corps more information about the congress his master had in mind. The czar hoped for a conference which would meet in open, public sessions to halt the race in armaments. Existing armaments were not to be disturbed, and no political or diplomatic questions were to be brought up. In no way were the powers bound to accept decisions of the conference, but if nothing else were accomplished, then an expert commission could continue discussion of arms questions. Governments accepting the invitation were to determine the time and place of meeting. Muraviev stressed that the invitation had been on initiative of his sovereign alone, that no other government had been consulted.

He told Hitchcock that he understood the isolationism of the United States, while hoping for American counsel and sympathy. Hitchcock wired Secretary Day an account of the interview.[9] Three days later Acting Secretary of State John Bassett Moore telegraphed acceptance of the imperial invitation. That famed authority on arbitration and problems of peace was not overly enthusiastic about the Russian proposal. He told Hitchcock that McKinley concurred with the spirit of the rescript and would send a representative, but made clear that the president would do nothing to limit American armaments. Moore explained that war with Spain rendered armament limitation impractical for the United States and that American armaments were, at any rate, far below those of Europe.[10] Secretary Day, briefly resuming his duties at the department, on September 14 sent Hitchcock a message much like Moore's: the state of war with Spain made it impossible for the United States to consider reductions in its military and naval programs.[11]

No one appears to have pointed out to either Moore or Day that hostilities with Spain had ended and that a state of war existed only in a technical sense. This excuse nonetheless was

[9] Sept. 3, 1898, in *FR, 1898*, pp. 542–543.
[10] Moore to Hitchock, Sept. 6, 1898, *ibid.*, p. 543.
[11] Sept. 14, 1898, *ibid.*, p. 545.

convenient for rejecting arms limitation. The numerical inferiority of American forces to those of other leading powers was a more valid reason, and at all times when the czar's proposal was under discussion the McKinley administration used it to forestall suggestions that the United States reduce its naval and military programs.

Leaders of other governments were, of course, as skeptical as McKinley. Publicly they praised the czar. Privately they suspected him. There was little speculation as to whether the American defeat of Spain had influenced Nicholas II; Europeans sought other reasons.

Within the Triple Alliance suspicion of Russian motives was particularly strong. The German emperor, while sending the czar warm congratulations, raged in private. He thought that Russia's financial difficulties accounted for the rescript, but he warned his foreign minister, Count Bernhard von Bülow, that there was a "bit of deviltry" in that document, for anyone who would decline the invitation could be accused of wanting to "break the peace." [12] The Austro-Hungarians, not so disturbed as their German allies, were offended by failure of the Russians to give them warning. The Italians, while not displaying resentment, wished no interference with their armaments.[13]

Russia's closest friends were as distressed as her enemies. Although the French may have learned of the rescript a day before everyone else, they had not been consulted. Fearful that

[12] G. Lowes Dickinson, *The International Anarchy, 1904-1914* (New York, 1926), pp. 347-348. Dickinson translates in part a note by the German emperor which was attached to a dispatch from Bernhard von Bülow to Wilhelm II, Aug. 28, 1898, in Johannes Lepsius, Albrecht Mendelssohn Bartholdy, and Friedrich Thimme, eds., *Die Grosse Politik der Europäischen Kabinette, 1871-1914* (Berlin, 1922-1927), XV, 149-150. Hereafter cited as *Grosse Politik*.

[13] Sir Horace Rumbold to Lord Salisbury, Sept. 8 and 14, 1898, in G. P. Gooch and Harold Temperley, eds., *British Documents on the Origins of the War, 1898-1914* (London, 1926-1933), I, 218, 219-220. Hereafter cited as *British Documents*.

limitation of armaments could wreck their dreams of avenging 1871, they regarded the rescript with distaste.[14]

In the Balkans several statesmen were disturbed. The Serbs, in particular, were displeased. One Serb leader bluntly declared:

The idea of a disarmament does not please our people in any way. The Servian race is split up under seven or eight different foreign Governments, and we cannot be satisfied so long as this state of things lasts. We live in the hope of getting something for ourselves out of the general conflagration, whenever it takes place.[15]

The Turks did not believe the Russians were sincere and feared that a conference could establish a league of peace which would hinder their usual policy of playing off one power against another.[16]

From the Far East came a calm, yet cynical reaction. The prime minister of Japan, Marquis Shigenobu Okuma, said that failure of the czarist scheme could cause a war—a war which Japan did not fear.[17]

Britain's recent advocacy of pacific means for settling disputes with America made it necessary for her statesmen to treat the Russian proposal with respect. Prime Minister Lord Salisbury declared that few nations "on grounds of feeling and interest" were more anxious for peace than Britain, but observed that the perfection, costliness, and horror of modern weapons served as a "serious deterrent" to war.[18]

In Russia there was skepticism toward the rescript. Leading newspapers at first commented enthusiastically upon the emperor's noble motives, but soon they were forbidden to discuss

[14] Sir Edmund Monson to Salisbury, Sept. 1, 1898, *ibid.*, pp. 215–216.

[15] Quoted in Ranald D. G. Macdonald to Salisbury, Sept. 15, 1898, *ibid.*, p. 220.

[16] *The Times* (London), Sept. 1, 1898.

[17] Sir Ernest Satow to Salisbury, Nov. 1, 1898, in *British Documents*, I, 221–222.

[18] Salisbury to Sir Charles Scott, Oct. 24, 1898, *ibid.*, pp. 220–221.

the matter. At the foreign ministry officials began minimizing the circular. Such behavior perplexed some foreign observers, but Herbert H. D. Peirce, who became American chargé when Ambassador Hitchcock left St. Petersburg in November to become McKinley's secretary of the interior, thought he understood. He told the new secretary of state, John Hay:

It should be remembered that the idea that a vast army is anything but a glory and a blessing is not only new, but is contrary to traditions instilled into the Russian mind, and carefully fostered since the time of Peter the Great. . . . Nor does the humanitarian aspect especially appeal to the ordinary Russian mind. The semi-oriental influences and traditions of the people have bred in them a slight regard for the value of human life and an apathetic fatalism which does not admit of the same point of view as exists in Western peoples.[19]

The emperor of Russia at the time of announcement of the rescript seemingly had little interest in his proposal. True, the circular drew attention to the Moscow ceremonies, but elaborate troop reviews contrasted with the rescript's pacific intent. From Moscow the czar went to Sevastopol to inspect troops and fortifications and review the Black Sea fleet.[20] If aware of this contradiction in his behavior, he made no attempt to correct it. Indeed one of his few reported remarks indicates that he found the idea of limiting armaments a trifle amusing. To a courtier who asked if it were true that he planned to reduce his army, he replied, with a wink: "I think that I could contrive to get along with a platoon or two less of them." [21]

2

While Nicholas II reviewed troops and accepted congratulations for his rescript, interested persons around the world were

[19] Nov. 9, 1898, in *FR, 1898*, p. 547.
[20] New York *Times*, Aug. 30, 1898; *The Times* (London), Sept. 5, 1898.
[21] New York *Times*, Sept. 4, 1898, requoted from the Cleveland *Plaindealer*.

trying to learn the origins of the document and discern its motives. There were reports that the czar had been inspired by one of his subjects, Ivan Bloch, author of *The Future of War*, and by pacific utterances of recent British prime ministers. Some thought the czar was following traditions of the Romanov dynasty. Alexander I at the close of the Napoleonic Wars had founded the Holy Alliance. Alexander II in 1868 had invited his fellow rulers to send military representatives to a conference in St. Petersburg to consider prohibition of certain kinds of projectiles; the conference had condemned explosive bullets. Alexander II in 1874 had called another conference to consider rules for reducing the horrors of war. That congress, meeting in Brussels, had adopted a code of laws of war, never ratified. So earnestly did Nicholas' father, Alexander III, work for peace that many called him the Peace Keeper of Europe. Was it not logical to think that the present Russian autocrat was acting in accord with the ideals of his house?

Most Russians accepted at face value Muraviev's statement that the rescript had come from the czar. They liked their ruler's idealism and concern for humanity. For nearly three years, it was said, the czar had been studying ways for preserving world peace. Statistics and special reports had assisted him. Nicholas' admirers thought of their young emperor's long hours of work while preparing his proposal. Many, too, gave praise to his empress, Alexandra Feodorovna. Surely that lady had stood beside her husband and sustained him in his efforts.[22]

It is not unlikely that the humanitarian aspect of the rescript did appeal to a certain mystical quality in the Russian emperor's character, but his idea did not derive from this quarter. Nicholas did not originate it. The truth was that the peace rescript had been conceived in fear, brought forth in deceit, and swaddled in humanitarian ideals.

It is by now a well-known story that the czar's minister of

[22] For a discussion of the various factors which may have motivated the czar, see Merze Tate, *Disarmament Illusion*, pp. 167–181.

war, General Alexei N. Kuropatkin, had set in motion the chain
of events which culminated in the circular of August 24. In
February 1899 he grew disturbed by reports that the Austro-
Hungarian army would adopt a new rapid-fire field gun. France
and Germany had adopted such a weapon, and descriptions of
new pieces disturbed the Russian general. The German gun apparently fired six rounds per minute. The Russian guns, firing
one round a minute, were no match. It seemed that Russia would
have to replace her field guns—and the new weapons would cost
at least fifty million dollars. Kuropatkin wondered where the
money would come from; the imperial treasury was almost
empty and loans from France were becoming difficult. Perhaps,
he thought, there was a way out. Austria, like Russia, was pressed
financially. If she could be persuaded to forego the new artillery
for at least ten years, could not Russia safely do the same? Why
not suggest this to the government in Vienna? Hesitantly
Kuropatkin brought up the subject with the czar. "Evidently
you still know me little if you suppose that I could reprove you
for such an idea," Nicholas told him. "I sympathize with it. For
a long time I was even against the adoption of new guns in our
army." [23]

Encouraged, Kuropatkin wrote Muraviev, explaining his
ideas. The foreign minister reacted enthusiastically. He probably
saw in Kuropatkin's proposal an opportunity for a brilliant
diplomatic maneuver. He took the war minister's letter to the
finance minister, Sergius Witte. That gentleman had little regard for either Muraviev or Kuropatkin. Always it seemed that
they were requesting money for some useless project—money
which he preferred to spend on railroads.

At first Witte thought that his colleagues were asking for

[23] Thomas K. Ford, "The Genesis of the First Hague Peace Conference," *Political Science Quarterly*, LI (1936), 364. Ford translates
from a czarist document in L. Telesheva, "Novie Materiali o Gaagskoi
Mirnoi Konferentsii, 1899," *Krasnyi Arkhiv*, LIV–LV (Moscow, 1932),
55.

more money in a roundabout way, but reading more closely he saw that he was mistaken. They wanted to save money—for once they were making sense. Witte relaxed, pleased. But he told Muraviev that Kuropatkin's plan was unworkable. Austria, he declared, would think that Russia was either admitting weakness or planning some dark scheme under cover of so pacific a proposal. In either case the Austrians would only go forward quickly in re-equipping their forces with the dreaded guns. It would be better, he suggested, to call upon all nations to disarm. Of course he did not wish to see his country placed at a disadvantage, and he promised that he would find the money for the new guns if nothing could be done to stay the race in armaments. He told his visitor:

But I often think that the unexampled prosperity of the United States of America is a direct effect of its immunity from militarism. Suppose each of the States there were independent as are those of Europe, would the revenue of North America exceed its expenditure as it does to-day? Would trade and industry flourish there as they now do? On the other hand, suppose Europe could contrive to disband the bulk of her land forces, do with a mere nominal army, and confine her defences to warships, would she not thrive in an unprecedented way and guide the best part of the globe? Can that ever be accomplished? Who knows? [24]

Muraviev put the vice-minister for foreign affairs, Count Vladimir Lamsdorf, to work on a draft of a circular note to the foreign representatives. When the matter came before a special ministerial council a few weeks later, Muraviev and Lamsdorf were ready. First they let Kuropatkin explain his idea of a ten-year Austro-Russian moratorium in the replacement of field guns. This project Witte attacked, stating objections already given the foreign minister. Lamsdorf and Muraviev supported him without reservation, and the council rejected the war

[24] E. J. Dillon, a British journalist who was a friend of Witte's, recorded these conversations in *The Eclipse of Russia* (New York, 1918), pp. 276–277.

minister's project. Then to the surprise of everyone Muraviev took out the draft circular and read it. It was really a version of Witte's suggestions, in diplomatic language. It appears that Muraviev gave Witte no credit; indeed the foreign minister had taken Witte's ideas so enthusiastically that he may have come to regard them as his own. The council in any event unanimously approved the draft.[25]

3

Such was the inspiration for the czar's famous rescript. In view of the circumstances the rescript made perfect sense to the czar's counselors. If they had known the precise reasoning behind it, it would have made sense to statesmen of the other powers of the world. There is admittedly an element of scheming in the diplomacy of any great nation, and in Russia in 1898 the czar and his advisers had simply carried that element to a higher state of perfection than was usual in international affairs. The offer to the nations of the world to meet for the purpose of limiting armaments was in truth a sort of masterpiece of diplomatic finesse, worthy of study by aspiring statesmen in the future.

There was a further advantage to the rescript, so far as the Russians were concerned. If it did no good in limiting the new artillery of the Western powers, hence reducing Russian army expenditures for the immediate years ahead, it would have the singular virtue of distracting attention of the powers from Russia's Far Eastern diplomacy. That diplomacy was causing much trouble in the courts and chancelleries of the West, and the court at St. Petersburg was willing to do almost anything to turn world attention elsewhere. After the Sino-Japanese War of 1894–1895 the Japanese had been ready to take large conces-

---

[25] *Ibid.*, pp. 277–278; Dillon's account agrees with the less-detailed version of the czarist government's actions in *The Memoirs of Count Witte*, trans. and ed. by Abraham Yarmolinsky (Garden City, N.Y., 1921), pp. 96–97.

sions in Manchuria; but Germany, France, and Russia in a
Triple Intervention in 1895 had told the Japanese that they could
take no concessions there; whereupon the Russians in the following year had concluded the Li-Lobanov treaty giving Russia
the very concessions denied the Japanese. The British were
furious at what they deemed Russian perfidy in the Far East.
The Germans were not altogether pleased. The Japanese were
angered at being cheated out of the fruits of a war. In the
months following the Li-Lobanov treaty the Russians moved
into Manchuria in earnest, constructing the Chinese Eastern
Railway as a short-cut across the hump of Manchuria to the
warm-water port of Vladivostok. By 1898 the situation in China
meanwhile had become critical, with the Chinese empire from
internal reasons on the verge of collapse. There was talk of the
partition of China. The Russians wished, naturally, to be first in
that field. It was best, therefore, to turn the attention of the
Western powers to other matters, and the rescript had, if nothing
else, that advantage.

Still, if it is true that Nicholas II's decision to issue the rescript
was in part moved by desire to distract attention from Russian
activities in the Far East, that famous document was quite unnecessary, for within a short time after its announcement, several international incidents occurred. An Anglo-Egyptian army
under command of Herbert Kitchener on September 2 smashed
a large Sudanese dervish force at Omdurman across the river
from Khartoum. This battle gave Britain control of the Sudan
and helped bring her near a clash with France. A few days after
celebrating Kitchener's victory, Englishmen learned that French
troops were occupying the Sudanese village of Fashoda on the
Nile. Salisbury demanded that France withdraw from Fashoda.
For weeks the Paris government refused, insisting on its right
to a Nile sphere of influence. From both sides of the Channel
came threats of war. But France, near civil war over the
Dreyfus case, could not long resist, and early in November
1898 the French Cabinet ordered its troops to leave Fashoda.

Tension between Britain and France remained high for months, and not until March 1899 was the dispute settled.

While Britain and France were quarreling, the German emperor was as usual creating his share of international excitement. Early in October, William II accompanied by Empress Augusta set out for a tour of the Near East, and en route they visited Emperor Francis Joseph in Vienna and King Humbert and Queen Margherita in Venice. Having given some appearance of strength to the Triple Alliance, they continued their journey. In Constantinople, Jerusalem, and Damascus the emperor courted the Moslems. He proclaimed himself the friend of all followers of Mohammed. Was he, in fact, threatening the ambitions of Britain, France, and Russia in the Ottoman Empire? So many observers feared.

Nicholas II, watching the Fashoda crisis, and reading reports of his Teutonic cousin's tour, was disgusted. Writing his mother, he complained:

How do you like England's behaviour towards France? Even after the French have made concessions, they still go on preparing their fleet against emergencies. What a clear and unmistakable answer to our proposals for a limitation of armaments; and how did you like the German Emperor's speeches during his visit to Palestine? Indeed, many strange things happen in the world. One reads about them and shrugs one's shoulders.[26]

The Russian monarch may have been shrugging his shoulders over the activities of American statesmen as well as those of European leaders. Negotiating peace with Spain at a conference in Paris, the United States gave other powers cause for concern. After a protracted struggle with its conscience, the McKinley administration demanded the Philippines, although the American army had gained control of only a small part of that archi-

[26] Nov. 8, 1898, in Edward J. Bing, ed., *The Secret Letters of the Last Tsar: Being the Confidential Correspondence between Nicholas II and His Mother, Dowager Empress Maria Feodorovna* (New York, 1938), p. 131.

pelago; indeed Manila itself had fallen to the Americans the day following the armistice. The Spanish peace commissioners denounced the American demands as unjust, but their efforts were futile and they yielded their country's rich Asian possession. Acquiring the Philippines, the United States became a colonial power, a nation whose voice would be heard in Asian affairs. Such new responsibilities indicated that the United States would expand, not decrease, her armaments.

The Paris Peace Conference of 1898 was important primarily for entry of the United States into the company of the colonial powers, but it was also of interest to those who wished the American Republic to take the lead in promoting international arbitration. The Spanish commissioners suggested that the United States and Spain arbitrate their conflicting interpretations of those articles of the peace protocol under which the Americans demanded the Philippines. At great length they reminded the delegates from the United States of their country's long and honorable record as a nation championing arbitration. The Spanish diplomats tried to refer a part of the peace settlement to arbitration. They asked that an arbitral tribunal determine what debts and other financial obligations should pass with the former Spanish possessions in both the Orient and the Caribbean to the United States. The Americans refused; questions between the United States and Spain had to be settled by negotiation, and that was that.

The American position remained firm. Spanish pleas found widespread sympathy in Europe, and even within the American commission they did not go without favorable reaction. On one occasion a member of that delegation, Senator George Gray of Delaware, wired Secretary Hay: "We have nothing to fear from arbitration, but have much to gain in moral prestige and maintenance of our preeminence in recognizing the obligations of international law." [27] But Gray's opinion found little support either in Washington or among his fellow commissioners.

[27] Nov. 25, 1898, *FR, 1898*, p. 960.

Another member of the peace commission, Whitelaw Reid, declared that the American delegation "made it clear that the rational place for arbitration is as a substitute for war, not as a second remedy, to which the contestant may still have a right to resort after having exhausted the first." [28]

This is a logical explanation of the American behavior at the Paris Peace Conference of 1898, and that conference was of course only one of the disturbing international events of the months following announcement of the czar's peace rescript— but it is necessary in the present essay to set out those peculiarly American details in some length. They have considerable bearing on the later behavior of the United States at the Hague Peace Conference of 1899. Many advocates of arbitration were disappointed by the American stand on arbitration in Paris. The Paris Conference was another blow to the reputation of the United States as a promoter of arbitration, one of the series of shocks which began with defeat of the Olney-Pauncefote arbitration treaty. In late 1898 it thus hardly seemed logical to expect the American government to take a strong stand on any measure to promote international peace.

4

In view of tensions among the great powers and the worldwide increases in armaments, it would not have been strange had the czarist government in 1898 dropped its proposal for a conference. Russian officials did for a time doubt the wisdom of pursuing the matter. Doubts found their way into the press, and it was reported early in December 1898 that a conference of ambassadors in St. Petersburg would be the only result. But a sympathetic reference in a speech by the German emperor encouraged the Russians to go ahead.

Resuming work, Foreign Minister Muraviev allowed himself

[28] "Some Consequences of the Last Treaty of Paris: Advances in International Law and Changes in National Policy," *Anglo-Saxon Review*, I (1899), 67.

to daydream a little, not of promoting peace but of improving his country's position in world politics. Several governments, he thought, would refuse a conference, and their refusal could be politically advantageous. He hoped for opportunity to put both Britain and America in a bad light. He knew that England would never consent to limit her navy and felt sure that the United States, acquiring an empire, would want to expand the American army. Perhaps an arms conference could unite the Continental powers against the Anglo-Saxon nations. And there would be Russia, standing gloriously in the middle.[29]

Muraviev prepared another circular for the foreign representatives in St. Petersburg. This document, which he gave the diplomatic corps on January 11, 1899, took note of responses to the rescript of August 24 while observing that since that time several governments had begun new armaments. The circular admitted that the question might be asked whether the time was opportune for discussing the original rescript, but the Russian government nevertheless thought the powers could exchange ideas on two topics: (1) limiting "the progressive increase of military and naval armaments"; (2) "the possibility of preventing armed conflicts by the pacific means at the disposal of international diplomacy."

The circular did not confine itself to generalities, but summarized subjects which the czarist officials thought a conference should discuss. To limitation of armaments, the only topic which appeared in the circular of August 24, were added seven others. Three recommended prohibition of new instruments of war or restriction on some already in existence. Two called for change in the laws of war at sea which would benefit neutrals and small-navy powers. One topic called for revision of the unratified declaration of 1874 on laws and customs of war. The final point

---

[29] William L. Langer, *The Diplomacy of Imperialism, 1890–1902* (New York, 1935), II, 588. Langer cites a memorandum by Muraviev in L. Telesheva, "K Istorii Pervoi Gaagskoi Konferentsii," *Krasnyi Arkhiv*, L–LI (Moscow, 1932), 89–96.

concerned improvement and extension of arbitration and mediation.[30]

The circular of January 11 created no such stir as that aroused by the rescript of August 24. Not that statesmen liked the second document better, for to arms limitation had been added mediation and arbitration and extension of laws of war at sea —topics which aroused dislike in Germany and Britain respectively. But diplomats by January 1899 had learned that Russian proposals for advancing peace contained more double-talk than sincerity. Moreover, the powers in early 1899 had too many problems to worry about Nicholas II's pacific whimsies. The United States in the Philippines had entered into its first armed conflict with a rebellious colonial people. Britain's dispute with the Boer republics bordered on war. Easing tension of the Fashoda conflict required care from both Britain and France. How could anyone give thought to the latest peace pronouncement from St. Petersburg? But perhaps the conference could handle all distasteful subjects in such a way as to hinder no one. With little further ado the powers agreed that the time for a conference was "opportune."

Thinking it wise that the conference not sit in the capital of a major power, "where so many political interests are centered which might, perhaps, impede the progress of a work in which all the countries of the universe are equally interested," the Russian government asked the Netherlands to act as host. Assenting, the Dutch invited to a conference at The Hague all governments having diplomatic representation at St. Petersburg, with addition of three other states—Siam, Montenegro, and Luxembourg. There were some minor troubles over invitations. Italy made clear that she would not participate if the pope were invited and, further, asked her allies, Germany and Austria-Hungary, to hold aloof should His Holiness send delegates. Upon intercession of the German foreign minister, Bernhard von Bülow, the Dutch sent no invitation. The Netherlands gov-

[30] For a translation of the circular, see Scott, II, 3–5.

ernment, for its part, caused some difficulty by desire to invite the Transvaal Republic, but, advised by the German Foreign Office, refrained from doing so.[31]

The Dutch Foreign Office received acceptance from all governments invited, save Brazil, and set May 18, 1899, Nicholas II's birthday, for the opening session of the conference.[32]

Everything thereby stood in readiness. The czar's rescript had been unexpected. Arising from financial and political difficulties of the Russian empire, it called upon other governments to adopt military policies at variance with their national interests and ambitions. The nations in accepting Nicholas II's invitation to a conference made clear that they would do little to achieve the announced purposes of the rescript. Yet the coming conference did offer an opportunity to advance pacific methods for settling international disputes.

[31] Luigi Albertini, *The Origins of the War of 1914,* trans. and ed. by Isabella M. Massey (London, 1952), I, 108. Albertini cites von Bülow to Prince von Radolin, Feb. 8, 1899, a memorandum by Count Pourtalès dated Feb. 21, 1899, and Bülow to Count Eulenburg, Feb. 25, 1899, in *Grosse Politik,* XV, 172–174.

[32] According to a diary excerpt dated June 1, 1899, in the *Autobiography of Andrew Dickson White* (New York, 1904), II, 284, an unidentified diplomat told White that Brazil's absence was due to "indifference and carelessness" rather than resentment over the omission of other South American states from the invitations. Of the Latin-American states, only Mexico, which, like Brazil, maintained a legation in St. Petersburg, was represented at the conference. Hereafter White's autobiography will be cited as A. D. White, *Autobiog.*

IV

Peace Workers and the Russian Proposals

PEACE leaders did not share the cynicism of statesmen toward the czar's rescript, and as soon as the circular of August 24 appeared, they welcomed it with almost mystic fervor. Their spokesmen in America, Britain, and Europe deluged Nicholas II with congratulatory messages. At last had come a clear vision of a time when

> the war-drum throbb'd no longer, and the battleflags were
> furl'd
> In the Parliament of man, the Federation of the world.

American peace spokesmen were slower than those of Britain and Continental Europe in making themselves heard. The day after announcement of the rescript, the New York *Times* reported peace leaders "jubilant," but not until September 26 did the American Peace Society formally take notice of the czar's circular. On that day the society approved two strong resolutions, one of these a congratulatory message which it sent to Nicholas II through his ambassador in Washington, Count Arthur Cassini, the other an address calling on President McKinley to instruct his delegates to the conference to present a general arbitration treaty.[1] The society's resolution preceded by several days similar resolves from the general convention of the Protestant Episcopal Church, meeting in Washington. The Episcopal Church convention probably was influenced by the Peace Society, for prominent among signatories to its resolutions was Robert Treat Paine. The church's resolution, addressed to President Mckinley, went farther than that of the Peace Society, calling not for a general treaty of arbitration but for a permanent system of "judicial arbitration." [2]

American peace workers' intentions were not altogether in line with those of the czar. So interested were leaders of the American Peace Society in arbitration and international tribunals that they seemed for a time to lose interest in Nicholas II's conference on armaments. It appeared useless to limit armaments of a nation which so recently had won victories with forces smaller than those of other leading powers. The time did seem opportune for renewing the campaign for an Anglo-American arbitration treaty. Britain's friendship for the United States during the late war had contrasted sharply with the hostility of Continental Europe. The new American secretary of state, John Hay, came to office in October after a pleasant experience as ambassador to the Court of St. James's. He soon received Robert Treat Paine and Chief Justice J. H. Stiness of Rhode Island, who urged a new and better arbitration treaty with England. Hay, although an ardent Anglophile, did not think the time ripe. He did not want the United States to suffer another treaty rejection, he said, and spoke so convincingly that he won his visitors to his viewpoint.

One would have thought that Paine and Stiness, having failed in their primary mission, would have urged Hay to back

[1] Edson L. Whitney, *The American Peace Society: A Centennial History* (Washington, 1928), p. 208.
[2] *Advocate of Peace*, LX (1898), 225.

up the peace rescript. If they did, they said nothing afterward about that part of their conversation.[3] Leading peace spokesmen in the United States seem to have done little to promote a conference until after publication of the Russian circular of January 11, 1899. There is no evidence, moreover, that the Universal Peace Union and other small peace organizations worked on the matter until after appearance of that document.

It is difficult to account for the slowness of American peace groups during the closing months of 1898 to promote the conference. Caution, not lack of enthusiasm, may have accounted for their inactivity. Then, too, it is likely that had the czarist proposal from the outset included an arbitration project they at once would have launched a campaign.

As for the American press, it did not lend itself readily to promotion of the rescript. Newspapers and magazines were finding stories about the late war more interesting than projects to maintain peace.

British peace spokesmen were under no such restraints as these and were quick to respond to St. Petersburg with resolutions and public meetings. Despite hostility from some newspapers and journals they made themselves heard so effectively that ranking members of the Salisbury ministry found it wise to listen.

Much of the strength of the English peace movement at this time was due to W. T. Stead. This famous editor, while not pacifist, was an extremely vocal champion of arbitration, peace, good British relations with Russia and America, and a strong British navy. Having favored the Olney-Pauncefote treaty, he was much disappointed by its defeat. The Russian circular of August 24 seemed to him the greatest opportunity for peace since the ill-fated arbitration treaty. He was getting ready for a trip to Russia when news of the rescript arrived. Ten years before, during a time of Anglo-Russian tension, he had been received by Czar Alexander III. At the close of that interview the

[3] Robert Treat Paine, address, in *Mohonk Conference, 1900,* p. 59.

emperor had invited Stead to come again, should relations between the two nations again become strained. Alexander III recognized Stead's value as a means for putting Russian views before the British people. In August 1898, tension between England and Russia was mounting, and the editor of the *Review of Reviews* hoped that Nicholas II like his father would grant an interview. But desire to do something to ease tension between Britain and Russia became a secondary object the moment Stead read the rescript of August 24. He determined to find out whether the czar was sincere and, if so, whether he would be strong enough to push his noble idea to realization.[4]

Stead left for Russia on September 15, hoping to interview King Leopold II of the Belgians, leaders of the French government, and the German emperor en route. At every turn he met disappointment. His requests for interviews were ungraciously refused; Stead learned that, courteous official messages to the czar notwithstanding, the rulers of the Continent disliked the rescript.[5] The usually buoyant editor was deeply discouraged when he arrived in St. Petersburg, and it seemed likely that further disappointment awaited him. The emperor was at his palace of Livadia, near the Crimean resort town of Yalta, and Muraviev was visiting the capitals of western and central Europe. But soon the Britisher's gloom lifted. Witte and Constantine Pobedonostsev, the procurator of the Holy Synod, did their best to welcome and convince him of their imperial master's devotion to the rescript. The publicist Ivan Bloch also received Stead and told his visitor of visits with the czar. The journalist left the author of *The Future of War* feeling that he had met a Russian Cobden; he was certain that the sovereign of Russia was a convert to Bloch's teachings.[6]

Stead learned that Nicholas would receive him at Livadia, and

[4] W. T. Stead, *The United States of Europe*, pp. 54–55, 65.
[5] Frederic Whyte, *The Life of W. T. Stead* (London, 1925), II, 129–134.
[6] Stead, *United States of Europe*, pp. 109, 127–137.

he arrived in the Crimea late in October. At once the pleasant young autocrat saw him. As they talked, Stead's estimate of the monarch rose. While in the Crimea he also met Muraviev, who had returned from Paris, where he had been trying to soothe the French, still resentful toward the rescript. Like his emperor, the foreign minister made a good impression on Stead.[7]

The British editor, convinced of Russian sincerity, set out to push the idea of armament limitation. He left the Crimea for London by way of Constantinople and Rome. In the Eternal City the papal secretary of state, Cardinal Rampolla, rebuffed him when he attempted to secure an audience with Leo XIII— an unexpected disappointment, for he had been informed that the pope was anxious to promote the czar's program.[8] Such treatment at the hands of the Holy See could not dampen his spirit. Returning to London, he told everyone that the circular of August 24 was "no mere flash in the pan" but "the carefully weighed and long considered expression of a reasoned conviction" of Nicholas II and his advisers.[9] He reported the supposed connections of the rescript to the ideas of Bloch and to the ideas set forth by the Budapest meeting of the Interparliamentary Union of 1896. Good Englishman that he was, he speculated on possible British inspiration for the rescript.[10]

Stead wanted to do more than testify to czarist sincerity, for he planned to mobilize public opinion in Europe and America in support of the proposed conference. He called a meeting at St. James's Hall in London for December 10, 1898, and many notables including Arthur Balfour attended. In their presence Stead dramatically proclaimed an International Peace Crusade. He declared that the English-speaking peoples, having fought two wars and threatened a third within recent months, should now promote peace strongly. His plans called for joint Anglo-American action, concerted with the work of Continental friends of peace. In every American and British town public meetings

[7] *Ibid.*, pp. 106, 147–167.   [8] Whyte, II, 140–146.
[9] Stead, *United States of Europe*, p. 195.   [10] *Ibid.*, pp. 114–117.

should select members of a joint Anglo-American committee to conduct the crusade. In February 1899 American participants in the pilgrimage were to leave San Francisco for Washington, adding members en route. At the White House they were to receive McKinley's blessing before they left for Europe. In London and principal Continental capitals they were to join more friends of peace. This reinforced international delegation would go to St. Petersburg to assure Nicholas II that he had support of the most enlightened public opinion in the world.[11]

American peace leaders liked the idea of such a medieval pilgrimage, yet few came forward to act upon Stead's proposal. They may have been annoyed to have an Englishman making plans which included Americans without their consent. They suspected Stead anyway. He had long been a prominent advocate of a large British navy, and had been so unwise as to point out that a limit on naval and military expansion in accord with the rescript would recognize a *status quo* which would leave Britain unchallenged on the seas for years to come. This was too much for the editor of the *Advocate of Peace*, Benjamin Trueblood, who wrote:

No, no Mr. Stead. The Conference will never recognize any such thing. If you go into the Conference, your English delegates, determined to maintain the *status quo* of the British fleet, you will kill the whole thing in less than a minute. The other nations are not going to concede to any one nation a supremacy which will forever thereafter make them inferior. They ought not to do so. Such talk is the talk of a man of war and not of a man of peace.[12]

Such suspicions probably disturbed Stead little. He hoped for support from the mass of American people, not just peace societies. Through the Associated Press he circulated his appeal and called upon civic leaders to conduct public meetings.[13] He

[11] *Ibid.*, pp. 202–208; *Review of Reviews*, XVIII (1898), 556–558.
[12] *Advocate of Peace*, LXI (1899), 6–7.
[13] Stead to Hay, Jan. 3, 1899, John Hay Papers, deposited in the Library of Congress.

probably pushed his hand too far. William E. Dodge of New York, who had worked for the Olney-Pauncefote treaty, received so many letters from Stead that he came to regard the Englishman as a nuisance. Dodge believed that the United States had need to expand its armed forces and the United States should have little to say about any foreign project limiting fleets and armies. He refused to initiate public meetings in support of the conference.[14] There were, in fact, no special meetings of professional and political leaders to support the peace rescript on a scale like those for the Olney-Pauncefote treaty.

Stead's appeal and his letters to prominent Americans brought few results. Americans simply did not respond. Stead asked Secretary Hay to help him by sending some word of benediction to publish in his new peace periodical, the *War against War*, which he began in February 1899. The secretary refused. Hay told him:

In my official capacity I am doing and shall do all in my power to bring about the realization of the beneficent projects of the Emperor of Russia, but I do not think it proper while I hold my present position to take part in any outside demonstration in a matter which has political and diplomatic relations.[15]

Stead finally was compelled to abandon his more ambitious plans. There was not support enough in two or three European capitals, it was said, and probably the lukewarm American response had something to do with dropping the project. Yet movements called peace crusades did come into existence in practically all European nations and in the United States. Sponsored by and connected with established peace groups, they spread propaganda. The veteran French peace leaders, Frédéric Passy and Emile Arnaud, were active. Peace crusades arose in central Europe, Scandinavia, and the Low Countries. European women were more active than men, and Princess Wiszniewsky of Paris, Mme. Waszklewicz van Schilfgaarde of The Hague, Frau Selenka

14 Dodge to Hay, March 6, 1899, Hay Papers.
15 Hay to Stead, Jan. 17, 1899, Hay Papers.

of Munich, Baroness Bertha von Suttner of Vienna, and England's Lady Aberdeen organized female demonstrations.[16] Baroness von Suttner traversed central Europe for support of political leaders as well as that of pacifists, and in Austria organized many public meetings.[17] The only important country without a campaign in interest of the conference was Russia, a nation which had no peace movement worthy of the name until after the close of the conference of 1899 at The Hague.[18]

In the United States there was a considerable campaign to promote the conference. After the czar's circular of January 11 proposed improvements in arbitration and mediation in addition to the question of armaments, American peace leaders seemed to waken. Some predicted that the conference would bring the abolition of war nearer. While others were more cautious, all became more interested as weeks passed and it was evident that the conference would meet. The American Peace Society, the Universal Peace Union, the WCTU, the Christian Endeavor, and churches embarked on campaigns which helped make up for earlier delay.[19] Peace workers even had a campaign poem. The aged Julia Ward Howe was as stirred about peace in 1899 as about the war to end slavery forty years before. She wrote "The Message of Peace."

> Bid the din of battle cease;
>   Folded be the wings of fire;
> Let your courage conquer peace,
>   Every gentle heart's desire.
>
> .   .   .   .   .
>
> For the glory that we saw
>   In the battle flag unfurled,

[16] Merze Tate, *Disarmament Illusion*, pp. 203–204.

[17] *Memoirs of Bertha von Suttner: The Records of an Eventful Life* (authorized trans., 2 vols.; Boston, 1910), II, 230–234. Hereafter cited as Bertha von Suttner, *Memoirs*.

[18] A. C. F. Beales, *History of Peace*, p. 215.

[19] Tate, *Disarmament Illusion*, pp. 211–213.

Let us read Christ's better law:
Fellowship for all the world! [20]

Boston peace workers were the most active of all American supporters of the czar. Inspired by Stead, they organized a Boston Peace Crusade under chairmanship of Edward Everett Hale. They could not have chosen a better leader. Hale delighted in the thought that the world's youngest emperor was leading mankind toward permanent peace. Speaking of Nicholas II in almost affectionate terms, he addressed meetings in thirteen states.[21] He inspired organization of a committee of prominent Philadelphians to promote the conference.[22] The Bostonians were almost as annoying to William E. Dodge and other moderates as Stead had been.[23] They wanted to hold public meetings, and working through an organization called the Massachusetts Good Citizenship Society they met each Monday noon at Tremont Temple during March and April of 1899. The American Federation of Labor's Samuel Gompers, the head of a leading publishing company, Edwin D. Mead, and Robert Treat Paine were speakers at these meetings. Hale delivered the opening address. Closing his speech, he shouted:

And the people of America, whose duty it is to speak first, because they are the great object lesson of the world, will insist upon it that the government which they have intrusted with the duty of administration shall speak, as it is only too glad to speak, in the voice which declares, "WE WILL HAVE A PERMANENT TRIBUNAL FOR THE TWENTIETH CENTURY!" [24]

[20] *Advocate of Peace*, LXI (1899), 145.
[21] Edward Everett Hale, address, in *Mohonk Conference, 1899*, p. 8. In an article entitled "Out of the Mouth of Czars," Hale prophesied concerning the conference: "The strong and the weak shall unite in the great procession of triumph by which the gates of peace are to be closed forever. And the youngest of emperors shall teach them" (*New England Magazine*, N.S., XIX [1899], 585).
[22] George G. Mercer, address, in *Mohonk Conference, 1899*, p. 39.
[23] Dodge to Hay, March 6, 1899, Hay Papers.
[24] *Advocate of Peace*, LXI (1899), 87.

One would have thought from this address that the czar's purpose in calling the conference was an international court—although the Russian peace circulars had not mentioned a court. Hale's speeches emphasized the conviction of American peace workers that a world court would enable mankind to avoid wars and, ultimately, to abolish war. Trueblood, a more precise, scholarly thinker, was equally anxious to persuade the McKinley administration to present at the conference a plan for an international court, and even to propose world parliamentary organization. The secretary of the American Peace Society collected some of his best essays in a volume published in February 1899 under the title *The Federation of the World*. By the time the czar's conference opened at The Hague on May 18, the aim of American peace workers had become world organization.

Peace workers hoped that speeches, periodicals, and pamphlets would inspire McKinley to instruct the delegates to the conference to promote their special projects. Were their efforts bringing results? Even Hale must sometimes have asked himself that question. McKinley's remarks about the rescript in his annual message of December 5, 1898, had fallen short.[25] Indication of interest at the White House was slight in early 1899. Even so, Hale told everyone that McKinley was so concerned about the conference that he wished to appoint former President Benjamin Harrison as head of the American delegation—and would have done so had Harrison not already agreed to represent Venezuela before a tribunal in Paris which was to try that country's boundary dispute with Britain during the coming summer.[26] Whether Hale's report about McKinley's wish to appoint Harrison was correct, the record does not reveal. It does indicate that thinking at the White House about the conference was not always as intense as that of peace leaders.

[25] *Ibid.*, p. 8.　　　　[26] *Mohonk Conference, 1899*, pp. 8–9.

V

The American Delegation

IN the working of any democratic government, and many governments of other sorts, the part of private individuals is often large, and such was the case in the McKinley administration in 1898 when the question arose of the Hague Peace Conference, especially appointment of an American delegation to that conference. Here a friend of Assistant Secretary of State David Jayne Hill took a large part. This individual was George Frederick William Holls.

I

Frederick W. Holls, as he was usually known, was a many-sided personage. An American of German parentage, he had risen to leadership among his fellow German-Americans in New York. As a lawyer Holls enjoyed respect, and Governor Theodore Roosevelt placed confidence in his advice in both legal and political matters. Holls's legal qualifications were not limited to the American scene. So skilled was he in questions of international law that the German government had employed him to handle several cases. His legal renown was equaled by his reputation as a scholar; he was the author of articles and books in both English and German. In the summer of 1898 the University of Leipzig awarded him an honorary degree of Doctor of Civil and Canon Law.[1] Few young Americans could claim so many honors and accomplishments, but Holls was far from satisfied, for he longed for fame as a diplomat.

When Holls visited Europe during the summer of 1898, he had in mind many other objects as well as acceptance of the Leipzig degree. He had sought to influence the course of relations between Britain, America, and Germany, and while in London presented himself to Arthur Balfour as authorized to speak for Washington; he told Balfour that Germany had asked for an island in the Philippines, but that McKinley would not act without British consent. Holls suggested that Britain should use good offices in Washington in Germany's behalf— if Germany would agree to cooperate with America and Britain in China. In return, he told Balfour, the United States wished to have the Clayton-Bulwer treaty of 1850 abrogated or modified. Balfour was impressed with Holls's opinions and suggestions, but he was in no position to give him answers.[2] The McKinley administration was aware of Holls's desire to participate in foreign affairs, yet it is doubtful that Holls was authorized to speak for McKinley, although within a few days after return to the United States he had an interview with the president which Holls described as "very satisfactory," and he wrote Balfour that the president was much in favor of the views he had expressed while in London. Holls thought that his plan would "indirectly contribute to that informal alliance or good understanding between the three great Anglo-Saxon Protestant powers which seems so very desirable." Close friendship of America, Britain, and Germany was one of Holls's dreams. He believed in the greatness of the Germanic race, and that in America that race was to achieve its destiny. He was anxious that

[1] "Our Delegation to The Hague," *American Monthly Review of Reviews*, XIX (1899), 555–557.

[2] Charles S. Campbell, Jr., *Anglo-American Understanding*, pp. 120–123. Campbell cites a memorandum by Balfour dated Aug. 16, 1898.

the three great nations which he loved should work in peace with the most important of the Slav nations, Russia. Hopefully he closed his letter to Balfour with the statement: "It is manifest moreover that the Czar's peace message was either preceded or must be followed by a check upon the attacks upon British influence in China." [3]

Holls became convinced that the proposed conference offered large opportunities to the United States. Two days after Christmas of 1898 he wrote McKinley urging that the American ambassador to Germany, Andrew D. White, head the American delegation to the conference. Holls referred to White as "our most experienced, most able and most highly trained diplomat"; he suggested that White might act as president of the conference. Ambassador White was one of Holls's closest friends; they had long consulted on political questions; White's interest in Germanic culture was as deep as that of Holls, and this common interest had resulted in their friendship becoming much closer than mere political friendship. Their closeness had increased during Holls's visit to Germany in the summer of 1898, when Holls and his wife had been house guests at the embassy in Berlin. But Holls was not thinking merely of friendship for White when he recommended him for the conference. He was thinking of his own diplomatic career, for his letter to McKinley closed with the delicate request that "nothing be done about the secretaryship of the said delegation until I can have a chance of speaking to you upon several aspects of the question, which cannot well be put in writing." [4]

Meanwhile plans for the conference went forward. A delegation called upon McKinley in January 1899 to urge appointment to the American commission of Northwestern University's

[3] Sept. 6, 1898, Frederick W. Holls Papers, deposited in the Butler Library, Columbia University. Holls explained his racist view of the future of the Germanic peoples in America in "The 'German Vote' and the Republican Party," *The Forum*, XX (1896), 589–590.

[4] Dec. 27, 1898, Holls Papers.

President Henry Wade Rogers. McKinley gave his visitors no encouragement; he did say he was thinking of Ambassadors Joseph H. Choate, Horace Porter, and Andrew White as American representatives. This utterance was one of the first indications that the chief executive was considering emissaries to the conference.

Assistant Secretary Hill was delighted that McKinley planned to send so strong a delegation, but thought the order of the ambassadors' names should be reversed, with Dr. White as chairman, for he, like Holls, was an admirer of the scholarly ambassador.[5] The assistant secretary was considering the part the United States should take at the conference. He thought it

would be well to magnify the proposition of the Czar from the political point of view, but there are reasons why the Government of the United States would not wish to take the lead in a matter which particularly concerns the countries of Europe. It looks to me, therefore, now as if the President would be likely to await developments before taking any action whatever.[6]

Holls had little reason for feeling that he had influenced the administration in regard to the proposed conference, but on February 17 wrote White that according to a Washington dispatch "all the points which I have tried to impress upon the President with regard to the Czar's Peace Conference have been adopted and the United States delegation is to consist of yourself, Mr. Choate and Mr. Tower, with probably General Miles and Admiral Sampson as military and naval Attaches." He had heard nothing about the secretaryship. He admitted interest in that office, but said that he feared he would be unable to accept it. Business and professional obligations were pressing.[7]

Early in March 1899 Holls visited Washington to urge his views upon anyone who would listen and there learned that the delegation would soon be appointed, for the conference would

[5] David Jayne Hill to Holls, Jan. 23, 1899, Holls Papers.
[6] Hill to Holls, Feb. 9, 1899, Holls Papers.
[7] Feb. 17, 1899, Holls Papers.

likely meet at The Hague during the coming summer. Secretary Hay intimated to Holls that White would head the delegation and that he would be accompanied by the new American ambassador to Russia, Charlemagne Tower, and by the minister to the Netherlands, Stanford Newel. Assistant Secretary Hill assured Holls that this course would be followed and that Holls would be appointed secretary and counsel. The New Yorker was not pleased. He wrote White that "nothing has been done however up to the time of this writing and it is quite possible that the President may change his mind." [8] He had no intention of giving the president an opportunity to change his mind. Newspapers had published reports that he was to be secretary. Holls saw Senator Mark Hanna. He plainly told that great personage:

You know the exact situation so far as I am concerned. I have not been and am not in the ordinary sense of the term a candidate. I have not looked for support and have spoken to nobody upon the subject beside Senator Platt, yourself and Assistant Secretary Hill of the State Department. I also had a few words of general conversation with Secretary Hay, in which he told me that he knew my name was under consideration. But now that the matter has gotten into the press—especially the German press—it is really of some moment to me and it may be of some importance in view of my work in the Party hereafter to have it known that I have the President's confidence.

With care Holls impressed upon Hanna the necessity of choosing delegates with an eye to the coming election. He suggested appointment of President Charles W. Eliot of Harvard or President Daniel Coit Gilman of Johns Hopkins. Holls pronounced Eliot the "sanest and fairest of the anti-imperialist cranks of Boston"; he thought such an appointment would quiet some of the anti-imperialist opposition to McKinley within the Republican party.

[8] *Ibid.*, March 9.

Along with such advice to Hanna, Holls presented his own case:

Now, my dear Mr. Hanna, you know as a shrewd politician that while there may be no practical result whatever from the Czar's Peace Conference, it is a splendid thing to talk about and that the President's attitude favoring it elaborately will be a splendid card for me to play. Moreover I can play it a great deal better and it will strengthen my position with the Germans a hundred per cent if I can speak with authority as one of the representatives of this country at this conference. Mr. Hay does not see this for he does not know what a political campaign among the Germans of this country means but you know it and the President knows it.

Holls insisted that he would withdraw at once if any other person representing the German-Americans could do as well as he, but he concluded that it would be a "stroke of political wisdom if the President would at once announce the names of the Special Embassy, with high military and naval attaches, and were to add my name as Secretary and Counsellor." He was anxious that the title of counsel be added to that of secretary. It was a title well known in French and German terminology and would give a "distinct rank in a diplomatic gathering." It would make it easier for him to leave New York if he could tell his disturbed clients that he had been retained by the federal government for so important a mission.[9]

Hanna talked with McKinley and reported that the president had arrived at no conclusion, and Holls wrote the president a long letter reiterating the arguments used on Hanna. He professed to suffer embarrassment since his name had been presented to the president for appointment to the special embassy. He insisted that his interest was largely moved by desire to further the nation's foreign policy—and the interests of the Republican party in the campaign of 1900. He doubted that the conference would have practical and far-reaching results. He thought it could be of value if it strengthened the peace party in Russia

[9] Holls to Hanna, March 15, 1899, Holls Papers.

and France. He cited reports that Germany had designated for her embassy some of her most illustrious statesmen. Holls thought that Britain and other great states would choose eminent statesmen as ambassadors. He told McKinley:

So far from being justified from taking such a course, I most respectfully submit that our government ought rather on the contrary to be, if anything more elaborately represented than Germany or Great Britain. We are the great power which has most recently been involved in war—a war, moreover, which in its brilliant success has revealed us to the world in a new light. We should therefore be among the most enthusiastic advocates of international peace and nothing should be left undone to impress the world with the fact that our government gladly welcomes every opportunity to show, in as conspicuous a manner as possible, its preference for peaceable means of settling international questions. It is all the more important we should show this very conspicuous courtesy to Russia on account of our good relations with Russia's greatest rival—England.

Holls, interestingly enough, offered advice on all aspects of the conference. He advised the president that the delegates should be "at least three special ambassadors . . . accompanied by a secretary, military and naval attaches and possibly, other minor officers." He suggested that the American representatives "enter into the discussions of the conference with eager interest," and that he could

think of nothing which would reflect greater glory upon your administration than to have it reported during and after the conference that your ambassadors were conspicuous by their strenuous efforts to make the conference a practical success. Whether they should succeed or not would then be a matter of minor importance.[10]

One wonders, of course, if William McKinley read this long letter.

2

Holls was not alone in seeking appointment to the Peace Conference. Many Americans with reputations and aspirations saw

[10] Holls to McKinley, March 21, 1899, Holls Papers.

in the conference a personal opportunity. The Very Reverend John Ireland, Catholic archbishop of St. Paul, was eager to secure a place on the mission. The Minnesota prelate was an ardent Republican within the hierarchy of the Roman Catholic Church in America. His enthusiasm for the party was almost as great as that with which he sought a cardinal's hat. His political views and activities made him a controversial figure within his church. His enemies abounded. The czar's call for a peace conference seemed to Ireland like a special blessing from Heaven; if only he could be a member of the American delegation. Writing from Rome he told McKinley: "Since my arrival in Europe, I see far more plainly than it could have been possible for me in America, that such an appointment from your hands would be of immense service to myself personally, and to all the ideas of state & church policies which seem to be connected with my name." He recognized that difficulties might stand in the way of his appointment, "but you can, if you desire, push them aside one way or another—& make the appointment which will be for me an act of supreme friendship on your part." [11] Membership in the American delegation would have aided Ireland at Rome. Leo XIII was disappointed that opposition of the Italian government had prevented Russia from inviting him to send delegates to the conference. Had Ireland been appointed to the American delegation, the Vatican could have felt that it had a spokesman. Perhaps a cardinal's hat might have followed. But McKinley, regardless of what may have been his feelings toward Ireland, did nothing; the archbishop failed to obtain a place.

Other aspirants secured intercession of highly placed friends. Although rules governing activities of members of the diplomatic corps forbade sponsorship of candidacies of friends, the American ambassador in Paris, General Horace Porter, wrote to Secretary Hay to urge appointment of General Daniel But-

[11] Feb. 6, 1899, William McKinley Papers, deposited in the Library of Congress. Certain personages at the Vatican frequently criticized Ireland for his support of democracy and separation of church and state.

terfield of New York. Porter got around the State Department rules by terming his letter of recommendation "unofficial." [12] Former Secretary of State William R. Day wrote McKinley to suggest J. Twing Brooks and John Bassett Moore. Although Moore was certainly the greatest American authority on arbitration and had just published his monumental study of that subject, the president does not appear to have paid much attention to the suggestion concerning Moore from his good friend, the ex-secretary of state. [13]

There arose the candidacy of Whitelaw Reid, publisher of the New York *Tribune*. M. G. Seckendorff, Washington representative of that paper, interviewed McKinley in March 1899, and he believed that the president was hinting that he would offer an appointment to Reid—if some interest were shown. Reid was one of the most ambitious place-seekers in the Republican party. He had sought appointment as ambassador to the court of St. James's in succession to John Hay, and great had been his disappointment when Joseph H. Choate had won that distinction. He had served McKinley as one of the commissioners to settle the war with Spain. Perhaps the president thought he could be further mollified by appointment to the Hague delegation. But Reid's representative appeared not to understand the hints which the president was making. He told McKinley that no one in the United States would regard the conference in any light other than a huge joke and that delegates to that congress would wink at one another in the manner of the Roman augurs. The president laughingly agreed. [14]

Meanwhile newspapers had predicted that Andrew White would head the delegation. All the urging of David Hill and of Holls was probably unnecessary to secure this honor for White, for no American diplomat abroad in 1899 had a better reputa-

[12] April 4, 1899, Horace Porter Papers, deposited in the Library of Congress.

[13] John Addison Porter to Day, April 4, 1899, McKinley Papers.

[14] Seckendorff to Whitelaw Reid, March 12, 1899, Whitelaw Reid Papers, deposited in the Library of Congress.

tion. White had served as minister to Germany from 1879 to 1881, minister to Russia from 1892 to 1894, and was again at the Hohenzollern court with the rank of ambassador. In comparison with White, Ambassadors Choate and Porter were novices. Nor were diplomatic honors White's only claim to fame. His career as an educator was even more distinguished than his service as a diplomat. He was one of the founders of Cornell University and first president of that institution. As a historian he enjoyed respect. He had become a center of much controversy among historians and theologians, for his thought had been profoundly influenced and directed by Darwinist theories; he considered history as the record of humanity's evolution toward a more perfect reality. Only a few years before he began service as ambassador to Germany, he had published his interpretation of history, *History of the Warfare of Science with Theology in Christendom*, presenting science as the source of human achievement and theology as cause of most of humanity's failures. Although White was a deeply religious man, his was a religion founded on a scientist's view of the universe and not upon traditional ideas. As a believer in the perfectibility of man he should have been an ideal delegate to The Hague, but he was far from happy over attending a conference whose failure was so freely predicted, and besides he was suffering from temporary financial embarrassment. A cable from President McKinley, however, persuaded the ambassador to accept this new task for his country.[15]

Hardly had the president decided on White's appointment when Holls again appeared in McKinley's office, and the president practically assured Holls that he would be appointed secretary—if White approved. Holls refrained from telling the chief executive that White had already approved.[16] He advised

---

[15] A. D. White to Fred White, March 16, 1899, Andrew Dickson White Papers, deposited in the Cornell University Library; A. D. White, *Autobiog.*, II, 251.

[16] Holls to A. D. White, April 4, 1899, Holls Papers.

McKinley and Hay to cable the ambassador. Hay sent the cable. White replied that Holls would be "especially agreeable." [17] McKinley made the appointment. "At least," the president observed to Secretary Hay, "we will get him out of the country for a while." [18]

The administration wished to associate with White a distinguished college president, and for a time it appeared that Holls's recommendation of President Eliot would have some result, for Hay talked about Eliot with Secretary of the Navy John D. Long and even sounded his Bostonian friend, Brooks Adams, concerning Eliot's attitudes on public questions. Adams, despite Eliot's well-known stand against imperialism, thought the Harvard educator "a pretty good jingo." [19] But McKinley offered the post to President Francis Patton of Princeton, who declined. President William Rainey Harper of the University of Chicago was considered, to the strong displeasure of Holls, who even before his own appointment urged the president to substitute President Charles Kendall Adams of Wisconsin. McKinley was not impressed by this last advice. He determined to appoint Holls's fellow New Yorker, President Seth Low of Columbia.[20] A handsome, urbane gentleman, Low had long been a power in New York politics. He had won recognition while serving as mayor of Brooklyn, and as president of Columbia he received new honors and proved an able educator—when he could spare time from his political activities. New York political leaders acclaimed his appointment.

There then arose the question of a military delegate. Reports had come to the State Department that other governments were appointing such delegates, and this course seemed a necessity for

[17] Hay to McKinley, April 5, 1899, McKinley Papers.

[18] Hay to Henry White, May 29, 1899, Henry White Papers, deposited in the Library of Congress.

[19] Hay to McKinley, March 18, 1899, McKinley Papers.

[20] Hay to Low, April 3, 1899, Hay Papers; Holls to A. D. White, April 4, 1899, Holls Papers; George B. Cortelyou to Thomas C. Platt, April 5, 1899, McKinley Papers.

the United States. Secretary Hay consulted the adjutant general of the army, General H. C. Corbin, and Corbin suggested an ordnance officer, Captain William R. Crozier.[21] Crozier's name was not well known to the general public. He was forty-three years old, and his rank was certainly not an exalted one. But few ordnance officers in the army were so highly regarded within the service. Crozier was the co-inventor of the Buffington-Crozier disappearing gun carriage, a device which had recently been adopted for use by coastal defense artillery.[22] Already Hay apparently had determined that decisions at The Hague restricting improvement of war equipment should not hinder the military development of the United States. Crozier would uphold his government with energy. McKinley approved and ordered his detail for service at the conference.[23]

Upon Hay's suggestion the president appointed Captain Alfred Thayer Mahan to represent the navy. Hay's idea appears to have been an afterthought, for he brought the matter to the chief executive's attention in a handwritten postscript to a typed letter in which he discussed problems of the impending conference.[24] Appointment of Mahan could lend prestige to the American delegation, for since publication of *The Influence of Sea Power upon History* in 1890 his fame had spread through Europe and to Japan, and during the recent war he had won distinction through work on the Navy Strategy Board. Despite Mahan's reputation it is difficult to understand why Hay should have desired the appointment. The captain opposed permanent systems of arbitration and the ancient American demand for freedom of private property on the high seas in time of war, and already Hay had considered using the conference to press American views on these subjects.

Captain Mahan, for his part, accepted this new honor re-

[21] J. A. Porter to Hay, April 6, 1899, McKinley Papers.
[22] "Our Delegation to The Hague," *American Monthly Review of Reviews*, XIX (1899), 554–555.
[23] J. A. Porter to Corbin, April 6, 1899, McKinley Papers.
[24] Hay to McKinley, March 18, 1899, McKinley Papers.

luctantly. Fearful that he would be put to large expense, he wrote the secretary of state an anxious letter. In his best style Hay answered:

While, as you know, in our relations to the Second Comptroller we are like the colored preacher, who told his congregation that "we are all in the hands of an unscrupulous Providence," I do not think we shall have any trouble in providing for your expenses, and also for the modest compensation which you mention. One way or another, in spite of the Second Comptroller, I am sure we can manage it. The President is greatly pleased to know that you will be able to go, and I hope you will find the service as agreeable as it will be interesting and important.[25]

After learning that none of the powers was naming its ambassador to St. Petersburg for the conference, Hay told McKinley that he was under no obligation to appoint Charlemagne Tower, and Tower's name dropped from consideration, but it was found necessary to appoint the minister to the Netherlands, Stanford Newel.[26] Newel was a Minnesota politician who had claimed his reward for faithful Republicanism in the form of the ministry to The Hague. He had earned a reputation as one of the most dissatisfied American representatives abroad. He was pleased by his appointment—but he could not resist the opportunity it afforded for new complaint to Washington. Newel, one should add, *was* underpaid. No other major power paid its representative in the Netherlands so little, and, besides, Newel received far less than his colleague in Brussels, where, Newel insisted, the cost of living was much lower. Washington officials were fully informed of these facts after Newel received his commission.[27]

At last the American delegation to the conference was complete, and the individuals appointed seem to have been fairly

[25] Hay to Mahan, April 4, 1899, Hay Papers.

[26] Hay to McKinley, March 18, 1899, McKinley Papers.

[27] Newel to Hay, April 14, 1899, Stanford Newel, Despatch Book, 1898–1899, preserved in the State Department files, National Archives. Hereafter cited as Newel Despatch Book.

happy. Frederick Holls could not wait for arrival of his commission to express appreciation. When announcement of his appointment appeared in the evening newspapers on April 6, 1899, he wrote McKinley to offer thanks.[28]

Everything generally seemed in order. The delegation was a strong one. Even Holls was satisfied. David Jayne Hill was similarly relieved, and writing Andrew White the assistant secretary said that "when he sees you Mr. Holls will tell you much, and I could tell you still more of the perils which we have fortunately passed of having the wrong men appointed."

3

To Hill was entrusted the difficult but welcome task of preparing instructions for the American delegates. In carrying out this assignment he told Ambassador White he was "anxious to cut off all chances for 'flapdoodle' and to open the way for our representatives to do the one thing that the nation will approve and which will, if adopted, as I think, help the administration and the world at large." [29] The "one thing that the nation will approve" was most likely advancement of a scheme for international arbitration.

In the matter of the instructions Holls also attempted to make his influence felt. He hoped that it would be possible to bring about an agreement "that before any declaration of war each nation agrees to appoint a second, as it were, in the person of the chief executive of some other nation and that the seconds shall have a certain time to arrange the quarrel, if possible." [30] This idea Secretary Hay considered foolish and refused to permit anything pertaining to it to go into the instructions.[31]

At this juncture there developed a small contretemps over the instructions which deserves some account—for it provided a

[28] April 6, 1899, Holls Papers.
[29] Hill to White, April 7, 1899, A. D. White Papers.
[30] Holls to A. D. White, April 4, 1899, Holls Papers.
[31] Hay to Henry White, May 29, 1899, Henry White Papers.

clear instance of Holls's touchiness in regard to his personal status at the conference. Holls had gone to Washington on April 17, 1899, at which locale, as he told White, "I have definitely assumed office and received instructions." Despite his delight in having entered office, he was disappointed when he first read his instructions. White, Low, Mahan, Crozier, and Newel were listed as delegates plenipotentiary. Holls was a mere secretary! True, he had desired this title—but he had hoped for it in addition to rank as delegate plenipotentiary. Why this slight? After all, the president had made the appointment by executive order; the Senate's approval had not been necessary.[32] He could have given Holls the rank he desired. The New Yorker feared that his humble status would prevent him from taking a seat in the conference. He went to see Hay, and the secretary of state, sensing his visitor's discomfiture, did his best to restore him to good humor. Hay told Holls that "the five delegates and you constitute the American commission, of which you are as much a member as any other, and which as a whole represents this country in the Conference." Having satisfied Holls on prestige, the secretary, who was suffering from dyspepsia, turned him over to Hill.[33]

As for the details of the instructions which Hill prepared, they gave the attitude of the administration toward points raised by the czarist rescript. Toward the proposal that the powers halt military increases, the instructions stated that this idea was,

at present, so inapplicable to the United States that it is deemed advisable for the delegates to leave the initiative upon this subject to the representatives of those Powers to which it may properly belong. In comparison with the effective forces, both military and naval, of other nations, those of the United States, are at present so far below the normal quota that the question of limitation could not be profitably discussed.

[32] Henry M. Wriston, *Executive Agents in American Foreign Relations* (Baltimore, 1929), p. 576.
[33] Holls to A. D. White, April 18, 1899, Holls Papers.

Nor were the instructions more favorable in regard to the Russian proposal that new kinds of weapons be forbidden and that certain existing weapons be restricted. Said the instructions:

It is doubtful if wars are to be diminished by rendering them less destructive, for it is the plain lesson of history that the periods of peace have been longer protracted as the cost and destructiveness of war have increased. The expediency of restraining the inventive genius of our people in the direction of devising means of defense is by no means clear, and, considering the temptations to which men and nations may be exposed in a time of conflict, it is doubtful if an international agreement to this end would prove effective.

The instructions took a much more cooperative attitude in regard to points in the czar's program concerned with suffering of individuals rendered helpless in battle; the American delegates were directed to support "any practicable propositions" for making more humane the laws of war. The eighth point in the Russian proposals, which asked that "the employment of good offices, of mediation and facultative arbitration," be accepted "in principle" in suitable instances, received warm approval from the State Department. Hay and Hill, both concerned, made certain that the delegates understood the importance the administration attached to international arbitration. The czar's suggestions on this point seemed "likely to open the most fruitful field for discussion and future action." Annexed to the instructions was a plan for a tribunal of international arbitration which the delegates were to propose.[34]

Discussion of this plan for an international tribunal marked one of the few disagreements between Hill and Holls. Holls opposed the part of the plan whereby members of the supreme courts of adhering states would choose the tribunal. He feared some of the great nations with more advanced cultures would have to present cases for trial by judges from inferior states. Hill

[34] For the instructions see James B. Scott, *The Hague Peace Conferences*, II, 6–16.

rejected Holls's contention, believing that it would not be possible for any state to be tried by judges whom it did not approve, and he reminded his critic that some of the world's authorities on international law came from nations with little power; the assistant secretary disposed of Holls's arguments with the words:

I feel, my dear Holls, that all small details will look after themselves if the great central principles are right. . . . Hence the one thought in preparing the Plan has been simplicity, with a secondary thought of generously trusting to the wisdom of nine or a dozen men who may some day be selected to constitute the great Tribunal to organize themselves effectively and sagaciously.[35]

In addition to these instructions on points in the program suggested by Nicholas II, one paragraph—the final paragraph—set out the American position concerning private property at sea in time of war. The instructions read:

As the United States has for many years advocated the exemption of all private property not contraband of war from hostile treatment, you are authorized to propose to the Conference the principle of extending to strictly private property at sea, the immunity from destruction or capture by belligerent Powers which such property already enjoys on land as worthy of being incorporated in the permanent law of civilized nations.

These instructions made certain that the United States would not participate in any moves concerning the major intent of the peace rescript, namely, control of armaments, but they did indicate desire by the State Department to regain for the United States its reputation as a champion of arbitration. An annex to the instructions traced the record of the United States as an exponent of international arbitration; it touched on the fate of the Olney-Pauncefote treaty; it advised the delegates that the "introduction of a brief resolution at an opportune moment . . . would at least place the United States on record as the friend and promoter of peace." [36]

[35] Hill to Holls, April 24, 1899, Holls Papers.
[36] Scott, II, 9–14.

VI

Opening the Conference

WITH appointment of delegates and writing of their instructions, much of the State Department's responsibility for American participation in the conference came to an end. There remained the arrangement of certain details. Since January 1899, when the Russian Foreign Office first requested the Dutch government to hold the conference at The Hague, diplomats in that capital had been concerned with those details.[1] To Stanford Newel preparation for the arrival of his fellow delegates became a trying task. Ambassador White asked Secretary Hay to secure the best available quarters for the American commission. This advice was hardly necessary, for the secretary of state was anxious that delegates of the United States make a favorable impression and instructed Newel to find good quarters.[2] Holls,

[1] Newel to Hay, March 11 and 22, 1899, Newel Despatch Book, pp. 125, 132.

[2] A. D. White, Diary excerpt, May 17, 1899, *Autobiog.*, II, 252. At The Hague, White followed his usual custom of keeping a diary in the form of short comments, but he also dictated or wrote at intervals the long diary, excerpts from which form chapters XLV–XLIX of the *Autobiography*. The original manuscript of the long diary has never appeared, but the short diaries were discovered in 1951 and were later placed in the White Papers in the Cornell University Library. Robert Morris Ogden, ed., *The Diaries of Andrew D. White* (Ithaca, 1959),

too, wrote Stanford Newel, stressing dignified rooms.[3] The American minister began making arrangements. But the English, Russian, German, Italian, and Austrian governments had taken the best rooms, and Newel feared he would compete with the Chinese and Siamese. Luckily he succeeded in finding quarters.[4]

In New York the secretary of the delegation was as occupied with the conference arrangements as was Newel. Holls planned for every contingency. He wrote Newel urging the need of a translator. He sent White a copy of John Bassett Moore's study of arbitrations to which the United States had been a party, and secured another copy for the delegates at The Hague. He was host for luncheons in honor of his fellow delegates, and together with Low, Mahan, and Crozier he discussed possible conference developments.[5] The other delegates had arrangements to make before leaving New York, but they learned to leave problems in the hands of the capable secretary.

Captain Crozier left for Europe on April 19, but Low, Mahan, and Holls did not leave until May 3.[6] Holls had secured passage for the party on the "St. Louis," one of the fastest ships of the American Line. That ship was, in fact, not only one of the finest of American merchant ships but an auxiliary vessel for the

---

includes only a few excerpts from the short diary of the conference period. Ogden doubts that White wrote the long diary while at the conference, although he notes a number of references in the short diary to a "Big Diary" or an "Extended Diary" (n. p. 357). He fails to note that White in his short-diary entry of June 3, 1899, wrote: "Dictating letters extended diary & c." On Jan. 27, 1900, White wrote Holls (Holls Papers) that he had been rereading and revising the long diary he had kept at The Hague. There seems little reason to believe that the published excerpts differ substantially from the original diary. The excerpts in the *Autobiography* compare closely in content and phraseology with the short diary.

[3] April 10, 1899, Holls Papers.

[4] Newel to Low, April 13, 1899, Seth Low Papers, deposited in the Low Library, Columbia University.

[5] Holls to Mahan, Holls to Newel, and Holls to A. D. White, all written on April 18, 1899, Holls Papers.

[6] Low to McKinley, May 2, 1899, McKinley Papers.

United States navy. The navy had helped finance its construction, and the vessel had performed brilliantly as a scouting ship during the recent war. It had been much in the news while engaged in spectacular cable-cutting exploits under fire at San Juan and Guantánamo.[7] But in May 1899 the deeds of a year before seemed remote as the ship carried American envoys of peace to the czar's conference.

The voyage to Europe was a pleasant one. Low, Mahan, and Holls were the most conspicuous personages aboard the "St. Louis," and many passengers sought places in the dining room near them.[8] The three delegates found themselves in the center of the ship's social activities. Naturally, consideration of conference problems was rarely absent from their minds. Holls speculated on the matters with which they would have to contend. He worried about conflicts between conference decisions and the principles of the Monroe Doctrine. It nonetheless was possible to enjoy the voyage and feel discreetly flattered by all the attention of fellow passengers.[9]

Arriving in London on Wednesday, May 10, after a week at sea, the American delegates received a friendly welcome. Although most Britons were less interested in the approaching conference than in celebrating Queen Victoria's eightieth birthday on May 24, several personages took care to honor their distinguished guests. Sir Julian Pauncefote, who came from Washington to head his country's conference delegation, conferred with Mahan and Low, and Balfour received Holls at the foreign office. On Friday, May 12, Ambassador Choate gave a luncheon in honor of the delegates, and almost all members of the British Cabinet and several leaders of the opposition were present.

[7] French Ensor Chadwick, *The Relations of the United States and Spain: The Spanish-American War* (New York, 1911), I, 32, 67, 242.

[8] Some people wrote the delegates several days before departure to secure dining room seats near them (Low to George Haven Putnam, April 22, 1899, Low Papers).

[9] Low to Mahan, April 3, 1901, Alfred Thayer Mahan Papers, deposited in the Library of Congress.

Mandell Creighton, bishop of London, and the historian W. E. H. Lecky were among the guests; Prime Minister Salisbury was not there.[10]

Presence of the delegates in London aroused speculation about Anglo-American cooperation at the conference, and journalists asked Low whether Britain and the United States would join in a proposal for international arbitration. He declined to answer. Holls was more cooperative and told reporters that much of the talk about common Anglo-American policy at The Hague was unofficial; that the delegates of the United States had instructions which they intended to carry out as far as possible with a minimum of red tape. An unidentified diplomat (perhaps Holls?) was reported as saying that while the English and American delegations did not have identical instructions it was probable that they would follow the same line at The Hague.[11]

There was, in fact, little evidence of Anglo-American cooperation, but the delegates did learn much about British attitudes toward armaments. Early in March 1899 the first lord of the admiralty, George J. Goschen, had declared in the House of Commons that Her Majesty's government would reduce naval building if other leading naval powers did the same. Goschen hoped the deliberations of the Hague Conference would make these reductions possible.[12] Britain thus was the only power which made any gesture toward limitation. Even so, while the American delegates were in London they heard little of this offer of two months before. During their stay only one member of the government, the duke of Devonshire, lord president of the council, had anything to say publicly about armaments. Speaking before a banquet of the Central Association of Bankers, he defended the exchequer's heavy spending for arms; he maintained that England's armaments had made possible solution of recent difficulties with Russia, France, and the United States; he

---

[10] New York *Times*, May 12, 1899.   [11] *Ibid.*, May 11.
[12] *Parliamentary Debates*, 4th ser., LXVIII, March 7 to March 20, 1899 (London, 1899), cols. 323–324.

emphasized that British power had made arbitration feasible between the United Kingdom and Venezuela and preserved relations with the United States.[13]

Soon after arrival in London, Holls went on to Berlin and
there engaged, together with Ambassador White, in some considerable diplomacy. The Berlin embassy had filled with guests,
and the Whites were unable to entertain Mr. and Mrs. Holls, but
the ambassador and the delegation secretary conferred at
length.[14] For some time White had carried on negotiations concerning a commercial treaty with Foreign Minister von Bülow,
and had been busy, but he had talked with German officials about
the approaching conference. A short time before Holls's arrival,
the emperor had summoned White to the palace, and after greeting the ambassador warmly William II had launched into the
subject of the conference. He made suggestions which White
later recognized as valuable, and indicated desire to work with
the United States. "What the conference will most need is good
common sense," the sovereign declared, and he said he was appointing his ambassador in Paris, Count Herbert von Münster,
to lead the German delegation "because he has lots of it." [15] His
Imperial Majesty said nothing about one of his appointments
which was arousing criticism. Among his delegates was a Baron
Karl von Stengel, professor at the University of Munich, who
recently had published a pamphlet entitled *Der Ewige Friede*,
in which he glorified war and characterized the approaching
conference as a daydream. Stengel's appointment had been denounced even in Germany, but the government refused to

[13] New York *Times*, May 11, 1899.

[14] A. D. White to Holls, May 8, 1899, Holls Papers. Holls had a talk
with Bülow in which he told the German foreign minister about unfavorable comments concerning Britain's Samoan policy, which he and
Choate had made at Choate's luncheon a few days before (Bülow to
Count Hatzfeldt, May 16, 1899, in *Grosse Politik*, XIV, 615; translated
in E. T. S. Dugdale, ed., *German Diplomatic Documents, 1871–1914*
(London, 1928–1931), III, 63.

[15] White, *Autobiog.*, II, 236.

change its mind. Bülow told W. T. Stead that Stengel had written no such pamphlet.[16] Stead told the foreign minister that the pamphlet was in its third edition. Holls and White would have received with interest an explanation of the appointment, but there was none.[17]

There was a mixed German reaction to the approaching conference. Many people prominent in the empire's public life shared the German government's distrust of the conference. Professor Theodor Mommsen said the congress would be "a printer's error in the history of the world." Professor Kuno Fischer, sometimes called the "Grand Old Man of Germany," predicted that the meeting would have no result.[18] The semiofficial *Kreuz Zeitung* had said on May 10, 1899, that "every impulse toward increased armaments during the present century has come from Russia and France: and there can be no sincere talk of disarmament by Russia, who would be the last power to call a conference in the interest of humanity and to cast the false mask away." There were nonetheless many Germans who hoped for achievement at The Hague. Reichstag members and professors and authors signed a manifesto urging support of the German delegates.[19]

The time came and the delegates began to assemble at The Hague. Ambassador White and Holls, accompanied by two members of the embassy staff, arrived on Tuesday evening, May 16, after a pleasant but tiring all-day journey from Berlin by way of Amsterdam, Haarlem, and Leyden. Mahan, Low, and Crozier arrived from London the same day. Representatives of other

---

[16] Bertha von Suttner, Diary excerpt, May 17, 1899, *Memoirs*, II, 247–248.

[17] At The Hague an unidentified diplomat told White that Stengel had been appointed, not because of his pamphlet, but to give Bavaria representation on the German obligation. Although Bavaria maintained her own diplomatic representatives in Russia, she was not invited to send a delegation to The Hague (White, Diary excerpt, June 1, 1899, *Autobiog.*, II, 284).

[18] New York *Times*, May 14, 1899.   [19] *Ibid.*, May 11.

nations had been appearing for several days. Newel took quarters for Low at a hotel some distance from the main part of the town. White, Mahan, Holls, and Crozier were to stay at the Hotel Oude Doelen. Some of the party may have doubted the wisdom of Newel's choice of rooms, but White had no doubts. He was delighted with his fortune, for thirty-five years before he had stayed at the Oude Doelen. He was pleased that so little had changed through the years; indeed an inscription over the hostelry's main doorway indicated only one rebuilding, in 1625, since the hotel was first constructed during the Middle Ages.[20]

The conference was scheduled to open formally on Thursday, the thirty-second birthday of the Russian czar, and only a few difficulties arose to bother the delegates and their governments. The Americans soon learned that the pope was attempting to create difficulties over the papacy's exclusion from the conference. To protest the refusal to invite the pope to send delegates, Cardinal Rampolla, the Vatican secretary of state, ordered the papal nuncio in Holland, Monsignor Tarnassie, to absent himself from the Dutch capital. The slight to the Holy See angered Catholics in the Dutch parliament.[21] Many Hollanders also were indignant because neither the Orange Free State nor the Transvaal received an invitation. Then trouble arose over Bulgaria. Delegates were present from that principality, technically subject to the Turkish sultan. The Turks were angered by what appeared recognition of Bulgarian independence.[22]

In addition to such small troubles there was abundant evidence of tension among the great powers. Everyone especially distrusted Russian desires. And many delegates considered distasteful the subjects they were to discuss.

There is not a single prominent diplomat in Europe who believes that the original purpose of the conference has the slightest chance

[20] A. D. White to Fred White, May 19, 1899, A. D. White Papers; White, Diary excerpt, May 17, 1899, *Autobiog.*, II, 252.

[21] New York *Times*, April 17 and May 16, 1899.

[22] *Ibid.*, May 14 and 16.

of realization. Disarmament was the keynote at the start. To-day the word is no longer mentioned. There is hardly a power that has not increased its forces by land or sea since the Czar invited them to diminish these.

So wrote Henry Norman, serving as London correspondent of the New York *Times*.[23]

Skepticism was everywhere. The head of the Russian delegation, for instance, the Baron de Staal, who was the czar's ambassador to London, was no more sympathetic to the armaments question than was any other diplomat. Six weeks before the conference he called upon Münster in Paris, and the two ambassadors agreed that it would be necessary to find a way around the armaments problem while making a few changes in the Red Cross statutes and international law so as to give appearance of achievement.[24] In The Hague, De Staal was naturally a center of speculation.

Like the Russian diplomat, Count Münster was distressed by assignment to The Hague. He wrote his good friend, Whitelaw Reid:

I could not refuse and have to obey orders, although I think it is a most difficult and ungrateful task. Beating empty straw is always a tiresome job, which may even be dangerous if it is, like in this case, Russian straw, that may conceal an apple of contention. As to disarmament, it is out of the question and it is ridiculous to have it proposed at this moment. The only important question to discuss would be arbitration and to come to an understanding on that point is, I fear, rather hopeless. . . . We can, in regard to Russia, not allow the conference to end with an entire fiasco and must try to cover it with a peaceful-looking cloak.[25]

The French foreign minister, Théophile Delcassé, was equally cynical. He had told Münster that his government's interests at

[23] *Ibid.*, May 14.
[24] Count Herbert von Münster to the German Foreign Office, April 4, 1899, in *Grosse Politik*, XV, 182–183; translated in Dugdale, III, 75.
[25] April 7, 1899, in Royal Cortissoz, *The Life of Whitelaw Reid* (New York, 1921), II, 258–259.

the conference would be the same as Germany's.[26] France had no desire to limit her armaments, but she had recovered from the apprehension and resentment which the peace rescript had aroused. She determined to help her Russian ally to save face. To head her delegation she sent former Premier Léon Bourgeois, a man sympathetic with peace. Associated with Bourgeois was one of France's famed peace leaders, the Baron d'Estournelles de Constant. These appointments, gestures to the czar, did not cause Münster to suspect Delcassé's sincerity. The German diplomat thought the two leading French delegates would use the conference as stepping stones to embassies. That would, he said, make them "prudent and amiable." [27] He was not to be disappointed, for Bourgeois and d'Estournelles followed the views of their government at the Hague Conference, and the French were interested but only in a negative way.

Some delegates even regarded the conference as a diplomatic picnic which would surely be the laughing stock of Europe. One prominent delegate openly predicted that it would be "a first class burial, attended by all the ceremony that any one could desire, but nevertheless a burial." [28] Another delegate was overheard lamenting his fate in being asked to attend the conference; he feared that his presence at The Hague would crown an otherwise honorable career with open failure.[29]

As for the American delegates, their views of the conference were not at first known. They did, however, appear privately. Several leading journals in the United States had predicted that Americans would take no part in questions with which their country was not concerned.[30] Their instructions did not indicate that the McKinley administration wished to depart from tradi-

---

[26] Münster to Prince Chlodwig von Hohenlohe, April 21, 1899, in *Grosse Politik*, XV, 186–187.

[27] Münster to Reid, April 7, 1899, in Cortissoz, II, 258–259.

[28] New York *Times*, May 21, 1899.

[29] White, Diary excerpt, May 18, 1899, *Autobiog.*, II, 256.

[30] *The Nation*, LXVIII (April 13, 1899), 270; New York *Times*, April 18, 1899.

tional principles of American foreign policy. On Wednesday afternoon, May 18, the delegation met at Newel's house and elected a chairman. White had been named first in the list of delegates, and it had been understood that the president wished him to be chairman, but the ambassador insisted that the chairmanship be determined by election. His fellow delegates unanimously elected him to that position. Having attended to this matter, they reviewed their instructions and decided that the plan for international arbitration was the document of most importance. Like delegates from other major powers, they had little desire to limit their country's armament program, but they did have interest in arbitration, which enabled them to begin their duties with more confidence than did most of their fellow envoys.

Certainly the Americans in general were not confident of success. On the evening of May 17 the first Dutch delegate, Jonkheer A. P. C. van Karnebeek, formerly a Netherlands foreign minister, gave a reception for members of the conference. The brilliance of the occasion much impressed the Americans, and they made interesting acquaintances. Yet Ambassador White concluded that "probably, since the world began, never has so large a body come together in a spirit of more hopeless skepticism as to any good result." [31] Gloom in this manner overhung the conference well before it got under way. A strange milieu confronted the diplomats of the world as they assembled —under this canopy of gloom—to open the conference for peace.

Fortunately the day of the conference's opening, May 18, 1899, was a beautiful spring day, a perfect day on which to begin a conference. The day began with a church service. The only ceremony of the morning was a mass at the Russian Orthodox chapel near Scheveningen in honor of the birthday of Nicholas II. Because that tiny building could hold barely a hundred people, the American commissioners did not attend. They missed

[31] Diary excerpt, May 17, 1899, *Autobiog.*, II, 256.

an impressive service. The famed Austrian pacifist, Baroness Bertha von Suttner, together with her husband, were among the few persons other than diplomats who were there. The baroness was confident that she was seeing an event which would begin a new epoch. The congregation appeared full of reverence as priests prayed for the autocrat of Russia. The baroness felt moved to address a silent petition to him:

O thou brave of heart, remain firm! Let not the ingratitude and the spite and the imbecility of the world penetrate to thee to disturb and paralyze; even if an attempt is made to belittle and misinterpret and even block thy work, remain firm! [32]

Afterwards the delegates gathered for their initial meeting. The Netherlands government had arranged for the conference to sit at the House in the Wood, a small summer residence of the royal family which was twenty minutes' drive from The Hague, and the delegates, newspapermen, and other interested people driving out to the little palace that afternoon made quite a procession. The Dutch parliament had appropriated $30,000 for the conference, and a goodly part of this sum had been spent on street decorations. [33] Flags of all nations were everywhere, and the bright orange of the Dutch flag predominated. Thousands of people lined the route. No police were present—or were necessary—to maintain order; at the palace gates a few soldiers and servants superintended traffic.

The scene at the palace that May day was assuredly impressive. For days painters, joiners, upholsterers, and cleaners had prepared the baroque halls of the House in the Wood, and everything was in order. [34] The opening session was to be in the great hall, under the cupola. At one end of the room, on a platform, were desks for the chairman and secretaries. On the other side of the room, divided by an aisle leading to the platform, were a hundred desks, each covered with a green cloth. A dozen

[32] Diary excerpt, May 19, 1899, *Memoirs*, II, 250.
[33] Newel to Hay, March 22, 1899, Newel Despatch Book, p. 132.
[34] *The Times* (London), May 17 and 19, 1899.

carefully chosen journalists were the first persons to arrive and they went to their seats in a small gallery. Baroness von Suttner and a British pacifist, Francis William Fox, the only peace leaders invited, went to seats in the gallery.[35]

Delegates began to enter at 1:45 P.M., Foreign Minister W. H. de Beaufort of the Netherlands being first to arrive. China's chief delegate, Yang Yu, was next. Sir Julian Pauncefote and Seth Low entered together, as did Andrew White and Captain Mahan. Soon all delegates had taken their seats.[36] Dutch protocol officers had assigned seats according to alphabetical rank of the French names of countries represented. *L'Amérique*, rather than *Etats-Unis*, was used in seating the Americans. White and his colleagues found themselves at the front of the room, before the platform and across the aisle from the representatives of Germany (*l'Allemagne*).[37]

Promptly at two o'clock Foreign Minister de Beaufort stepped to the platform and declared the conference in session. He welcomed the delegates in the name of Queen Wilhelmina. In flowery, courtly language he praised the humanitarian spirit of the Russian emperor and ascribed the same motives to his young sovereign's willingness to act as hostess for the conference. Pointing to a painting over the door, done by one of Rubens' pupils, he observed that it was an allegorical representation of the Peace of Westphalia. He hoped that the painting would be an omen of fortune for their deliberations. He proposed two motions: that the conference send a congratulatory telegram to the czar and that the presidency be conferred upon M. de Staal.

The conference unanimously passed De Beaufort's motions, and De Staal took the chair. He had never before presided over a meeting conducted by parliamentary procedure. He appeared

[35] Francis William Fox, *Some Historical Incidents in Connexion with Establishment of the International Tribunal of Arbitration at The Hague in 1899 and International Arbitration* (London, 1901), pp. 12–13.

[36] New York *Times*, May 19, 1899; *The Times* (London), May 19, 1899.

[37] White, Diary excerpt, May 18, 1899, *Autobiog.*, II, 257.

bewildered as he assumed the presidency, yet he handled the situation fairly well.[38] Having known beforehand that he would be named president, he had prepared a speech praising his ruler and Queen Wilhelmina. He referred to the Netherlands as a cradle of international law and mentioned the treaties of peace concluded on Dutch soil. Like the foreign minister, he hoped the conference would attain success. Closing his address De Staal proposed a message of thanks to Queen Wilhelmina and that De Beaufort be named honorary president and Karnebeek vice president. These motions carried, and then came election of official secretaries. The posts went to members of the staffs of the French, Dutch, German, Belgian, and Russian delegations.[39] President McKinley had hoped that Holls would be one of the secretaries of the conference, and Holls would have accepted such an honor, but no nomination came as he sat beside Ambassador White.[40] On that first day there were no special honors for the United States.

With almost no further ceremony the session came to an end. De Staal proposed a resolution declaring sessions of the conference closed to the public, and it was quickly carried. The conference thereupon adjourned until eleven o'clock on Saturday morning, May 20, 1899. The first session had lasted only thirty minutes.[41]

[38] A. D. White to Joseph H. Choate, Feb. 24, 1912, Joseph H. Choate Papers, deposited in the Library of Congress.

[39] James Brown Scott, ed., *The Proceedings of the Hague Peace Conferences: The Conference of 1899* (New York, 1920), pp. 13–16. Hereafter cited as *Proceedings, 1899.*

[40] Holls to A. D. White, April 4, 1899, Holls Papers.

[41] Frederick W. Holls, *The Peace Conference at The Hague and Its Bearings on International Law and Policy* (New York, 1900), pp. 52, 57.

VII

First Labors

THE opening ceremony had been a gracious affair and relieved the forebodings of some of the delegates. Nicholas II, reading of the conference's first session, could feel that the meeting would not hurt his prestige. His cousin the German emperor appeared to give the meeting full support. Speaking in Wiesbaden, William II declared that Germany's aims at the conference were the same as Russia's. And from Washington came indication of American pleasure—a wire from President McKinley congratulating the Russian sovereign on his birthday and upon the conference's auspicious beginning.[1]

I

Such interest was heartening, but diplomats at The Hague had to solve many problems before they could feel that the conference was underway. To consider these matters the delegation chiefs met in one of the large rooms of the Oude Doelen at eleven o'clock, Friday morning. M. de Staal presided. Not recovered from influenza and suffering from a toothache which was to send him to a dentist several times within a few days, he

---

[1] *The Nation*, LXVIII (May 25, 1899), 385; A. D. White, Diary excerpt, May 19, 1899, *Autobiog.*, II, 258–259.

could not conceal a certain discouragement behind his usually amiable manners. His unfamiliarity with parliamentary rules, apparent on the preceding day, was now a serious handicap. He did not know how to present a motion, and when someone offered to amend a motion he had no idea what to do with it. Through the tact of his colleagues, most of whom had years of parliamentary experience, the president got through the morning.[2]

Before the conference assembled, it had been reported that delegates would divide into three commissions to consider points of Muraviev's circular of January 11. This scheme was followed, but it was difficult to work out. The Russians since issuing their tentative program had given little consideration to the manner in which the conference was to function. A Dutch scholar, A. van Daehne van Varick, had prepared a collection of documents which the Netherlands Foreign Office gave to the delegates; there were selections from treaties, letters, and speeches concerning armaments, the laws of war, and arbitration. The collection was no help in organizing the conference. Soon the more experienced statesmen drew together and decided that one committee, the first commission, would concern itself with the first topics suggested in Muraviev's circular. These dealt with armament limitation. Upon the first commission would fall responsibility for at least a gesture toward the armament problem. The second commission was to discuss articles five, six, and seven of the Russian program, possible changes in the rules of war. The third commission was to deal with the final item in the circular —article eight—good offices, mediation, and arbitration. Each delegation could have representatives on all three commissions if it desired. Although there was no limit to the delegates a country could have on a commission, no state was to have more than one vote. To this rule there was a single exception. Montenegro, ap-

[2] Stead to Nicholas II, May 28, 1899, in Frederic Whyte, *W. T. Stead*, II, 155; White, *Autobiog.*, II, 258–259; A. D. White to Choate, Feb. 24, 1912, Choate Papers.

parently reluctant to incur the expense of a delegation, sent no representative of her own and requested the Russian delegation to act for her.[3] There was no conflict between the points of view of Russia and Montenegro.

Sitting among his fellow heads of delegations, Andrew White began to hope for good results, for as diplomats tackled organizational problems there appeared desire to achieve at least some success. Talking with statesmen throughout the day, White noted a spirit of cooperation. That evening De Beaufort gave a reception, and at that function the change in attitude was fully discernible. Even the Germans displayed good will, for Count Münster assured White that his delegation would as far as possible stand with the United States. Encouraged, the chief delegate of the United States did not allow himself to be optimistic, for he was still convinced that nothing could be done to limit armaments. He was certain that it would be impossible to make arbitration compulsory. He hoped that the meeting might establish regular arbitral machinery and make the rules of war more humane. He had some hope that his delegation could introduce proposals concerning immunity of private property on the high seas.[4]

The conference again came together at eleven o'clock Saturday morning to listen to telegrams from Queen Wilhelmina and Nicholas II thanking the assemblage for its messages of two days before. De Staal then addressed his fellow delegates. He confined himself almost exclusively to arbitration and mediation:

Peace is the crying need of the nations, and we owe it to mankind, we owe it to the Governments which have entrusted us with their powers and in whose care is the welfare of their people, we owe it to ourselves to do a useful work by specifying the method of employing some of the means of assuring peace.

Skillfully he sidestepped armaments until near the end of his speech. He then remarked:

[3] James B. Scott, *The Hague Peace Conferences*, I, 149.
[4] White, Diary excerpt, May 19, 1899, *Autobiog.*, II, 259–260.

It might be well to investigate whether a limitation of increasing armaments is not required for the well-being of nations. In this matter, it is for the Governments to weigh in their wisdom the interests which they have in charge.

Closing, De Staal announced decisions made the day before by the delegation chiefs. Requesting that commission assignments go out to the secretaries of the conference, he adjourned the session.[5]

2

This brief meeting gave evidence that the conference was studying its problems. Optimism increased, and on the following Sunday from pulpits in Europe and in America sermons were heard which forecast achievement. In the English church at The Hague, Dean O'Foley took as his text: "And your old men shall see visions and your young men dream dreams." He told his hearers, among whom were several English and American delegates, that Gladstone typified the older generation of peacemakers, who had framed the Geneva conventions, and that the delegates at the conference were dreamers of a new generation, seeking to substitute law for force in relations among states.[6]

His opinions were like those of peace leaders gathering in the Dutch capital. From all over Europe and from the United States had come peace spokesmen. They conducted themselves as though they were official members of the conference, and they sought to make their influence felt. Ready to praise developments which they approved, they were ready to disapprove steps contrary to their wishes. The Baroness von Suttner had been among the first peace leaders on the scene. Accompanied by her lovingly obedient husband, she was one of the most conspicuous personages at The Hague. Giving luncheons and dinners, conferring with statesmen, and writing for journals, she worked harder than many delegates. Most diplomats treated her

[5] *Proceedings, 1899*, pp. 17–20.
[6] New York *Times*, May 22, 1899.

with respect; she believed that a few welcomed her advice; with
the French and American delegations she found particular favor.
Through peace work she was acquainted with D'Estournelles of
the French commission, and they had long, earnest conversations. Holls and White frequently discussed the work of the
conference with the Austrian lady.[7]

Peace leaders still had their troubles. Some diplomats, for example, ignored the Baroness von Suttner and her friends. She
complained:

The German delegation is the only one from which no one does
me the honor of greeting me. Count Münster treats me as if I were
a rattlebrain. When Professor Stengel spoke in his pamphlet of the
"comical persons" of the peace movement, from whose grotesque
behavior and ideas he could not sufficiently warn people, he evidently included me in the number.[8]

Notable among the peace leaders was Ivan Bloch, the Russian
publicist, who arrived on the second day of the conference and
remained until its adjournment. Peace spokesmen welcomed him.
The delegates, too, were careful to show him deference, for they
believed that his *The Future of War* had helped persuade the
czar to propose the conference. Bloch denied that his book suggested to the emperor the idea of a conference, yet he never
wearied of telling of long interviews with Nicholas II and of
the czar's interest in *The Future of War*.[9] Bloch brought with
him trunks of copies of his six-volume work, and he gave books
to everyone in sight. He gave lectures, to which he invited delegates, peace leaders, and reporters. Although he served supper
in the middle and at the end of his lectures, they could hardly
have been pleasant affairs. Illustrating his talks with lantern
slides and drawing from his experiences as a transportation officer during the last Russo-Turkish War he sought to make war

[7] Bertha von Suttner, Diary excerpts, May 22 and June 15, 1899,
Memoirs, II, 258 and 294.
[8] *Ibid.*, May 25, 1899, p. 266.
[9] *The Times* (London), May 23, 1899.

appear impractical. After hearing these lectures, Benjamin Trueblood wrote: "I never saw any one more absolutely possessed of
his subject. He did not, would not, and I suppose could not talk
about anything else." [10] But Bloch was not carried away by his
own enthusiasm. He told an English newspaperman that the
conference would be satisfactory if it did nothing more than get
the powers to study the problems laid before it.[11]

Receiving less notice than Bloch and the Baroness von Suttner
were other leaders of the European peace movement whose
prestige was, in reality, as great as theirs. From Paris came two
noted arbitration exponents, Dr. Charles Richet of the University
of Paris, who represented the French Arbitration Society, and
Emile Arnaud, president of the International League of Peace
and Liberty. Frédéric Passy, dean of French pacifists, had longed
to attend, but a surgical operation prevented him. A. H. Fried of
Berlin represented several German peace groups. Fredrik Bajer
of Copenhagen was present in behalf of the International Peace
Bureau of Bern. Dr. W. Evans Darby, the renowned secretary
of the London Peace Society, was a spectator. Recently Darby
had published a scholarly book entitled *International Tribunals,*
and Baron de Staal ordered a copy for each delegate.

Some peace leaders came bearing memorials for action on disarmament and arbitration. Munich's Madame Selenka brought
one of the most impressive petitions, which bore the signatures of
millions of women in eighteen countries. She asked for an interview with De Staal. This interview the president of the conference granted, but he warned his visitor to limit her call to
five minutes. Madame Selenka charmed the aged Russian. As a
gift she had brought an album containing, among other interesting things, a peace poem written by Queen Elizabeth of Rumania under her pseudonym of Carmen Sylva. So interested did
De Staal become that he talked with Madame Selenka for thirty

[10] Benjamin F. Trueblood, "The International Peace Conference at
The Hague," *New England Magazine*, N. S., XX (1899), 666.
[11] New York *Times*, May 20, 1899.

minutes. Other memorialists were not so fortunate, but they too received attention. Madame Wazklewicz, organizer of the Dutch Peace Crusade, brought a petition signed by 200,000 Nether- landers. Senator Henri Lafontaine of Belgium had a memorial with signatures of more than 100,000 of his countrymen.[12]

American peace leaders, while not so prominent as those of Europe, were present in force. The Universal Peace Union claimed at least twenty of its members and leaders were at The Hague, although this number included several individuals more identified with other American peace organizations and some distinguished European pacifists who accepted membership in the Philadelphia organization. The Reverend George Dana Boardman and Howard M. Jenkins, who was editor of the *Friends' Intelligencer*, were among Philadelphia pacifists at The Hague early in the conference.[13]

The outstanding American peace leader to appear that summer was Dr. Trueblood, secretary of the American Peace Society. Representing both that society and the Universal Peace Union, he could claim to be spokesman of the most powerful American pacifist groups. He arrived on May 19 and remained four weeks, observing the proceedings with an intelligent eye. The Quaker scholar received every courtesy from delegates and Dutch of- ficials. European pacifists welcomed him as one of the world's great leaders of the peace movement. Hardly had he arrived when he began circulating news that he knew for a certainty that the United States had ordered its delegates to submit a de- tailed plan for a court of arbitration. Trueblood helped focus pacifist interest on the official American representatives.[14]

Other Americans, less closely associated with the peace move- ment, also made the Hague Conference a high point on Euro- pean tours that spring and summer. Archbishop Ireland, despite

[12] Trueblood, pp. 666–667; *Advocate of Peace*, LXI (1899), 153–154; New York *Times*, May 26, 1899.
[13] *The Peacemaker*, XVIII (1899), 4; George G. Mercer, address, in *Mohonk Conference, 1899*, pp. 39–40.
[14] Von Suttner, Diary excerpt, May 21, 1899, *Memoirs*, II, 225.

failure of the McKinley administration to appoint him a delegate, did not lose interest in the conference, and interrupted a speaking tour to visit it.[15] The historian, James Ford Rhodes, anxious to see the making of history, visited the conference.[16] (Apparently he was little impressed by what he saw; he failed to mention the conference in his *History of the McKinley and Roosevelt Administrations*.) But the most distinguished American to visit The Hague during the conference was Thomas B. Reed, speaker of the House of Representatives.[17]

Talking with peace enthusiasts and with other spectators added greatly to demands on the time of the delegates, and this was especially true with the Americans. No delegation received more attention from the "unofficial representatives" than did that of the United States. And White and his colleagues were not concerned with pacifists at The Hague alone; at no time were they permitted to forget that many groups at home were following their every movement. As long as the conference sat, the Universal Peace Union held three meetings weekly to lend moral support to the gathering across the sea.[18] Boston was likewise a center of support for the conference. There Edward Everett Hale led a group which from early March to late August published a special journal entitled the *Peace Crusade*.[19] Conferences of several leading denominations prayed for success of the Hague deliberations. The Woman's Christian Temperance Union and women's suffrage groups were active.

Americans with interest in the conference felt it necessary to make their opinions heard, and messages went to the czar, to

[15] *The Peacemaker*, XVIII (1899), 4.

[16] The historian—who was Mark Hanna's brother-in-law—thanked Holls warmly for courtesies shown him at The Hague (Rhodes to Holls, June 15, 1899, Holls Papers).

[17] White, Diary excerpt, June 18, 1899, *Autobiog.*, II, 316.

[18] Journal of Alfred Love, XXII, May 18, 1899, pages not numbered (unpublished MS in the Swarthmore Peace Collection).

[19] So far as can be determined, the only surviving copies of the *Peace Crusade* are in the New York Public Library.

the conference officials, and to the American delegation. Every mail brought telegrams and letters to the envoys of the United States. Holls as secretary had to answer these messages and found the task extremely arduous. He was careful when talking with a peace leader to give the impression that he and his colleagues felt strengthened and sustained by evidence of interest in America.[20] Actually the delegates of the United States were irked by the peace zealots. While many peace messages were helpful, some were stupid indeed. "If these good people only knew how all this distracts us," White said, "from the work which we have at heart as much as they, we should get considerably more time to think upon the problems before us." [21]

3

In addition to the pacifists there were the spokesmen for the discontented minorities. The American delegates were favorites with some of these people. After all, was not the United States the great exponent of liberty? Boers from South Africa, Armenians from Turkey and Russia, Macedonians and Young Turks from Turkey, Finns and Poles crowded into The Hague. Presence of these people was embarrassing to Britain, Turkey, and Russia. The Americans, annoyed by not even one Filipino, listened to what seemed endless pleas for sympathy and support. Despite reports which may have been fictitious that former President Cleveland had written the delegation in behalf of the Armenians, and rumor that President McKinley had ordered the delegates to present Finland's grievances against the czar, the

[20] According to the minutes of the American commission, kept by Holls, at most formal meetings of the delegation, some time was devoted to consideration of messages from peace, church, and woman suffrage groups. The minutes are preserved in the State Department files in the National Archives, hereafter cited as American Commission, Minutes. The American delegation was officially styled "commission," and this term is used in their minutes. This term was used to refer also to committees of the conference.

[21] Diary excerpt, May 21, 1899, *Autobiog.*, II, 262.

American envoys could only listen to the claims of these distressed people.[22] Conference officials at the behest of the Russian government determined that the conference should discuss only topics listed in Muraviev's January circular. Further, to talk about woes of subject nationalities would be not only embarrassing but dangerous, for the Hague meeting was a peace conference and the nationality issue raised questions that could lead toward war.

No group with a grievance was more outspoken than the Young Turks. They received scant respect from the diplomats, for everyone knew that their leaders lived luxuriously in Paris by blackmailing the sultan. To be rid of them, after many entreaties for an audience, the American delegates finally one evening granted them a few minutes. "Your excellencies, ve are ze Young Turkeys," began their spokesman. The Americans, highly amused, hardly heard the ensuing tirade against the Turkish government.[23]

At other times the Young Turks were not so amusing, and one evening one of them, Ahmed Riza, delivered an unusually violent speech against the Porte. A Turkish diplomat challenged him to a duel. Ahmed declined. Thereby passed the only threat of bloodshed at the conference. His refusal won him admiration of the pacifists.[24]

Then there were the reporters. Through this milieu of pacifists, diplomats, and nationalist minority leaders wandered journalists from most of the leading papers in England and the Continent, but few from the United States. News was not easy, for regulations for secrecy, frequently violated, made reporting difficult. Disgusted with red tape, many newsmen left the Netherlands before the conference had sat a week. Those who remained secured information from meager handouts of an official news

[22] New York *Times*, May 19, 1899; *The Nation*, LXVIII (May 18, 1899), 365.

[23] White, Diary excerpt, June 8, 1899, *Autobiog.*, II, 288.

[24] *Advocate of Peace*, LXI (1899), 154–155.

bureau established at the second plenary meeting. The American delegation, known to disapprove of secrecy, received many reporters, and they proved almost as troublesome as the nationalist minorities. But it was not long before most American delegates stopped seeing the journalists, turning them over to Holls.[25] The secretary, while finding the newsmen a burden, was never reluctant to talk; several journalists distrusted Holls for quibbling and evasiveness, but so much did he have to say that it was rare that a news story from The Hague failed to mention his name.[26]

Among the journalists was W. T. Stead, who came from St. Petersburg, where he had another interview with the czar. Naturally he thought himself fitted to represent the views of the Russian ruler. Establishing his family in a villa near Scheveningen appropriately named "Pax Intrantibus," he prepared to bring his power to bear on the conference. He persuaded the leading Hague paper, the *Dagblad*, to let him use its presses, and he turned out a regular chronicle of the conference in French and Dutch. The Manchester *Guardian* opened its columns, and English readers soon found in that paper the most interesting if not the most accurate accounts of the Hague deliberations. As was to be expected, Stead's *Review of Reviews* and its sister publication, the *American Monthly Review of Reviews*, carried his version of the more important conference developments.

Stead was not at all dismayed by secrecy regulations. Although he announced that he would be "hunting the hard fox," the foxes were not difficult to find. The first Serbian delegate, Chedomil Mijatovich, gave confidential information.[27] Others did likewise. Stead pronounced Holls "the most powerful and active of the American delegates here." The Englishman asked Holls to join in efforts to dispel the almost universal distrust of Russian intentions, and to this the American assented.[28] Holls did not fully

---

[25] Holls to Hill, May 31, 1899, David Jayne Hill Papers, deposited in the University of Rochester Library.

[26] Trueblood, p. 662.   [27] *Ibid.*, p. 653; Whyte, II, 153–154.

[28] Stead to Nicholas II, May 28, 1899, in Whyte, p. 156.

return Stead's admiration. "That irrepressible nuisance" was the American secretary's term for his self-appointed friend.[29] Other conference members found Stead annoying. Controllers of the conference were horrified to find him flouting their secrecy, and considered action against him. But such a course seemed unwise; after all, no one knew the extent of Stead's influence with Nicholas II, and he did write the Russian ruler letters about the conference.

4

Interrupted by pacifists, nationalist leaders, and reporters—especially W. T. Stead—it is no wonder that the conference sometimes moved slowly. The American delegates conferred among themselves and with representatives of other powers about arbitration schemes and the question of immunity for private property on the seas. It seemed likely that both Britain and Russia would oppose the United States should its delegation introduce a resolution on private property, but some support did appear. Count Welsersheimb, head of the Austrian delegation, favored the American view. Meanwhile interest in an arbitration scheme increased. The American representatives, pleased to note this, feared that some plan would appear which would conflict with the Monroe Doctrine. They considered a request to the State Department for instructions, but decided to await developments.[30]

Appointment of the commissions came at this time. At ten o'clock Tuesday morning, May 23, the delegation heads met to consider the organization of the commissions, and at noon the entire conference met to hear the commission assignments. Auguste Beernaert, president of the Belgian chamber of representatives and head of his country's conference delegation, became president of the first commission. Münster and White were honorary presidents. White, Crozier, and Mahan represented the United States. Feodor de Martens, the second Russian dele-

[29] Holls to Hill, May 17, 1899, Holls Papers.
[30] White, Diary excerpts, May 22 and 23, 1899, *Autobiog.*, II, 262–263.

gate, was to head the second commission; associated with him as honorary presidents were Spain's duke of Tetuan and Turkey's Turkhan Pasha. White, Mahan, and Crozier were on this commission, and Newel joined them. Heading the third commission was Léon Bourgeois of France. This announcement created some disappointment, for advocates of arbitration had been certain that Pauncefote would preside over this committee.[31] That diplomat was named an honorary president of the commission, a distinction also accorded the first Italian delegate, Count Nigra. White, Low, and Holls were American representatives.[32]

That afternoon the three commissions met for the first time. Sessions of the first and second commissions were brief. Beernaert and Martens had perfunctory remarks. Having announced that the commissions would meet again on May 26, they adjourned their groups.[33] Léon Bourgeois, opening the third commission, did so with an emotional flourish, obviously intended to ease disappointment. He declared that he would have preferred to see someone presiding with greater experience and distinction, but that he would bring wholehearted devotion to his task. As if to please his government's Russian allies, he cautioned his colleagues to keep their proceedings secret, but Baron de Bildt of Sweden urged that the conference news bureau give out full accounts of the deliberations. Recognizing that their work would call for study of previous arbitration developments, the first delegate from Luxembourg, M. Eyschen, suggested that a recent book by the Chevalier Descamps of Belgium, a fellow commission member, be made available to each member. Descamps agreed to make his book available. The commission took note of the fine work of the Netherlands government in compiling documents for the conference, and upon motion of Count Nigra a message of appreciation went to the Dutch officials.[34]

The conference thus was at work, but the hopeful thinking of a few days before seemed to diminish. There was criticism

[31] Manchester *Guardian*, May 24, 1899.
[32] *Proceedings, 1899*, pp. 21–26.   [33] *Ibid.*, pp. 271, 383–384.
[34] *Ibid.*, pp. 581–582.

of Russia. It was said that the czar's purpose in calling the conference was to gain time to increase his armaments. The American delegation, not inclined to criticize Russian motives, had cause to be provoked, for Ambassador White gave Martens a memorandum on exempting private property from seizure on the high seas, only to have that expert on international law reject it. The subject was not on Muraviev's program, the Russian insisted, and Russia would oppose its introduction and Great Britain, France, and Italy undoubtedly would do likewise. White reminded Martens of President McKinley's determination to press the matter. He insisted that his delegation should at least have opportunity to present its views. Martens refused. The ambassador suggested that a paper on the subject be submitted to the diplomats present but that its consideration be referred to a future conference. Martens' reply was that he would take the matter into consideration.

More troubling were indications that Germany would oppose systematizing arbitration. Münster said that arbitration would injure Germany, for it would give enemy powers time to mount an attack. Germany, he thought, could mobilize her army in ten days. Why give up this advantage? White's efforts to dissuade him were in vain. And even among the American delegates there were doubts. They met twice on May 24 and talked over possible conflicts between the Monroe Doctrine and arbitration. They decided to cable the State Department for permission to depart from their original instructions, should such conflicts appear likely.[35]

Still on Wednesday evening pessimism again lifted, for that night came one of the most brilliant social events of the conference. From her house in the country, Queen Wilhelmina came into The Hague to hold a reception for the conference members. De Staal called on the queen to present her with the Russian Order of St. Catherine, set in diamonds.[36] Promptly at

[35] White, Diary excerpt, May 24, 1899, *Autobiog.*, II, 264–266.
[36] *The Times* (London), May 25, 1899.

5:00 P.M. the first delegates arrived at the queen's apartment. Less than a year before the eighteen-year-old sovereign had ended her minority and taken over the royal duties. This reception was one of the most difficult tasks she had yet performed. She was evidently timid, and her slender blonde beauty contrasted with the bearded faces of aging diplomats. As she passed from diplomat to diplomat she gained confidence. Conversing in French, German, and English, she spoke with all present. Ambassador White did his best to find topics which would interest the young ruler. He thanked Her Majesty for having placed the House in the Wood at the disposal of the conference. At length he dwelt on the artistic beauties of that palace, but the queen liked the House in the Wood for different reasons—its pools were splendid for skating.

Leaving Wilhelmina's rooms, the delegates went to the apartments of her mother, Queen Emma. That lady received them with all the poise of her long regency, and she too was able to speak with each delegate in a language the delegate could understand.[37]

At 9:30 P.M. the chief delegates, accompanied by their colleagues and by members of the diplomatic corps, again went to the palace for another presentation and a ball. It was, Dr. Trueblood said, the "most 'brilliant' function" seen in the Netherlands for a generation.[38] Most diplomats and military and naval officers appeared in uniform. China's Yang Yu was the only individual to appear in outlandish costume; his rich robe of peacock blue and his cap, adorned with the red coral button of a mandarin of high rank, had been subject of comment since the conference's opening. The Turks with their red fezzes, and the Persians with their black, gave to the occasion an added Eastern touch. The Americans, somberly dressed in evening clothes, were as conspicuous as these representatives of the Orient. But European courts had long since become accustomed to eccentric

[37] White, Diary excerpt, May 24, 1899, *Autobiog.*, II, 266–268.
[38] Trueblood, p. 665.

American notions of diplomatic dress, and there were no untoward comments.

Low and Holls were impressed by their regal reception. Low later reported that "there, as in everything relating to the Conference, was the predominating fact of unity." [39] Ambassador White, accustomed to court functions, was not so aware of a spirit of unity. He enjoyed the music and studied the architecture of the palace, built for King Louis Bonaparte and Queen Hortense, but he remained alert for diplomatic comments. Talking with the British naval delegate, Sir John Fisher, he at first believed that the Englishman would support American proposals. Recently Fisher had been in a naval skirmish in China. Going ashore with eleven hundred men he had returned with only five hundred. Fisher was for peace. Would he support the American proposals on private property at sea? The answer was No. [40]

Largely ceremonial and organizational had been the first labors of the conference, but much had been accomplished. Old acquaintances had been renewed and new ones made. At the close of the first week few diplomats had fully recovered from the gloom which had marked their arrival, yet several delegations hoped to achieve good results in regard to arbitration and the laws of war. Unfortunately, few individuals hoped for action on the czar's proposal to limit armaments.

[39] Seth Low, "The International Conference of Peace," *North American Review*, CLXIX (1899), 627.

[40] White, Diary excerpt, May 24, 1899, *Autobiog.*, II, 267–268.

VIII

The Problem of Armaments

IN retrospect few aspects of the First Hague Peace Conference appear unhappier than the deliberations of the first commission concerning armaments. "Among the tasks of high importance which lie before the Conference," so declared the president of the commission, Auguste Beernaert, "our First Commission has perhaps the most sacred." [1] Few delegates agreed with the Belgian statesman. Suspicious of Russian intention, fearing any restriction on armaments, they conducted themselves as though nothing were sacred save the sovereignty of their governments.

It is sad, too, to reflect that no nation went into the First Hague Conference with greater determination to defeat its original, primary objective than did the United States of America. Sincere in desire to establish a permanent international tribunal, the Americans would countenance no agreement hindering improvement in their army and navy.

The American representatives would not budge from a narrow construction of their country's national interest. The State Department's instructions had stated the McKinley administration's attitude fully and accurately, and the two American military representatives on the first commission, Captains Mahan and

[1] *Proceedings, 1899,* p. 272.

Crozier, were in accord with their government, but they interpreted the delegation's instructions more strictly than Secretary Hay intended. They saw dangers in utterly harmless resolutions. The blunt, undiplomatic vigor with which Crozier and Mahan maintained what they thought to be correct policy dismayed Ambassador White, yet the latter always yielded to Mahan's cold arguments. White was a member of the first commission and one of its honorary presidents, but he left presentation of American views on armaments entirely to Mahan and Crozier. Through their efforts the United States soon stood forth as one of the powers most interested in defeating the czar's arms proposals.

I

The first four of the Muraviev circular's eight points formed the agenda for the first commission. The initial point, which called for suspending increases in military and naval effectives and budgets, was the most controversial of the four, and at Beernaert's suggestion the commission postponed that point until two subcommissions had time to discuss the second, third, and fourth points.[2] The full commission did not meet between May 26 and June 22. Meanwhile a subcommission on land armaments and a naval subcommission held five meetings each in which they buried most of the Russian proposals. Beernaert as chairman of the first subcommission and Karnebeek presiding over the second may well have felt that their tasks were difficult, for both were anxious to promote peace whereas most members of their groups were military and naval officers interested in better ways for waging war. Only the Russian representatives had detailed proposals and they presented them poorly. Like De Staal and other members of their delegation they had no experience in parliamentary bodies. Colonel Gilinsky, czarist spokesman in the first subcommission, had been an attaché with the Spanish army in Cuba. He was fully acquainted with the horrors of the most recent war, yet he made little use of this knowledge to promote

[2] *Ibid.*, pp. 273–275.

his sovereign's pacific objectives. He presented his arguments without enthusiasm.[3]

The second article in the Muraviev circular had called on the nations "to prohibit the use in the armies and fleets of any new kind of firearms whatever, and of new explosives, or any powders more powerful than those now in use, either for rifles or cannon." [4] In the opening meeting of the first subcommission on May 26, Gilinsky stressed his government's interest in this point. He urged prohibition of new guns for a term of years; particularly was he anxious that nothing be done to turn existing guns into automatic weapons. Gilinsky was so concerned about this possibility—not directly stated in the Muraviev circular—that he failed to mention his government's desire to outlaw new explosives and powders. Captain Crozier, listening to unfavorable reactions to Gilinsky's efforts, turned discussion to that topic. He observed that prohibition on new powders could run counter to the Russian wish to reduce military expenditure, for new powders could prove less expensive—and more effective—than those in use. The co-inventor of the Buffington-Crozier gun carriage did not intend to permit restriction on military invention if he could help it.

Beernaert saw that no progress could be made unless the delegates stated their positions on restriction of guns. Asking his colleagues to declare their views, he received a variety of answers; most delegates tried to make it appear that their governments favored restriction—with reservations which would nullify the restriction. Only the Siamese, Persians, and Bulgarians were willing to accept the czarist proposal in entirety. Only the Serbian and American delegates rejected it completely. Crozier lessened the bluntness of his statement by announcing that the United States had no present intention of changing its small arms.[5]

[3] Crozier to Corbin, July 19, 1899, copy in Hay Papers; New York *Times*, June 27, 1899.

[4] From the translation in James B. Scott, *The Hague Peace Conferences*, II, 4.

[5] *Proceedings, 1899*, pp. 331–336.

Despite unfavorable reaction to Gilinsky's first efforts, the Russians did not immediately abandon their proposals on guns. They made more strenuous attempts to win acceptance of their views. At the second meeting of the subcommission, on May 29, Colonel Count Barantzew of the Russian army presented an elaborate plan to limit the weights and calibers of small guns, weights and velocity of bullets, and rapidity of fire. Only the Netherlands General J. C. C. den Beer Poortugael gave him support, by proposing a more general statement which would have allowed improvements in existing guns. Poortugael became a more effective exponent of the czarist proposals than were the Russians. On one occasion he spoke so eloquently that the subcommission voted to have his speech printed. But admiration was all Den Beer Poortugael obtained. The Russian and Dutch proposals were lost in a mire of reservation and objection.[6]

Turning to artillery, the czar's representatives found the subcommission as intractable as in regard to small arms. Because the Russian government had first conceived the idea of a conference while worrying about Austro-Hungarian plans for new, rapid-fire field guns, one would expect to find the Russians making their strongest effort to secure restriction on those guns. This they did not do. They appeared little concerned about this problem. Gilinsky, while asking for an agreement not to change existing cannon, declared that armies which had not yet adopted the new guns should be permitted to do so. Most delegates seemed favorable to this mild restriction, but when Beernaert reminded them of the principle involved, namely renunciation of the right to change weapons for a period of time, they reversed themselves. All delegations with exception of the Belgians and Russians cast negative votes. The Belgians and Russians failed to vote.[7]

It did appear necessary to secure agreement at least on some point relating to the second point of the Muraviev circular, and opportunity to do this appeared at the first session of the sub-

<hr />

[6] *Ibid.*, pp. 337–338, 349–353.   [7] *Ibid.*, pp. 311–332, 339–341.

commission. While discussing restriction on small arms, Colonel Künzli of the Swiss delegation asked if it would not be wise to prohibit projectiles which cause extremely painful wounds. He referred to the notorious dumdum bullets used by the British in Africa and India.[8] The British had found the dumdums, as originally designed, to have inadequate "stopping power" and to make the bullets effective they had perforated their casings. The perforated bullets expanded in the bodies of victims, causing wounds which were often denounced for their needless cruelty. A German professor had conducted experiments with expanding bullets which seemed to confirm those accusations. General Poortugael favored Künzli's proposal, and the Russians, never reluctant to embarrass Englishmen, took up the suggestion.

No topic before the subcommittee on land armaments created more interest. With relief a majority of the military delegates discovered that here was something on which they could agree— and at the same time have the pleasure of making the British uncomfortable. General Sir John Ardagh, the chief British military delegate, fought to prevent this aspersion on his country, although at first he pretended to take little notice of it. When Gilinsky and Künzli presented texts for a declaration outlawing the dumdum, Ardagh even accepted the Russian text *ad referendum*.[9] As discussion warmed, he abandoned his conciliatory attitude. At the third session of the subcommittee, on May 31, he told his colleagues some unpleasant truths about fighting savages:

> In civilized war a soldier penetrated by a small projectile is wounded, withdraws to the ambulance, and does not advance any further. It is very different with a savage. Even though pierced two or three times, he does not cease to march forward, does not call upon the hospital attendants, but continues on, and before anyone has time to explain to him that he is flagrantly violating the decision of the Hague Conference, he cuts off your head.[10]

The subcommission nonetheless voted to prohibit expanding bullets. Even Captain Crozier found himself supporting a restric-

[8] *Ibid.*, p. 332.   [9] *Ibid.*, p. 338.   [10] *Ibid.*, p. 343.

tive declaration. Only Ardagh voted against it. The Austro-Hungarian delegate abstained from the vote. The first subcommission's actions on the second point of the Muraviev circular had been devoid of serious achievement—the restrictions on dumdums had been more anti-British than antiarmament.

Turning to the third point, the group found a subject on which something could be done. That point called for agreement "to restrict the use in military warfare of the formidable explosives already existing, and to prohibit the throwing of projectiles or explosives of any kind from balloons or by any similar means." [11] The first clause of this point caused no difficulty; everyone except the Russians and a few minor powers opposed restriction of existing explosives; the matter was quickly forgotten. The subject of balloons, however, was intriguing.

Balloons had been used in warfare only for observation before 1899. There had been suggestions that they might be used for throwing projectiles, and some individuals had predicted that such use would turn them into inhuman military devices. Few delegates regarded the balloon as having much military potential. Why not restrict the use of something no one would want to use?

Nor did the delegates show much concern about "any similar means." Of course everyone knew that experiments with heavier-than-air flying ships were in progress. Samuel P. Langley of the Smithsonian Institution was attempting to build an airplane for the American army, but he was meeting with slight success.[12] At no time did members of the land armaments subcommission mention his work or that of other experimenters with heavier-than-air flying craft. In fact only Colonel Gross von Schwarzhoff

[11] Scott, II, 4.

[12] The American government was perhaps more interested than any other government in the military possibilities of aircraft. President McKinley had asked Langley to build an airship for the War Department, and Congress in 1898 had appropriated $50,000 for that purpose (Archibald Black, *The Story of Flying* [New York, 1940], pp. 46–47; Charles H. Gibbs-Smith, *The Aeroplane: An Historical Survey of Its Origins and Development* [London, 1960], pp. 26–27).

of the German delegation expressed interest in the czarist proposal's ambiguous closing phrase. He feared that it could be construed as applying to mortars and other high-firing guns and he thought it wise to limit the prohibition to five years.

The subcommission approved almost unanimously a draft declaration to prohibit throwing projectiles from balloons or similar devices. Even Schwarzhoff voted without reservation, but other delegates were not so cooperative. General Ardagh abstained from the vote, and Colonel Coanda of Rumania voted for the declaration with the proviso that it be limited to five years.[13]

Again Captain Crozier voted for restriction in an area in which new inventions might occur, but in a subsequent meeting he reopened discussion, wishing the prohibition limited to five years. He explained his change of front in words which set forth the American attitude toward any restriction on invention. He said:

We are without experience in the use of arms whose employment we propose to prohibit forever. Granting that practical means of using balloons can be invented, who can say that such an invention will not be of a kind to make its use possible at a critical point on the field of battle, at a critical moment of the conflict, under conditions so defined and concentrated that it would decide the victory and thus partake of the quality possessed by all perfected arms of localizing at important points the destruction of life and property and of sparing the sufferings of all who are not at the precise spot where the result is decided. Such use tends to diminish the evils of war and to support the humanitarian considerations we have in view.

Nothing came of this effort. After Crozier had explained his belief in the humanitarian qualities of more effective means for killing, Beernaert prevented reconsideration of the declaration by observing that the subcommission had already disposed of the matter. If he wanted to bring it up again he could do so before the full commission. Beernaert did consent to inclusion of Crozier's speech in the subcommittee's minutes.[14]

[13] *Proceedings, 1899*, pp. 341–342   [14] *Ibid.*, pp. 353–355.

2

In the second subcommission, as in the first, the second point in the czarist circular was a major topic of debate. Russia's Captain Scheine in the group's first meeting on the afternoon of May 26 called for a halt in new firearms and explosives. Like Gilinsky in the first subcommission he was at first unprepared to offer a specific plan for attaining his government's wishes, but this fact did not delay objections. At once the delegation demanded explanation of the term "new firearms." Scheine said that the term should mean "an entirely new type" and that it did not apply to weapons transformed and improved. This generous interpretation of the phrase satisfied few delegates. Mahan thought that a new type should be considered "an acquired notion" and that the subcommission should examine independently whether they wished to prohibit new inventions. The British delegate, Admiral Sir John Fisher, protested that restriction on new weapons could work to the disadvantage of civilized nations in war against less civilized people and savage tribes. The Englishman thought it impossible to restrict invention of new weapons without establishing a committee of control, but feared that the nations would consider such a body a threat to their sovereignty. Admiral Péphau of France and Captain Siegel of Germany immediately declared that a committee of control could not be established. The idea died, as Fisher perhaps intended it to do.

Karnebeek brought up the question of explosives. He thought it would be easier to reach agreement on new explosives than to outlaw firearms. Fisher and Péphau disabused him of this idea. No nation, they said, was willing to reveal the composition of its explosives, and without this knowledge as a starting point nothing could be done. Karnebeek pressed on to discuss limitation of existing explosives, but it was plain that the Russians could expect no more for this restriction than for prohibition on new inventions. It was becoming obvious that subsequent meetings of the second commission would result only in rejection of the czarist proposals.

Despite the discouraging trend of the subcommission's first meeting, Scheine worked out a plan for arresting invention in naval guns, which he presented to the group on May 29. His scheme was as elaborate as that for limiting small arms which Barantzew was presenting to the first subcommission on that same day. It met an identical fate; Scheine was no more effective in debate than Gilinsky or Barantzew. Indeed Péphau made stronger efforts to secure agreement than did Scheine. The French admiral suggested a general statement prohibiting for a short time any radical changes in naval guns. This declaration could easily have been interpreted by naval powers to please themselves, yet few were willing to adopt even this measure and it was abandoned.[15]

Siegel, Fisher, Captain Sakamoto of Japan, and Captain Hjul-hammar of Sweden found fault with the Russian and French proposals, but few people in the subcommission were more adroit in opposition than Captain Mahan. Scheine's plan among other things called for limitation on gun calibers, and Mahan took responsibility for defeating this part of the proposal. He pointed out that if calibers were limited it would also be logical to limit armor plate. Hearing Mahan advance this idea, Karnebeek praised him. Such praise was premature. If the Dutch diplomat thought that Mahan was in favor of extending limitation to armor he was mistaken, for after several delegates had expressed views on the subject the American said he doubted they could discuss armor after all, for it was not on the program.[16]

Russian representatives were not as much concerned as Mahan about agenda for the first commission's program. Realizing that Scheine's scheme had failed, they devised another and in this plan incorporated a restriction on thickness of armor plate. The new plan seemed more detailed and complex than the earlier. Its complexity must have delighted the subcommission, for Mahan, Siegel, Count de Serallo of Spain, and even Péphau found it an

[15] *Ibid.*, pp. 359–364.   [16] *Ibid.*, p. 364.

excuse for agreeing to nothing. Again the Russians had failed.[17]

Failure to attain agreement under the second heading of the Muraviev circular was not complete; poison gas proved a convenient weapon to outlaw, even as in the first subcommission the dumdum bullet proved a useful subject for prohibitive declaration. At the third meeting of the naval subcommittee Karnebeek asked Scheine if his government intended to frame a restriction on new explosives. Apparently the Russians had decided to make no strong effort in this direction, for Scheine's answer was negative, but he did state that his government desired outlawing of projectiles containing explosives which could spread "asphyxiating and deleterious gases."

Here was an interesting subject, in view of what happened in the First World War. Prior to 1899 poisonous gas had not been used in warfare. Certain experts had suggested it, but many famous military and naval leaders thought otherwise. Even Sir John Fisher believed gas an unlikely weapon, and the British admiral was willing to support prohibition against asphyxiating gas provided that the restriction related only to such gases. Mahan opposed the Russian idea. Admitting that he had made no study of explosives, the American declared that asphyxiating gases might prove more humane than projectiles which killed or crippled by tearing the body, and he observed that poisonous gases could produce decisive results. Within the American delegation Mahan's stand caused some controversy. White, always desirous of advancing humane practices in warfare, wished to support the prohibition, but Mahan had his way. Determined to support no kind of restriction on invention, he alone in the naval subcommission opposed the declaration.[18]

The third point in the Muraviev circular did not concern the naval subcommission, for balloons seemed less applicable to naval warfare than to land engagements. The fourth point, however,

[17] *Ibid.*, pp. 371–374.
[18] *Ibid.*, pp. 365–367; A. D. White, Diary excerpt, June 22, 1899, *Autobiog.*, II, 319–320.

was exclusively the concern of the naval experts. That point read: "To prohibit the use, in naval warfare, of submarine torpedo boats or plungers or other similar engines of destruction; to give an undertaking not to construct, in the future, vessels with rams." [19]

This point promised extensive debate. In fact, it was disposed of with little discussion. The result was entirely negative.

Submarines had been rarely used, by 1899, and their future did not seem promising. The Russian representatives had no specific proposal for prohibiting them; they merely declared that Russia would not introduce submarine torpedo boats if other powers would not. British, German, Italian, and Japanese representatives also believed their governments willing to adopt such restriction, provided it were unanimous. The Austro-Hungarian and French delegates thought that submarines could have large defensive uses, and the delegates from small powers were quick to side with them, for they recognized the importance of any primarily defensive weapon. Mahan expressed no opinion as to defensive or offensive value of submarines; he announced that his government wished full liberty to use them. So many were the objections that Karnebeek made no attempt to bring a restrictive declaration to a formal vote.

The subcommission gave slightly more attention to rams, for this device was a weapon which had occasionally appeared in naval warfare since ancient times. It also was easier to discuss weapons with rather extensive histories than those which had not advanced beyond the experimental stage. When the matter first arose, Scheine as usual was ready with no specific proposal, but Karnebeek after listening carefully to the preliminary discussion proposed to prohibit rams but not existing ram-equipped ships or those under construction, nor ships merely equipped with bows re-enforced to withstand shock. Only on this occasion did Mahan favor a restrictive measure. He thought that Karnebeek's proposal should be acceptable—if it could be uni-

[19] Scott, II, 4.

versally accepted. British, Japanese, and French delegates held similar opinions. Captain Siegel made no statement as to whether the German government would accept a prohibitive declaration, but he dwelt on the impossibility of changing construction plans then underway. Count Soltyk of Austria-Hungary, alone of representatives from major powers, declared that his naval high command would not commit itself on this question. The Scandinavian delegates protested against restriction, for they thought it would be harmful to small powers likely to wage defensive warfare. These objections destroyed possibility of agreement, and without protest from Scheine the subcommission ended its discussion on rams.[20]

3

The subcommissions presented their reports to the full commission on June 22. At that meeting and at another on the following day the commission considered prohibitions against expanding bullets, asphyxiating gases, and throwing of projectiles from balloons. General Ardagh made another effort to have the bullet resolution less specific. Captain Crozier, regretting his vote for that resolution in the subcommission, supported the Englishman's demand. Their arguments failed, and only Britain and the United States voted against the declaration. Crozier again demanded a five-year limit on the resolution against throwing projectiles from balloons. This time he received support from the British, French, and Rumanian delegates, and the commission yielded to his demands. Mahan, too, found it necessary to present some of his views to the full commission; despite entreaties from other delegates he stuck to his position on asphyxiating gas; only the American delegation cast a negative vote on that restriction.[21]

There followed considerable speech making. After the declarations prepared in the subcommissions had been adopted, Beernaert at the meeting of June 23 tried to obtain agreements

[20] *Proceedings, 1899*, pp, 367–369.   [21] *Ibid.*, pp. 276–281, 283–284.

to prohibit submarines and warships equipped with rams. Failing, he opened discussion on the first point in Muraviev circular. The Belgian statesman lauded Nicholas II for his grand design, and then asked De Staal to speak. The president of the conference ignored the sad record of the first commission as he called upon it to adopt a plan for holding down military budgets and the size of armies and navies. The aging diplomat emphasized the reasonableness of his government's proposal:

Is it necessary for me to declare that we are not speaking of Utopias or chimerical measures? We are not considering disarmament. What we are hoping for, is to attain a limitation—a halt in the ascending course of armaments and expenses. We propose this with the conviction that if such an agreement is established, progress in other directions will be made—slowly perhaps, but surely. Immobility is an impossibility in history, and if we shall only be able for some years to provide for a certain stability, everything points to the belief that a tendency toward a diminution of military charges will be able to grow and to develop. Such a movement would correspond entirely to the ideas which have inspired the Russian circulars.[22]

Nothing came of this effort. Such a movement would not have corresponded entirely to the ideas which had inspired the Russian circulars, but there were few individuals in the conference who believed that the Russians were moved either by humanitarianism or common sense. Only General den Beer Poortugael in a stirring speech supported De Staal. Other delegates were interested in giving this most spectacular proposal a decent funeral. This they did, although it required three more full meetings to complete the obsequies.

Gilinsky and Scheine presented proposals of their government—simple, clear-cut programs, contrasting favorably to their complex and confusing proposals on guns. Gilinsky asked no increases for five years in armies and military budgets and a limit to the troops maintained by all governments in time of peace, excluding only colonial troops. Scheine's proposal was

[22] *Ibid.*, p. 301.

more modest. He asked that governments determine their naval budgets for a three-year period and that they refrain from increasing the total sums of their budgets during that period. He also asked for advance publication during that same period of total warship tonnages, numbers of officers and men, and the expenses of coastal fortifications. As soon as Scheine had presented this plan, the commission adjourned for the day.[23]

Two days elapsed before the commission met, and those days were busy for all delegates who planned to vote against the czarist proposals. Within the American delegation there was much discussion about the Russian plans. There was no doubt as to the American attitude: the United States would agree to no part of them. Mahan and Crozier secured permission from their colleagues to abstain from voting or even from entering into discussion on naval limitation.[24] Both Mahan and Crozier prepared speeches should it prove necessary to defend the American position.[25]

But the American delegates worried needlessly about the czarist proposals, for other military and naval officers determined that no agreement should be reached, and objections of only one man were sufficient to wreck the Russian efforts. At the June 25 meeting Colonel von Schwarzhoff of Germany in a ten-minute speech refuted all the Russian arguments and scorned the idea that armaments were ruinous to his country. "I have no mandate to speak for my honored colleagues," he said,

but as far as Germany is concerned, I can reassure her friends completely and dissipate all benevolent anxiety regarding her. The German people are not crushed beneath the weight of expenditures, and taxes; they are not hanging on the edge of the precipice, they are not hastening towards exhaustion and ruin. Quite the contrary; public and private wealth is increasing, the general welfare, and *standard of life*, are rising from year to year. As for compulsory

[23] *Ibid.*, pp. 302–306.
[24] American Commission, Minutes, June 27, 1899.
[25] Crozier to Corbin, July 19, 1899, Hay Papers.

military service, which is intimately associated with these questions, the German does not regard it as a heavy burden, but as a sacred and patriotic duty, to the performance of which he owes his existence, his prosperity, his future.[26]

Crozier and Mahan did not have to use their speeches.

Newspapers around the world described the Schwarzhoff speech as a sudden, dramatic surprise. Few members of the commission were much surprised. They had not expected the Germans to reveal their feelings so boldly and quickly, but Schwarzhoff had stated with honesty what everyone knew to be the common position.[27]

Gilinsky sought to answer Schwarzhoff, but it would have been better had he kept quiet. The commission referred the czarist proposals to its military members for technical examination. Those individuals—with the exception of the Russian military and naval delegates—concluded that limitation was impractical.[28] The commission had to admit failure, but it did make a gesture designed to help the Russians save prestige. It unanimously adopted a resolution framed by Léon Bourgeois of the French delegation that restriction of military charges would be "extremely desirable for the increase of the material and moral welfare of mankind." [29]

Adopting the Bourgeois resolution, the first commission virtually had completed its work. Preparation and adoption of reports remained. In trying sessions the commission had defeated the primary objective which the Russians had announced for calling the conference. There had resulted a few meaningless restrictions on armaments, and even those restrictions had passed with difficulty.

[26] *Proceedings, 1899*, pp. 308–309.

[27] Crozier to Corbin, July 19, 1899, Hay Papers.

[28] *Proceedings, 1899*, pp. 89, 313, 315, 358. Captain Crozier was one of the experts called upon to examine the Russian proposals, but in his report to the American delegation he made no mention of his work in this connection. For this report, see Scott, II, 29–35.

[29] *Proceedings, 1899*, p. 319.

IX

The Rules for War

WHILE the first commission was ending its talks on armaments, the second commission was concluding its work on the laws of war, finishing at about the same time as the first group. But it presented a comprehensive report to the full conference long before either of the other commissions. The report included texts of two proposed international conventions. One extended the Geneva rules of 1864 to maritime war, while the other revised the Brussels Declaration of 1874 on the laws and customs of war.[1]

These proposals seemed likely to find acceptance in the conference. There was no skepticism about the second commission's objectives such as that which had wrecked the czar's proposals on armaments. An international agreement on war regulations and protection for victims of marine battles seemed eminently practical. During the preceding half-century there had been attempts to codify the laws of war and to assure humane treatment for the sick and wounded and prisoners of war. Drawing up its conventions, the second commission therefore faced no new problems and could simply bring to conclusion a work long in progress.

[1] *Proceedings, 1899,* pp. 27–44.

I

Many members of the first commission also served in the second committee, and many of the military and naval experts attended its sessions, but these individuals did not dominate the meetings of the second commission as they did the first, for the international lawyers regarded the second commission as their special responsibility. Under their guidance the second commission produced some of the peace conference's most important documents.

The most famous international lawyer at The Hague was Professor Feodor de Martens of St. Petersburg. Author of numerous books on the law of nations, Martens had represented Russia in several international conferences and for years had been a counselor of the czarist foreign ministry. Twenty-five years before he had taken part in the Brussels Conference called by Alexander II to codify the laws and customs of war. It was fitting that Martens should preside over the second commission and its second subcommittee charged with revision of the still unratified Brussels rules. These tasks he performed well; he was soon recognized as the strongest person in the Russian delegation.

Duties in the second commission were part of Martens' work that summer. He was his government's spokesman in the third commission. Moreover, when the conference slowed, he rushed off to Paris, where he was presiding over the arbitral court trying the Venezuela–British Guiana boundary dispute.[2]

There were other experts in international law on the second commission. Among them were Professors Louis Renault of Paris, Heinrich Lammasch of Vienna, Baron Karl von Stengel of Munich, Philipp Zorn of Koenigsberg, and T. M. C. Asser, a Hollander who was at the time president of the Institute of

[2] Frequently sittings of the Paris arbitration tribunal were delayed by Martens' activities at The Hague, to the annoyance of the chief counsel for Venezuela, former President Benjamin Harrison (Harrison to J. M. Quigley, June 23, 1899, and Harrison to W. H. H. Miller, June 23, 1899, Benjamin Harrison Papers, deposited in the Library of Congress).

International Law. At the first meeting of the second commission Martens honored Asser by nominating him for the presidency of the first subcommission, and the Dutch scholar received unanimous election.

It was unfortunate that two of the greatest maritime powers, Great Britain and the United States, had no eminent lawyers on a commission which was to spend much time on rules for sea warfare. General Ardagh and Admiral Fisher in the second committee, as in the first, represented Britain. Mahan and Crozier bore primary responsibility for presenting American views in the second group, while at the same time they were so zealously guarding their nation's armaments in the first commission. It had not been intended that Crozier and Mahan should have such heavy burdens, for Newel, too, was a member of the second commission. As a lawyer that diplomat should have been able to contribute to the group's discussions, but at no time did he say anything in the commission—or any other part of the conference—which reporters thought worthy of recording.

White, while content to leave most of the work in the second commission to Mahan and Crozier, kept an eye on their activities. Since youth he had revered the name of the Dutch pioneer in international law, Grotius, and he was delighted to think that the conference could realize some of his hero's ideals. The second commission was important to White for another reason: only through its sessions could he hope to make another effort to present American proposals for exempting private property, not contraband, from capture in naval wars. It was obvious that if those proposals were presented at all he would have to take charge, for Mahan, who was the logical person to present them, considered the traditional American views on private property outmoded and unrealistic. The captain was willing to join in formal presentation of the delegation's demands, but intended to do nothing that might indicate personal approval. Despite Mahan's arguments, White remained convinced of the righteousness of traditional American views toward private property. Rebuffs he received on this subject during the first week of the conference did not lessen his determination to bring the matter up again. He decided to wait until the struggle for a permanent court in the third commission seemed near victory before making another attempt in behalf of private property at sea.[3]

2

While White waited, Mahan found much to do in the second commission's first subcommittee. That group's program called for discussion of the fifth and sixth articles in the Muraviev circular. The first article proposed extension of the Geneva rules to the sea, on the basis of the Additional Articles of 1868; the sixth article called for neutralization of all lifesaving ships and boats. The Russian foreign minister had needlessly separated these topics, for the unratified Additional Articles of 1868 included provision both for extension of the Geneva rules and for neutralization of hospital ships and lifesaving craft. The Additional Articles were so comprehensive that the subcommission's work was essentially revision of them. Their existence probably accounts for the fact that the subcommittee completed its deliberations more rapidly than any other division of the conference. It required only five meetings between May 25 and June 15 for lawyers and naval experts to agree on a new convention, in many respects like the Additional Articles.[4]

At first it seemed that small quarrels about competency of the conference on certain subjects would hinder extension of the Geneva rules. Colonel Gilinsky presented Russian proposals to a plenary meeting of the commission on May 25; he called for

[3] A. D. White, Diary excerpt, June 19, 1899, *Autobiog.*, II, 317; Low to McKinley, June 13, 1899, McKinley Papers.

[4] For the slight differences between the convention and the Additional Articles, consult *Proceedings, 1899*, pp. 31–44, and A. van Daehne van Varick, *Documents Relating to the Program of the First Hague Peace Conference Laid before the Conference by the Netherland Government* (Oxford, 1921), pp. 27–30.

revision of the Geneva Convention and establishment of an International Red Cross Bureau to supervise volunteer medical assistance and relief in wartime. These proposals troubled the Swiss, for they had proprietary interest in the Geneva Convention and disliked the idea of a revision they had not initiated. The chief Swiss delegate, Edouard Odier, pointed out that revision would require medical and sanitary experts and presence of representatives of all signatory governments. Faced with these arguments, Martens declared that the subcommission must limit itself to topics in the Muraviev circular; in effect the president of the commission ruled against his compatriot.[5]

The conference had to leave the Geneva Convention untouched, but the second commission's naval subcommittee had little difficulty incorporating its principles, together with provisions from the Additional Articles, into an agreement guaranteeing humane treatment for the wounded and prisoners of war at sea. It was easy, too, to decide upon markings for hospital ships, for the Additional Articles provided an excellent system. There was only one small difficulty. The Turks and Persians demanded the right to use a crescent instead of a red cross. Mahan tried to compromise between Moslems and Christians by suggesting a device with no religious meaning to replace the red cross. Neither the Moslems nor Mahan could get the subcommittee to act, for it was pointed out that the Geneva Convention recognized only the red cross on land; it seemed wise to use the same emblem at sea. The Moslems made it clear that no red-cross flag would fly from ships sent to relieve their sailors.[6]

The subcommission encountered its most serious problem in determining the status of relief ships outfitted by private benevolent groups or neutral powers. The Russians and the French thought that such ships should be under authority of a belligerent. Mahan went farther; he declared that such a ship ought to fly a belligerent flag as requirement for admission to a battle area. No one agreed with the American delegate. It was said that

[5] *Proceedings, 1899*, pp. 385–386.   [6] *Ibid.*, pp. 454, 461.

such a regulation would infringe on the sovereignty of neutral governments which had registered relief vessels. The subcommission decided that neutral relief ships would carry commissions from one belligerent while reporting their names to other warring governments.[7]

So rapidly did the subcommission work that at its second meeting Asser appointed Fisher, Renault, Scheine, and Siegel to a *comité de rédaction* to prepare a draft convention. Renault did most of the work, for he was a far more experienced writer than the three naval officers who served with him, and on June 13 he presented to the subcommission a draft containing ten articles. Most members of the subcommission were satisfied, but the report failed to please Mahan. Reading his copy, the American commissioner found fault with its sixth article that neutral ships having on board persons sick, wounded, or shipwrecked could not be captured for carrying them but could be captured if violating neutrality. Mahan did not take issue with what he found in the article but with what he did not find. He thought the status of men rescued by neutral ships should be determined. A veteran of the Civil War, he remembered the rescue of the "Alabama's" captain and crew by the British yacht "Deerhound," and that those men had been declared under protection of the neutral British flag. To Mahan it seemed unfair that victors should be robbed of their captives in such a manner. Mahan could not convince the subcommittee that it should add to the sixth article, but it was agreed that he should appear before the *comité de rédaction* prior to revision of the draft convention.

While waiting to appear the captain found another questionable omission. The sixth article concerned neutral merchantmen which entered a battle zone by accident, and Mahan now found that the third article failed to define the status of men picked up by hospital ships flying neutral flags. He could hardly believe he had overlooked this error, but now that he could aim

[7] *Ibid.*, pp. 391–392, 462–471.

attacks at two articles he seemed to have a stronger case. He had no more success with the *comité de rédaction* than with the full subcommission. Two hours of discussion failed altogether to make the changes he desired.[8]

At the last meeting of the subcommission, on June 15, he repeated his demands, but declared in a spirit of conciliation that he would not insist on them and would advise his government to accept the proposed convention.

Mahan actually was far from ready to surrender. He found another article to oppose. The tenth article imposed on neutrals the obligation to guard victims of war landed at their ports so as to prevent them from reentering combat. Although the article stated that expenses for guarding and entertainment should be borne by belligerents, strong objections arose. Representatives of small states likely to be neutral in a large-scale conflict declared that the article placed too heavy an obligation on neutrals. Mahan and Japan's Ichiro Motono were the only great-power spokesmen to join delegates from minor powers in voting against the article, and, of course, they did not defeat it. Neither Motono nor Mahan explained his vote, but it is obvious that the article, like articles three and six, made it too easy in Mahan's way of thinking for seamen and their officers to escape capture.[9]

Mahan then took another tack. Speaking before a session of the full second commission on June 20, he defended his stand and proposed additions to the convention. He urged that sick, wounded, or shipwrecked belligerent personnel on board any kind of neutral ship be given up to their enemies on demand. If no demand came, Mahan said, then those individuals should remain in neutral custody for remainder of the conflict. At the request of Asser and Renault, Martens referred Mahan's pro-

[8] Mahan gave a full account of his difficulties with the *comité de rédaction* in a report to the American delegation, dated July 31, 1899. For this report see James B. Scott, *The Hague Peace Conferences*, II, 39–44.

[9] *Proceedings, 1899*, p. 471.

posals to the *comité de rédaction* with instruction to consider them and report back to the commission.[10] The *comité de rédaction* never reported on the Mahan articles.

A plenary meeting of the conference on June 20 provisionally adopted the draft convention without mention of them, and it seemed unlikely that further action would be taken. Apparently few persons cared much for Mahan's opinions, although he was the best-known naval authority present.

3

Mahan's role in the first subcommission stood in sharp contrast to Crozier's participation—or lack of participation—in the second subcommission. That group met eleven times between May 25 and June 20, and the American rarely took part in its discussions. One might have expected him to have much to say, for this group debated the seventh Muraviev topic—a call for revision of the Brussels Declaration on laws and customs of war—and the United States had pioneered in codification of those laws and customs. During the Civil War, Francis Lieber of Columbia College had written a code which the Union army issued as "General Order No. 100." Martens told the subcommittee that the American code had inspired much of the work of the Brussels Conference of 1874, yet Crozier said nothing to indicate American interest in an international code.[11] Evidently he had come to The Hague without copies of General Order No. 100 and its revisions. On June 13 he wired Washington for them.[12] After receiving copies he did little but compare decisions of the conference with his army's code so that he could write his report.

While Crozier listened, the second subcommission revised the laws of war in the Declaration of Brussels. Only when discussion turned to invasions did Crozier take interest. Delegates

[10] *Ibid.*, pp. 391–392.   [11] *Ibid.*, pp. 505–506.
[12] Crozier to Corbin, June 13, 1899, files of the Adjutant General's office, deposited in the National Archives.

from small states, led by Beernaert of Belgium, held out for utmost protection for invaded populations, while the Germans demanded as few restrictions as possible. Crozier later wrote that in this matter he "took the guiding principle that the United States itself did not fear invasion but could afford to be as humane towards invaded countries as anybody." [13] He voted with small-power delegates to suppress those articles of the Brussels Declaration which offended them—and some of those articles were suppressed.

In only one other respect did Crozier make a contribution to discussions on the laws of war. The thirteenth article of the Brussels Declaration among other things forbade unnecessary seizure and destruction of enemy property. When this clause came before the subcommittee on June 1, Crozier brought up the question of private property at sea. He stated that he knew the group could not debate the matter, since they were charged only with the laws of war on land, but he asked that the subject be referred to another division of the conference. Martens hedged, and why should he not? Already he had tried to convince the Americans that private property at sea, since the Muraviev circular did not mention it, was beyond the scope of the conference. Yet Martens' resistance was wearing down, for he permitted Crozier's remarks to be included in the minutes and said that the full commission would decide whether to propose that the conference take up the subject.[14]

4

White was disturbed when he learned of Martens' reaction. Did this mean that the time had come to push proposals on private property? Talking the matter over with other American delegates, White decided to wait, for the arbitration court plans were far from secure. While he waited, the ambassador at-

[13] Crozier to Corbin, July 19, 1899, Hay Papers.
[14] *Proceedings, 1899*, pp. 491–492; American Commission, Minutes, June 1, 1899.

tempted to win support. He talked with everyone who would listen. He found that the chief objection was that while immunity for private property, not contraband, was acceptable—who could define contraband satisfactorily? White passed on. Only one representative of a great power, Count Münster, promised support, and this promise the ambassador distrusted, for he feared that the Germans were trying to drive a wedge between Britain and America. There was unquestionably sincere support from the Dutch and Swedes. White had long talks with their delegates, and they advised him that the best way to get the matter before the conference would be to send De Staal a memorial.

White decided to follow this advice. Consulting the Dutch, Scandinavians, and Germans, he carefully prepared his petition. By the time he had completed that document, success seemed certain, and on June 24 he sent the memorial to De Staal.[15]

Evidently the memorial broke down Russian objections to letting the Americans say what they wished about private property, for at its last meeting on July 5 Martens called the second commission's attention to White's letter. From Martens' kind words one would never have suspected how he had tried to ignore the subject. He recalled that Russia had expressed sympathy for the idea as early as 1823, and he declared that it deserved everyone's interest. Was it possible for the conference to settle the question? Martens said that it was not possible, and the subject should be referred to a later conference.

The chief British delegate, Pauncefote, had no desire to discuss private property at the Peace Conference or any other conference, but it is apparent that he disliked Martens' method of disposing of the subject, for he suggested that the commission vote on whether it could debate the question. White declared that the conference had already discussed subjects not on the Russian program and that it could, if it wished, also talk about

[15] White, Diary excerpts, June 3, 5, 13, 15, *Autobiog.*, II, 287, 290, 296, 297, 301.

private property. He proposed that a plenary session of the conference decide the question of competency. At the same time he virtually conceded defeat by agreeing with Martens that the moment for debate was not opportune. It was well that White made no strong effort to force discussion, for the commission voted only to recommend that the conference adopt a formal recommendaton, or *voeu,* that a future conference consider the matter.[16]

That same day a plenary meeting of the conference adopted the second commission's report on the laws and customs of war, and proceeded to minor problems connected with that commission's work. Among these lesser questions was that *voeu* on private property. Martens moved that the *voeu* be adopted, and White in a seconding speech explained the reasons for his country's interest in the subject. Of course the *voeu* carried, and many were the congratulations White received on his address.[17] But not everyone was happy with his remarks: Admiral Péphau told Lieutenant Colonel Charles À Court, a British military attaché, that the Americans, having destroyed the Spanish navy and commerce, only wanted to make sure that no one would destroy theirs.[18]

That insignificant *voeu* was the smallest kind of triumph, and it was one of two small triumphs for White that day, for he was instrumental in righting a wrong to Switzerland. He learned that the Dutch had been trying to usurp Swiss claims to sponsorship of future conferences on the Geneva Convention. In behalf of the Swiss the Rumanian delegate, Alexandre Beldiman, had proposed a *voeu* to prevent this misdeed. The *voeu* expressed desire that Switzerland call a conference to revise the convention. This proposal had failed, and among those voting against it was Mahan. White, learning from Beldiman the reason for the motion, prevailed upon Mahan to change his vote in the com-

---

[16] *Proceedings, 1899,* pp. 411–413.   [17] *Ibid.,* pp. 46–50.
[18] Charles À Court, note on limitation of armaments, enclosed in Pauncefote to Salisbury, July 31, 1899, *British Documents,* I, 229–231.

mission. This Mahan did, and White explained that the original vote had been due to misunderstanding. A new vote was called and the motion carried. At the plenary meeting of the commission on July 5, the ambassador was pleased by adoption of the *voeu*.[19]

As the work of the second commission drew to a close White had reason for being happy with his part in it. He had won no great victories, but he had done his best to carry out his instructions. Mahan and Crozier too were satisfied, although it is apparent that they realized that their parts in both the first and second commissions had been negative, for late in the conference Crozier wrote General Corbin:

Mahan and I have had little or no constructive work, that has nearly all fallen to the lot of the people attending to arbitration, but we have had to be constantly on guard that something unfavorable to the United States should not find its way into the agreements. Sentinel duty is fatiguing.[20]

[19] White, Diary excerpts, June 30 and July 5, 1899, *Autobiog.*, II, 324–326, 328; *Proceedings, 1899*, pp. 393–394.
[20] July 19, 1899, Hay Papers.

X

Mediation

MOST delegates seemed to ignore the failures of the first commission and the easy, undramatic successes of the second commission. They watched the third committee. Could it bring a permanent international court? Here was the great question at The Hague, and from late May to the close of July the third commission labored to answer it.

The second meeting—the first serious session—of the third commission was scheduled to take place on the afternoon of May 26, and all the delegates anxiously awaited it. Among the American delegates, White and his colleagues hoped to present their plan for a permanent court. As the time for the meeting neared, they wavered in their decision. The first sentence in the plan's third section read: "The contracting nations will mutually agree to submit to the International Tribunal all questions of disagreement between them, excepting such as may relate to or involve their political independence or territorial integrity." [1] All members of the delegation agreed that there was no chance that the conference would approve this provision for obligatory arbitration, even with wide exceptions. Why, then propose such a thing? And if a provision of this kind should be incorporated

[1] James B. Scott, *The Hague Peace Conferences*, II, 15.

into a final treaty, would the United States Senate ratify the agreement? Remembering recent history, the delegates concluded that objection would come from every side. Indeed had a treaty with a clause like this been in force in 1898, the United States might have been bound to submit its dispute with Spain to an arbitral court. To negotiate a treaty on this basis only a year later would be a tacit admission that the Republic, if not guilty of wrong, had been at least not zealous in upholding principles of peace and international law. Such an agreement in 1899 would be impolitic. And there were other objections to the ambitious plan, all of them concerning its wording. The delegates could not present a plan features of which they considered unsatisfactory. They cabled Secretary Hay on May 24 to eliminate the obligatory features of the plan and for permission to make such changes in its text as they saw fit.[2] A reply came on the morning of May 26. To their relief the secretary of state gave permission to make changes. Of course, it was too late to alter the plan before the meeting of the third commission a few hours later.[3]

It was unfortunate that the Americans could not present their plan that day, for other advocates of arbitration quickly distinguished themselves. Hardly had the commission assembled when Bourgeois read a Russian proposal for establishing rules for mediation, arbitration, and international commissions of inquiry. The czarist plan made no provision for an international court. This omission disappointed a number of delegates, and Bourgeois shared this disappointment for he moved at once to provide an opening for exponents of a tribunal. Suggesting that they take the Russian proposal as a guide for the order and topics of deliberation, the commission president proposed that the group should also consider whether it would be preferable

[2] Telegram from the American Commission to Hay, May 24, 1899, copy in American Commission, Minutes, May 24, 1899, and dispatch from the Commission to Hay, May 26, 1899, copy in the Minutes, May 26, 1899; A. D. White, Diary excerpt, May 23, 1899, *Autobiog.*, II, 263.

[3] *Autobiog.*, May 26, 1899, pp. 271–272.

to extend arbitration by inserting arbitration clauses into international acts or by establishing an international organization which could (1) act as an intermediary, reminding disputing states of the existence and possible application of arbitrating conventions, (2) serve as a means of conciliation before beginning judicial procedure, (3) act as an international tribunal.

The commission approved Bourgeois's recommendations as its order of business, but opponents of a tribunal were chagrined to hear their president introduce the idea.

They soon had additional cause for alarm, for Sir Julian Pauncefote became unduly specific. He declared that he could not see how new codes and rules could advance their cause. "If we want to make a step forward, I believe that it is absolutely necessary to organize a permanent international tribunal which may be able to assemble at once upon the request of the disputing nations." Sir Julian asked Bourgeois to sound the commission for its views on this subject before going further.[4]

Silence greeted Pauncefote's request, and then one delegate exclaimed: "Good heavens, but things are getting serious indeed."[5] And they were. Few persons present were wholeheartedly in favor of a court, and most wished to postpone discussion of so difficult a topic as long as possible. Count Nigra said that he would be grateful to Pauncefote if he would not insist upon priority for his proposal in discussion; the Italian diplomat declared that they should follow the order of discussion agreed upon. To his support came Belgium's Beernaert, an earnest friend of arbitration, who protested that Pauncefote's proposal found the commission unprepared.

Pauncefote did not insist upon immediate discussion of proposals for a court. He said that he had only desired to learn the sentiments of the commission. Then Bourgeois suggested that since it would be difficult for the whole commission to discuss the Russian and British proposals at once, a *comité d'examen*

[4] *Proceedings, 1899*, p. 584.
[5] Manchester *Guardian*, May 27, 1899.

should give them preliminary examination. The commission agreed to this suggestion and entrusted appointment of the special committee to Bourgeois and its other officers.

The commission recessed to permit its officers to select the members of the special committee. Those officials simplified their task by limiting their choice to lawyers, and consequently only eight men received appointments: Asser of the Netherlands, Descamps of Belgium, D'Estournelles of France, Lammasch of Austria, Martens of Russia, Odier of Switzerland, Zorn of Germany, and Holls of the United States.[6]

The Russian and British proposals and appointment of the special committee had been quite enough for most delegates for one day, but before adjourning they had a further surprise. Bourgeois received a communication from De Staal supplementing the original Russian proposal by calling for an international court! Apparently the Russian representatives had waited to learn whether there would be much demand for a tribunal. Now they made known their determination not to be outdone by the British in championing peace and arbitration.[7]

At the close of the third commission's session, the special committee organized under Bourgeois's chairmanship. Descamps became reporter and president, D'Estournelles secretary, and an attaché of the French embassy, Jarousse de Sillac, acted as assistant secretary. The group resolved to follow the plan of discussion already determined by the commission. They received one new proposal—Count Nigra introduced a plan for mediation like that of the Russians except that mediation should not require suspension of preparations for war or military operations. The committee set Monday, May 29, for its next meeting and specified as the topics for that day the first six articles of the Russian draft, all of which concerned good offices and mediation.[8]

[6] The officers of the commission first asked Newel to serve on the *comité d'examen*, but he declined. Thereupon they asked Holls, who gladly accepted (Holls to Hill, May 31, 1899, Hill Papers).

[7] *Proceedings, 1899*, pp. 583–585.   [8] *Ibid.*, p. 687.

No one at first realized the importance of appointment and organization of the *comité d'examen*, for it had been expected that the third commission, unlike the other great committees, could handle its work without division into subcommittees. The *comité d'examen* became the heart of the conference. Bourgeois usually presided over its sessions, leaving Descamps little more than his job as reporter. Karnebeek, De Staal, and another distinguished Russian, Chamberlain de Basily, frequently attended, and other delegates were often invited to its sessions, usually held in the Hall of the Truce in The Hague rather than at the House in the Wood.[9]

Failure of the American delegates to present their court plan disappointed arbitration advocates, but the delegates let it be known that they would redeem themselves.[10] While Low undertook revision of its text, it was decided that Mahan, Crozier, and Newel should make no strong efforts in the other commissions until there was substantial success for arbitration.[11] There was no rush to present the plan, for mediation was certain to occupy the *comité d'examen* for a few days.

To Holls the forthcoming debate seemed a special opportunity to present his proposal for mediation by "seconding powers." He had not understood as a flat rejection Hay's refusal to incorporate the idea in the delegation's instructions, for while in London he had talked the matter over with Choate and Balfour and believed they approved. He met opposition within his delegation. Low doubted the wisdom of introducing the proposal, and Newel strongly disapproved. White sided with the secretary, and Holls had his way.[12]

[9] Frederick W. Holls, *The Peace Conference at The Hague*, pp. 169–173. Basily, while serving as consul general in Budapest, had attended sessions of the 1896 conference of the Interparliamentary Union. It was believed by some individuals that his reports on that conference had helped inspire the calling of the peace conference (Merze Tate, *Disarmament Illusion*, pp. 77, 95).

[10] Manchester *Guardian*, May 27, 1899.

[11] Holls to Hill, May 31, 1899, Hill Papers.

[12] Holls to Hill, June 5, 1899, Hill Papers.

But Holls had placed himself in a difficult position in regard to his fellow delegates. A majority of the group had come to dislike him and watched with distaste while he thrust himself to the fore. Should his project, unauthorized by the State Department, bring embarrassment, the secretary could expect difficulties with his colleagues. Even White who remained his constant friend, years later described Holls's methods as "pushing ways." [13] Animosity toward the secretary grew, a fact of which he was aware, but he concealed it until the close of the conference, writing his friends of perfect harmony within the delegation.

Taking the Russian proposals as a basis for deliberation the *comité d'examen* in two sessions, on May 29 and 31, worked out rules and definitions for good offices and mediation. These kindred practices had long been a part of diplomatic procedure. The Congress of Paris of 1856 had expressed desire that quarreling states "before taking up arms, should have recourse, in so far as circumstances would allow, to the good offices of a friendly Power." [14] Despite this declaration, there had been no instance in which powers on the verge of war had asked mediation by neutrals. There had been instances, most of them unsuccessful, in which neutral governments had offered their services, and there had been examples of neutral mediation to end wars. The Russian proposals sought to reaffirm the principle of the Declaration of Paris by calling on the nations to agree that they would ask for good offices or mediation before declaring war, "so far as circumstances admit"; the czarist program also called for a declaration that the powers "consider it useful" for neutral states to take the initiative in proposing a settlement even without invitation from a disputant. At the same time the Russians wished

[13] A. D. White to Choate, Feb. 24, 1912, Choate Papers.

[14] This *voeu* of the Congress of Paris was included by A. van Daehne van Varick in *Documents Relating to the Program of the First Hague Peace Conference*, p. 76.

to protect mediating states from suspicion of meddling by declaring that their intervention would "have strictly the character of friendly advice and no binding force whatever."

The Russian articles were largely acceptable to the *comité*, although the group rearranged and reworded them. Only one clause caused difficulty and that was the expression "so far as circumstances admit." Asser noted that this qualification had appeared in the Declaration of Paris, not in the Act of Berlin of 1885. To include it in a new convention would be a step backward. Nigra and Descamps supported the Dutch delegate, but others could not agree. Lammasch sought to retain the substance of the clause while making it less pointed. He thought it should read: "unless exceptional circumstances render this method manifestly impossible." Descamps persisted in demanding that the clause be dropped altogether, while Zorn insisted that the Russian text be retained. The Russian delegate, Martens, did not care. He sensibly observed that governments would not have recourse to good offices if circumstances did not permit. Bourgeois, implying that it was hardly fair to regard inclusion of the clause as a retrogressive step, observed that the Act of Berlin concerned only Africa. Bourgeois, Holls, and Zorn approved the Lammasch version, but those delegates favoring deletion carried the vote.

Soon the committee reversed itself. Zorn had voted for the Lammasch wording as a lesser of two evils, and lost. He announced that at the next meeting of the full commission he would propose restoration of the original Russian clause. Faced with this threat, the committee reconsidered and adopted a modification of Lammasch's language.[15]

The Russian proposals were retained, but to them were added two features. One was Count Nigra's amendment and the other was Holls's idea of "seconding powers."

Holls presented his proposal on May 29; to his delight delegate after delegate rose to offer praise, and two days later the com-

[15] *Proceedings, 1899*, pp. 691–696, 835–836.

mittee unanimously approved it.[16] Friendly colleagues christened the proposal "La Proposition Holls." [17] The Germans liked the idea, for it reminded them of their "courts of honor." In the European press were kind comments.[18]

Holls sought at once to capitalize on this achievement. He was quick to make his new glory known at home. To Governor Theodore Roosevelt he sent a copy of the article's French text, and he cabled Albert Shaw to hold open the July number of the *American Monthly Review of Reviews* for an article he intended to write.[19] Unfortunately "La Proposition Holls" brought its author no credit in Washington. Newspapers reported that Holls had presented the proposal as a substitute for the plan for a permanent tribunal, and great was the anger at the State Department. "That unutterable ass of a Holls," was Hay's comment, and the secretary of state feared that White was giving Holls too much authority.[20] Even Assistant Secretary Hill was disappointed in his friend, and of course President McKinley was highly displeased.[21]

From Washington to The Hague went a telegram in which Hay told the delegates that they ought not urge the proposal for fear it might hurt the chances of the court plan. This communication distressed Holls and White, and they cabled back that this success had in fact strengthened the delegation. They nonetheless offered to withdraw "La Proposition Holls." [22]

It was lucky that McKinley and Hay did not order withdrawal of Holls's proposal, for on June 5 a plenary meeting of the third

[16] *Ibid.*, pp. 696–698.

[17] Andrew D. White, address, *In Memoriam, Frederick William Holls* (privately printed, 1904), pp. 22–23.

[18] White, Diary excerpt, May 29, 1899, *Autobiog.*, II, 274.

[19] Holls to Theodore Roosevelt, June 24, 1899, Theodore Roosevelt Papers, deposited in the Library of Congress; Albert Shaw to Holls, June 8, 1899, Holls Papers.

[20] Hay to Henry White, May 29, 1899, Henry White Papers.

[21] Hill to Holls, June 15, 1899, Holls Papers.

[22] A. D. White to Hay, June 2, 1899, McKinley Papers.

commission adopted it. On that occasion Holls said nothing; he left support of the measure to others.[23]

The mediation plan seemed a success of minor proportions. Agreement on the mediation proposals concluded one part of the *comité*'s work. Debate on mediation, moreover, had given the delegates time to consider the court schemes of the American, Russian, and British delegations—time to plan the most important part of their deliberations.

[23] *Proceedings, 1899*, pp. 591–592.

XI

The Tribunal Crisis

HOLLS had little time to lament his difficulties with the State Department, for even before "La Proposition Holls" won approval by the full third commission the *comité d'examen* was at work on a draft of an arbitration convention.

For the American delegation the first question to arise in this connection concerned the Russian plan's tenth article, by which the powers would submit certain minor quarrels to arbitration. The Americans, having decided to omit from their plan all references to obligatory arbitration, still hoped to appear as exponents of so exalted a conception.[1] When they learned the details of the Russian plan, they found reason to be glad they had abandoned their own obligatory arbitration scheme, for the Russians wanted to include monetary disputes, interoceanic canals, and international rivers on the compulsory list. To the Americans extension of obligatory arbitration to these topics was offensive. They thought that fixing monetary standards and issuing money were, as Holls later explained, "peculiarly appurtenant to the sovereignty of the State itself," and no international act should touch upon such subjects. They were even more opposed to inclusion of disputes about international rivers and interoceanic

[1] Holls to Hill, June 26, 1899, Hill Papers.

canals. The American delegates knew that few of their fellow citizens would care to have a court of Europeans try cases involving the St. Lawrence, Columbia, Yukon, or Rio Grande. Above all they disliked the thought of a multinational treaty which could interfere with their government's plans for a Central American canal.[2]

Holls on June 3 demanded exclusion of the clauses on money, canals, and rivers. So emphatically did he declare his government's opposition that few committee members opposed him, and those items were struck from the list.[3]

Buffeted by this attack, the principle of compulsory arbitration nearly collapsed. Several of the conference delegates disliked it even when applied to insignificant matters, and so it was decided to drop the topic for a time and to begin consideration of the tribunal plans at the next meeting, scheduled for two days later.

I

Pauncefote and Holls had laid their delegations' court plans before the *comité d'examen* on May 31, and for several days leading delegates had been discussing these projects and also that of the Russians. The Americans were unhappy to hear their plan receive more criticism than either of the other proposals. To many delegates the American idea of a continuously sitting court was objectionable. Some individuals feared that such a tribunal would be a threat to national sovereignty. Even earnest supporters of arbitration thought a court of this kind unwise, for, they pointed out, if it at first would have little to do it would be scorned as a needless expense. The clause calling for appointment of judges by the supreme courts of signatory powers likewise was condemned. It was pointed out to the Americans that few nations had supreme courts like their own, and that few

[2] Frederick W. Holls, *The Peace Conference at The Hague*, pp. 227–229.

[3] *Proceedings, 1899*, pp. 702–703.

high European tribunals could assume such responsibilities.[4]

While hardly anyone outside the United States delegation approved the American proposal, most delegates found merit in the Russian and British projects. These plans were similar in several respects. Neither envisioned a continuously sitting court. The Russians thought that the conference should give five powers authority to name one judge each whenever there should be a demand for an arbitration and that these five powers should retain this appointive power until a new conference. The British suggested that each signatory government name two jurists to a list, and that from this list parties to an arbitration should choose judges. Both plans permitted disputing powers to name a judge not on the list and called for a permanent bureau to carry on administrative work for the court.[5]

Although these plans, particularly the British project, were weak on points in which the Americans were strong, their weaknesses were merits in the eyes of most delegates. Indeed Ambassador White soon felt compelled to admit that he favored the British plan for practical reasons while continuing to prefer the American project from the theoretical standpoint.[6] Accordingly White and his colleagues decided to support the British plan as a basis for committee discussions while hoping to secure modifications containing features of their own proposal. Pauncefote's friendly attitude doubtless helped make this decision easier. He

[4] A. D. White, Diary excerpt, June 2, 1899, *Autobiog.*, II, 286; Low to McKinley, June 13, 1899, McKinley Papers; American Commission to Hay, June 16, 1899, copy of dispatch in American Commission, Minutes, June 22, 1899.

[5] For the principal arbitration plans presented to the *comité d'examen*, see the annexes to the minutes of that committee in *Proceedings, 1899*, pp. 797–817, 833–834. Pauncefote's proposal was similar to the plan of the Interparliamentary Union, adopted at its conference in Brussels in 1895. The Union's plan was among the documents laid before the Hague Conference by the Dutch government. It is reprinted in A. Van Daehne van Varick, *Documents Relating to the Program of the First Hague Peace Conference*, pp. 87–88.

[6] Diary excerpt, June 1, 1899, *Autobiog.*, II, 280.

virtually assured White that he would not oppose omission of one feature of his plan to which the ambassador objected—the clause which permitted appointment of judges not on the court list.[7]

2

The Russians, like the Americans, were willing to adopt the British proposal as a basis for deliberation, and on June 9 began the most serious debates of the conference. Bourgeois, Pauncefote, and Descamps made optimistic speeches, but the mood of hope disappeared quickly when Zorn rose to speak. He declared that he personally desired ultimate success for the czar's "noble wish," but, he said:

I cannot, I must not, surrender myself to illusions; and such is, I am sure, the opinion of my Government also. It must be recognized that the proposition now proposed and submitted to the judgment of the committee is but a generous project; it cannot be realized without bearing with it great risks and even great dangers which it is simple prudence to recognize. Would it not be better to wait the results of greater preliminary experience upon this subject? If these experiences prove successful, and if they realize the hopes reposed in them, the German Government will not hesitate to co-operate to that end, by accepting the experiment of arbitration having far greater scope than anything which has been in practice up to this day. But it cannot possibly agree to the organization of the permanent tribunal before having the preliminary benefit of satisfactory experience with *occasional* arbitrations.[8]

There followed an embarrassing scene. Zorn moved that Article 13 of the original Russian draft be the basis of deliberation rather than the court plan, "inasmuch as this plan accurately represents the views of the Imperial German Government upon the subject." Consternation spread through the group. Asser reminded him that there already had been abundant experience

[7] *Ibid.*, June 6, 1899, pp. 290–291.
[8] *Proceedings, 1899*, pp. 712–713.

with arbitration. The German delegate, seeming to contradict his previous statements, admitted the validity of this argument, but reminded the *comité* that the Russian government had modified its first project—to which Germany had assented—by introducing its tribunal proposal.[9] Here the Russians were vulnerable, for they were opposing introduction of other topics in the second commission on grounds that they were not on the program. Luckily no one other than Zorn alluded to this embarrassing fact. Nigra, representing a German ally, urged Zorn to abandon his opposition. Even Lammasch announced his willingness to take part in debate on court plans—although he said that he could not bind the Austrian government on this subject. Martens attempted to explain away Zorn's objections, and Holls, too, tried to persuade the German to alter his course. Holls recalled that recently a conference on protection for labor had met in Berlin at the emperor's invitation. Purely Platonic resolutions had been the only accomplishment of that conference. "Public opinion," Holls warned, "expects more this time." [10]

Holls's warning ended discussion on Zorn's declaration, and without voting on the German motion the committee took up the Pauncefote plan. For the remainder of that session and at a meeting on June 12 the *comité d'examen* discussed the British proposal. It was decided that The Hague should be the seat of the permanent tribunal and its bureau and that judges should serve on the court list for terms of six years. Holls asked that judges be selected by supreme courts, but, as he expected, the *comité* voted down his motion. Holls served notice that the United States, while willing to take part in debate on the Pauncefote plan, had not ceased to prefer its own proposal and that his delegation reserved the right to introduce its court scheme at a later date should such a course become desirable. The American delegates had heard rumors that they had completely abandoned their plan, and Holls's announcement reflected their irritation.[11]

[9] *Proceedings, 1899,* pp. 713–714.   [10] *Ibid.,* pp. 715–716.
[11] *Ibid.,* pp. 718, 720; American Commission, Minutes, June 12, 1899.

But these rumors were minor annoyances only, for anxiety over the German position was upsetting the nerves of all arbitration exponents. The German attitude was steadily growing more obstinate. The conference had entered a major crisis, for, should Germany persist in opposing the court, would not Italy and Austria-Hungary join her, despite the friendly attitude toward arbitration displayed by their delegates? De Staal, Pauncefote, and White discussed the situation in long, earnest talks, and for a time it seemed unlikely that much could be done. White wired the State Department, but the department could do little.[12] Pauncefote informed the British Foreign Office, and Lord Salisbury instructed his ambassadors in Rome and Vienna to bring pressure on the Italian and Austro-Hungarian governments.[13]

Secrecy rules had long since collapsed, and reports of crisis spread through the Dutch capital and then around the world. Worried comments of peace spokesmen at The Hague added to the gloom.[14] Would there be a way to bring Germany into line?

The American proposals regarding immunity for private property gave White an opportunity to exert the strongest kind of pressure on Count Münster. The head of the German delegation seemed to think that he could please the Americans by siding with them on this subject despite his delegation's opposition to arbitration. Early on the morning of June 15 the aged statesman called on White to tell him that the Wilhelmstrasse had just directed him to give full support to private-property proposals. White listened carefully to his visitor, but when they finished talking about private property the American turned discussion to arbitration. Münster denounced it in scathing terms. Especially did he condemn compulsory arbitration, pointing out that those obligatory features opposed by the United States

[12] White, Diary excerpt, June 9, 1899, *Autobiog.*, II, 294.

[13] Sir G. Bonham to Salisbury, June 13, 1899, and Rumbold to Salisbury, June 13, 1899, *British Documents*, I, 228–229.

[14] Manchester *Guardian*, June 14, 1899; New York *Times*, June 14, 1899.

had been stricken out. He condemned the idea of a permanent bureau as an opportunity for troublesome professors to interfere with diplomacy. White countered by telling him that compulsory features objectionable to Germany could also be eliminated and that Pauncefote was planning to offer a change in his bureau proposals. The British statesman intended to suggest that the bureau be under control of a council of the diplomatic corps at The Hague; White, himself, was suggesting that the foreign minister of the Netherlands be president of that council. Receiving this information Münster's protests became less ardent.

The American ambassador told Münster that the German emperor had told him that he was sending the count to The Hague because he had good common sense—and the conference needed common sense more than anything else. The American talked of the virtues and abilities of the young emperor and he strongly implied that no statesman with common sense would permit William II to encounter the hatred of the world for blocking the court proposals. Münster seemed to weaken, yet he called the conference a detestable trick designed to embarrass Germany and to glorify the czar. To this White answered:

If this be the case, why not trump the Russian trick? or, as the poker-players say, "Go them one better," take them at their word, support a good tribunal of arbitration more efficient even than the Russians have dared to propose; let your sovereign throw himself heartily into the movement and become a recognized leader and power here; we will all support him, and to him will come the credit of it.[15]

White promised that he and his friends would do everything to make German assistance fully known to the world. He said that France had never really wished arbitration and that the Russian statesmen had little interest in it. If only Germany could come out for a court—and continue to support immunity for private property—then, said the ambassador, the German emperor could be the "arbiter of Europe."

[15] Diary excerpt, June 15, 1899, *Autobiog.*, II, 303.

White noted that Münster was disturbed; relentlessly he continued his arguments. The French socialist, Jaurès, had told D'Estournelles that the conference would surely fail—and that failure would help socialism. White repeated this story, warning that to contribute to the failure of the conference would only give "socialists, anarchists, and all the other anti-social forces" a club, while alienating middle classes and religious people everywhere. Knowing that the German emperor opposed arbitration as a derogation on his sovereignty, White pointed out that the emperor would have to submit to the tribunal only those questions he wished. Regardless of the present emperor's attitude, Germany was already committed to arbitration in principle, for William I had acted as arbiter between America and Britain in the northwest boundary question, and Bismarck had even asked the pope to arbitrate the Caroline Islands dispute.

White did not confine his arguments to the bad effects on world opinion certain to come from German intransigence and the absurdity of the emperor's fear of encroachment on his sovereignty. The ambassador dwelt on the practicality of arbitration in German-American relations. He pointed out that there were minor yet acrimonious disputes between the two countries and that they were of the kind that could be settled easily—if it were not for interference of quarrelsome individuals in the Reichstag and Congress. Arbitration would settle these questions without opposition from noisy legislators.

When Münster left, White felt there was a possibility the count would urge his government to reverse its stand. The ambassador, nonetheless, decided to proceed at once to enlist every possible ally in his campaign to force Germany to change her policy. Attending a tea given that afternoon by D'Estournelles, he met Baroness von Suttner. He told the Austrian noblewoman that Germany had brought the conference to a turning point. He urged her to do everything possible to win support of journals in Austria, Italy, and Germany for the court. This she promised to do and also said she would try to secure the aid of a friend, then at The Hague, who was a favorite of the grand duke of Baden, an uncle of the German emperor. In the evening White saw Stead at a reception given by Ambassador Okolicsányi of Austria. The American told Stead of the seriousness of the crisis and urged him to employ his persuasive powers through the press. He told the journalist of D'Estournelles's encounter with Jaurès and asked him to make every use of it.[16]

White did not have to wait for journalistic influence to bring result, for the next morning Münster again called. This time the count was excited. He had just received word that the emperor had decided to have nothing to do with the tribunal; White's arguments had convinced Münster of the unwisdom of this course; the count had asked De Staal to postpone the session of the *comité d'examen* scheduled for that day. Münster said that if the session did take place as scheduled, Zorn would have to make the declaration in behalf of Germany and that such a statement would be a misfortune. Gladly White joined the German diplomat in requesting postponement. De Staal acceded and announced that the meeting would not occur because D'Estournelles was too much occupied with other matters.

Later that day Münster told White he was sending Zorn to Berlin to lay the matter before the Foreign Office, and he urged White also to send an emissary. The ambassador agreed, choosing Holls as his messenger. In the American delegation this decision was denounced by Newel, Crozier, Mahan, and, in particular, Low. The ambassador persisted, stating that he was taking this step on his own responsibility and in his capacity as ambassador to Berlin. Ending his arguments with his colleagues, White wrote a long letter to Bülow, setting forth the arguments used with Münster the day before.[17] He gave this letter to Holls for delivery, and also gave his envoy a copy of a pastoral letter by the Episcopal bishop of Texas. The bishop's letter called for prayers

[16] *Ibid.*, pp. 305–307; Bertha von Suttner, Diary excerpt, June 15, 1899, *Memoirs*, II, 294–296.

[17] White included a copy of his letter to Bülow in a diary excerpt dated June 16, 1899, *Autobiog.*, II, 309–314.

in behalf of the conference. White hoped this document would help convince German officials of the importance of arbitration to the religious people of America.[18]

Münster, like White, sought to arm his emissary with written arguments. He wired the Wilhelmstrasse that Zorn was coming to explain why the German delegation wanted to change course. He told his superiors that the provisions on obligatory arbitration could be eliminated and that there was no possibility the conference would accept the idea of a permanent court capable of intervention. In a letter to the imperial chancellor, Prince von Hohenlohe, Münster repeated these contentions. He declared that he personally continued to regard the idea of a court with repugnance, but he thought it better to join in establishment of a harmless tribunal than to risk offending other nations, particularly Russia, the United States, and England.[19]

Zorn and Holls left late that afternoon for Berlin. Soon many delegates were aware that decisions of moment were at hand, for nothing was said about immediate resumption of work in the *comité d'examen*. A few arbitration supporters were irritated. Pauncefote was angry. He said that the *comité* could get along without Zorn and that if Germany did not want to go with the conference's decisions she could stay out as far as he was concerned. The British statesman ignored the fact that if Germany opposed the court she could be joined by Italy and Austria. Pauncefote had not learned that Holls was on the mission, and White said nothing about his friend's journey, trying only to soothe the irate Englishman.[20]

3

In Berlin, Zorn did his best to change his government's attitude. He told Bülow that the Americans were so anxious for German participation in the tribunal that they would urge the conference

[18] *Ibid.*, June 23, 1899, p. 322.
[19] Münster to the Foreign Office and Münster to Hohenlohe, both dated June 16, 1899, in *Grosse Politik*, XV, 284–285.
[20] White, Diary excerpt, June 16, 1899, *Autobiog.*, II, 314.

to drop the compulsory arbitration proposals. He stressed that should Germany continue her uncompromising opposition she would endanger her good relations with Russia. Noting that Germany's allies, Austria-Hungary and Italy, like Britain and France were showing interest in arbitration, he warned his superiors that their policy could lead to diplomatic isolation. To good effect he repeated Jaurès' remarks to D'Estournelles. Despite the urgency with which he presented his arguments, Zorn advised his government to make no immediate announcement of a change in policy. He believed it best to wait until the *comité d'examen* had presented a complete court project to the conference.[21]

Both Hohenlohe and Bülow received Holls. The latter was no stranger to the foreign minister, for they had met only a month before.[22] Friendly were the greetings extended to the American, yet he spoke with bluntness. He predicted that the project for a tribunal would fail without German cooperation, although he soon contradicted himself, declaring that Britain, America, Russia, and France could found the court without the help of Germany. As Holls wrote on return to The Hague his "central proposition was that *the train was going to start,* and that any one who did not choose to get aboard when it was time would find himself left on the platform in no very desirable or dignified position." [23] He showed Bülow and Hohenlohe the Texas bishop's prayer. That document seemed to touch the hearts of the German officials.[24]

[21] Zorn to Münster, June 18, 1899, in *Grosse Politik,* XV, 293–296.

[22] In a diary excerpt dated June 20, 1899 (*Autobiog.,* II, 317), Ambassador White stated that he had received a telegram from Holls in which the latter told of his reception by Hohenlohe and Bülow. An editorial comment on a telegram from William II to Bülow of June 19, 1899 (in *Grosse Politik,* XV, 298), doubts that Bülow saw Holls, but on June 21 Holls wrote the German foreign minister a letter which refers to recent conversations between the two. A copy of this letter is preserved in the Holls Papers. A letter from Holls to David Jayne Hill of June 26, 1899, in the Hill Papers, also refers to conversations with Bülow.

[23] Holls to Roosevelt, June 24, 1899, Roosevelt Papers.

[24] White, Diary excerpt, June 23, 1899, *Autobiog.,* II, 322

Bülow asked Holls to appear before a meeting of the foreign ministry's legal counselors. The foreign minister told Holls that he hoped the meeting could result in some agreement, but the counselors considered themselves instructed only to listen to him and to state objections. Holls hinted that American domestic politics made necessary a record of achievement at The Hague. Admitting that his countrymen had at first shown little interest in the czar's rescript, he said that they were now overwhelmingly in favor of an international tribunal. Blaming the Irish-Americans for defeat of the Olney-Pauncefote treaty, the erstwhile German-American said that it was now time for German-Americans to assert themselves in the right direction. The counselors raised several legal and theoretical objections to the court project. They feared that the court could place restrictions on the sovereignty of member states. Holls refuted these objections to his own satisfaction. He admitted that even an American could have qualms about the proposed tribunal, but he stressed the voluntary character of its jurisdiction and declared his belief that in practice the court would acquire no power by which it could interfere with the sovereign functions of states.[25]

He received no assurance that Germany would retreat from her position, but he had been in Berlin less than a day when he sent White a hopeful wire. His optimism may have been due in part to a promise by Bülow to arrange an imperial interview for him; the staunch Republican from New York had long wished to meet the German emperor. William II was aboard his yacht in the North Sea, but his arrival in Hamburg was expected momentarily.

The interview in fact failed to materialize. After two days in Berlin, Holls went to Hamburg while Zorn returned to The

[25] Holls to Bülow, June 21, 1899, Holls Papers. Holls told Bülow of his meeting with the counselors, and he strongly reaffirmed his delegation's desire for a tribunal with no power to interfere with the sovereignty of nations. In a report dated June 19, 1899, one of the counselors, Hellwig, gave his impressions of what transpired during the meeting (in *Grosse Politik*, XV, 298–300).

Hague. Unfortunately the yacht did not arrive as soon as expected, and Holls waited many hours. Finally an officer of the imperial household assured him that the interview would indeed be arranged upon His Majesty's arrival. Holls felt that he could delay return to The Hague no longer; he told the official that he would come back to Hamburg whenever the emperor should send for him.[26]

It was, in sum, difficult to draw conclusions about the success of Holls's mission. Holls arrived at The Hague railway station in the evening of June 19, and in the waiting room he met Baroness von Suttner and a group of her friends. They wanted to know what had happened in Germany. "I cannot tell you anything yet," he said. "Only I will mention the title of one of Shakespeare's plays, 'All's well that ends well.' "[27] Had everything ended well? It was too soon to know.

No one was sure that the Germans would yield, but it was expected they would do so—while asking modifications in the court plan. The *comité d'examen* resumed work on June 21 with the obvious intention of giving the Germans encouragement. Sir Julian Pauncefote moved to amend his bureau proposals along lines discussed with White. The *comité* approved this change, and Zorn observed that this innovation should facilitate acceptance of conference decisions by participating governments. Zorn's remarks indicated that Germany would drop opposition to the court.[28]

Foreign Minister Bülow on June 22 wired Münster that Germany would support a tribunal, but she would ask modifications. The foreign minister instructed the German delegation to demand: (1) a larger number of judges; (2) elimination of the term "tribunal" and its replacement by "list of arbitration judges" or a similar term; (3) omission of all references to obligatory arbitration; (4) restriction of the activities of the permanent

---

[26] Holls to Bülow, June 21, 1899, Holls Papers.
[27] Von Suttner, Diary excerpt, June 19, 1899, *Memoirs*, II, 301–302.
[28] *Proceedings, 1899*, pp. 725–729.

bureau to care of documents concerning court business (a demand which had in fact been partly met the day before). The foreign minister said that Germany might consent to some expression of hope by the conference that nations refer to arbitration those types of disputes included in the Russian proposal for compulsory arbitration—but he hoped that Russia would not insist upon this concession.[29]

Reports that Germany had yielded spread through The Hague on June 23. Of course it was expected that Germany would demand concessions, but few individuals knew the extent of her demands. There was rejoicing in the Dutch capital. Supporters of the projected tribunal believed victory in sight.[30]

Holls could no longer expect his interview with William II, but even this fact did not lessen his joy. He believed that his appearance in Berlin had been largely responsible for changing the mind of the imperial government. Writing Governor Roosevelt and Assistant Secretary Hill he told of his mission to Berlin —never once mentioning that a German delegate had gone on a similar mission. But Holls did try to share his glory. He told Roosevelt that Ambassador White was "easily the most influential" delegate, and he declared that the American position from the first had been "one of influence and power, which is no doubt due in a large measure to all you heroes of the Spanish war." [31]

Did Holls deserve credit for ending the crisis? His friends accepted his claims, but the truth seems to be that pressure from several sources caused the Germans to reconsider and that they were in process of changing their minds before Holls and Zorn journeyed to Berlin. Both Italy and Austria-Hungary favored a tribunal provided it should be optional rather than obligatory. The Italian foreign minister, Marquis Visconti Venosta, on June 9

[29] Margaret Robinson, *Arbitration and the Hague Peace Conferences, 1899 and 1907* (Philadelphia, 1936), pp. 80–81. Robinson translates in part the message from Bülow to Münster, June 22, 1899, in *Grosse Politik*, XV, 307–308.

[30] White, Diary excerpt, June 23, 1899, *Autobiog.*, II, 321–322.

[31] Holls to Roosevelt, June 24, 1899, Roosevelt Papers.

asked the German government to reconsider its position.[32] In reply the Wilhelmstrasse restated its policy, but it did hint that there was a possibility that Germany would modify her position if firm guarantees could be given that the court would be impartial.[33]

Representations in Rome and Vienna by the British ambassadors seemed to strengthen Germany's allies in support of the proposed tribunal. The Austrian foreign minister, Count Goluchowski, on June 13 told British Ambassador Sir Horace Rumbold that Austria still favored the court but feared the plan could not succeed should even one great power oppose it. Goluchowski assured Rumbold that in this matter Austria was not acting in concert with Germany. Two days later Austria asked Germany not to oppose a voluntary arbitration tribunal.[34] In the meantime the German ambassador in London, Count Hatzfeldt, learned that Lord Salisbury, while desiring establishment of the court, favored sending only disputes of minor importance to it for settlement. The prime minister believed that it could never intervene in a great international question, such as Egypt or Alsace.[35] The attitudes of Italy, Austria, and England caused reconsideration of policy in Berlin even as Münster received the order to oppose the court project.

But the German government was more concerned about the effects of its policy upon relations with Russia than with the wishes of other great powers. While Holls and Zorn were in Berlin, the German ambassador in St. Petersburg, Prince Radolin, negotiated with officials in the czarist foreign ministry. Radolin

[32] Marquis Visconti Venosta to Count Lanza, June 9, 1899, in *Grosse Politik*, XV, 266.

[33] Unsigned memorandum for the Italian government, June 10, 1899, *ibid.*, pp. 273–274.

[34] Rumbold to Salisbury, June 13, 1899, *British Documents*, I, 228–229; note by Undersecretary von Richthofen, June 15, 1899, in *Grosse Politik*, XV, 283.

[35] Hatzfeldt to the Foreign Office, June 14, 1899, *ibid.*, pp. 279–280; translated in E. T. S. Dugdale, *German Diplomatic Documents*, III, 78.

on June 19 warned that continued opposition to the court could be harmful to German-Russian relations and could hurt Germany in world public opinion. He also warned that should Germany not enter the court she could find it difficult to control negotiations among powers participating in the tribunal.[36]

Pressure from her allies and from Britain and realization that continued opposition could hurt German relations with other powers—particularly Russia—caused Germany to waver in her opposition to the tribunal and led to the decision to support a weak court project. Holls's appearance in Berlin was not decisive, and probably the American was no more influential than Zorn. Yet his efforts may not have been altogether without effect. Bülow warned William II that rejection of the whole court idea could mean the loss of the fruits of his policies toward both Russia and the United States. The foreign minister declared that he was convinced that if Germany would join in establishing the new tribunal her new stand would make a "fresh leaning" of the United States toward England difficult and could even turn America toward Germany. In this hope the emperor concurred.[37]

[36] Radolin to the Foreign Office, June 19, 1899, in *Grosse Politik*, XV, 296–298.

[37] Bülow to William II, June 21, 1899, *ibid.*, pp. 300–306; Dugdale translates part of this document in III, 80–81.

XII

Completing the Arbitration Convention

FOR a time the Germans did not make known the price they intended to make the conference pay for their support. For several days Prince Radolin negotiated with Muraviev and and Lamsdorf. The Russians avoided giving Radolin a definite promise that they would not oppose German demands, but Lamsdorf assured Radolin that he hoped the conference would accept German wishes.[1] While these conversations were in progress the *comité d'examen* discussed the Russian proposals for commissions of inquiry and arbitration procedure.

I

Without difficulty the *comité* reached agreement on international commissions of inquiry. On occasion such commissions had proved useful in determining facts in minor disputes. Everyone agreed that it would be wise to set up regulations to govern their organization and use. There was some debate on the word-

[1] Radolin to the Foreign Office, June 23 and 24, 1899, and Radolin to Hohenlohe, June 22, 1899 in *Grosse Politik*, XV, 309–311.

ing of the Russian draft, for in effect it would have made resort to commissions of inquiry obligatory. Lammasch opposed this feature of the draft. To his support came Holls. Zorn agreed with Lammasch and Holls, and on June 21 the *comité* adopted a draft in accord with their ideas.

At its sessions on June 23, 26, and 30 and July 1 the *comité* discussed arbitration procedure. In drafting a permanent code of procedure the group debated not only the Russian plan but also the code which the Anglo-Venezuelan arbitration was following. It required little effort to agree upon details and provide for the form of agreement (*compromis*) which nations were to conclude before sending disputes to arbitration.[2]

Debate on arbitration procedure offered Holls an opportunity to introduce an important feature of the American plan—revision of arbitral awards. He suggested that parties to an arbitration should have three months to appeal for a rehearing. Martens objected that unless awards were accepted as final then arbitral tribunals would lose respect. Holls explained that he wished only to provide for rehearings in case new facts should be discovered after the decisions, but Martens still objected. Holls modified his proposal to extend the waiting period from three to six months, making this change to please the Siamese and other nations at great distances from The Hague. Supported by Pauncefote, Asser, Zorn, and Odier, Holls won the *comité*'s approval for his modified proposal, although it was obvious that Martens again would oppose this measure should opportunity arise.[3]

On July 1 the *comité* returned to the subject of an international tribunal. Zorn announced withdrawal of German opposition, making clear that his government expected the project for a tribunal to be made less ambitious. He served notice that when the *comité* would again discuss compulsory arbitration he would have objections, but for the present he demanded that the name "Permanent Court of Arbitrators" replace "Permanent Tribunal

[2] *Proceedings, 1899*, pp. 730–744.   [3] *Ibid.*, pp. 741–742, 749–755.

of Arbitration," which the *comité* had been using. Most members of the group disagreed, for it was apparent that Germany wished to deny the proposed institution recognition as an international tribunal. They did consent to the name, "Permanent Court of Arbitration." Zorn agreed to this compromise, even though the mere substitution of "court" for "tribunal" could not accomplish his government's purpose.[4] Two days later he brought up another proposal to weaken the tribunal. He asked that each power appoint four judges to the list rather than two as provided in the Pauncefote plan. Holls protested that this amendment would cause the list to be too long, but the *comité*, probably feeling that it was wise to placate the Germans, accepted Zorn's motion.[5]

A chance thereupon arose to strengthen the court in another way. Even as Zorn was endeavoring to weaken the court plan, the French were considering a proposal to strengthen the court's moral authority. At the meeting of June 9 Bourgeois had said that the permanent bureau ought to be empowered to urge arbitration on disputing powers, and on July 1 he revived this idea, declaring that nations should not consider such actions unfriendly.[6] Such a proposal would have been contrary to German wishes, and the French probably realized this, for they soon suggested their new idea. D'Estournelles on July 3 proposed an article by which signatory powers were to consider it their duty to remind quarreling states of the existence and uses of the court. This proposal won praise for the French; in fact it was soon called "Article D'Estournelles." Zorn found merit in the idea. But Holls announced that the United States would have to examine the proposition to see whether it could affect the distinction established by traditional American policy between American and European questions. He reserved right to return to the subject and said the United States might have to make a declaration explaining its views. American doubts notwithstanding, the

[4] *Ibid.*, p. 755.   [5] *Ibid.*, p. 764.   [6] *Ibid.*, pp. 710–711, 757–758.

comité unanimously approved the article, and as Article 27 it became an important part of the convention.[7]

On the afternoon of July 4 the *comité d'examen* met for what its members believed would be the last session. One matter remained—the list of topics for compulsory arbitration in Article 10 of the Russian draft. Zorn asked suppression of Article 10. He said Germany could go no further and believed she had done much by accepting the list of arbitrators and the Permanent Court. Martens suggested a compromise proposal. Zorn rejected it. The other members bowed to Germany's wishes. With this decision it became clear beyond all doubt that the principle of compulsory arbitration would not be incorporated into the convention.[8]

Closing the meeting, Bourgeois thanked the *comité* for the energetic way in which it had pursued its tasks and for the conciliatory spirit which had marked its work. The *comité* in truth had accomplished much. Surmounting a crisis which had threatened to wreck the conference, it had drafted a convention for a permanent court, arbitration procedure, and commissions of inquiry. Defeat for compulsory arbitration was a disappointment—but in any event the convention would have applied it to only unimportant matters. The *comité* could announce accomplishments far greater than those of any other subdivision of the conference.

2

The *comité d'examen* ended its meeting of July 4 on an almost happy note. Friendship seemed to rule. Could the remaining work of the conference be concluded in conciliatory fashion?

For the good will shown in the *comité* on July 4 the Americans

[7] *Ibid.*, pp. 759–764. Holls did not report his reservation to the American delegation, and his failure to do so was to be the source of much trouble for him. See below, pp. 176–177, 194–195, n. 28.

[8] *Ibid.*, pp. 767–772.

were in part responsible; that morning they were host to the entire conference at a remarkable celebration. Early in June, White had conceived the idea of celebrating the Fourth of July by honoring the memory of Hugo Grotius. It would be fitting, the ambassador thought, to lay a wreath on the tomb of the great pioneer in international law in Delft Cathedral.[9] Securing Secretary Hay's approval and permission from the Dutch authorities, White planned a ceremony. From a Berlin silversmith he ordered an elaborate wreath of silver and gold, and he asked a number of prominent persons to make speeches.[10]

The Fourth dawned rainy and unpleasant, yet most members of the conference and many other guests journeyed to Delft. For White there was an anxious moment that morning, for after arriving in the cathedral he could not find Holls. He finally espied his friend seated at the organ. Holls had replaced the church organist and was giving a splendid rendition of religious hymns and national airs.[11] After he had played several numbers, Karnebeek, De Beaufort, Asser, and Low spoke briefly. White placed the wreath on Grotius' tomb and delivered the main address. He told his audience that he seemed to hear a voice from the tomb telling the conference to go on with its work "of strengthening peace and humanizing war" and to "give to the world at least a beginning of an effective, practicable scheme of arbitration."[12]

The American delegates had planned events for the entire day. They entertained their guests at luncheon in the Town Hall of Delft. That afternoon Newel gave a reception, and in the evening an orchestra gave an "American concert" at Scheveningen.[13]

[9] A. D. White, Diary excerpt, June 6, 1899, *Autobiog.*, II, 291.
[10] *Ibid.*, July 2, 1899, p. 326.
[11] Andrew D. White, address, in *In Memoriam: Frederick William Holls*, pp. 28–29.
[12] Holls included the texts of the speeches in his account of the Delft celebration which he published as an appendix to *The Peace Conference at The Hague*, pp. 535–562.
[13] White, Diary excerpt, July 4, 1899, *Autobiog.*, II, 327–328.

The Grotius celebration dramatized the work of the *comité d'examen* and lent prestige to the American delegation—obscuring the defeat of compulsory arbitration that day. Two days later at a banquet in Amsterdam, Queen Wilhelmina thanked White for the honor accorded her country.[14] President McKinley and Secretary Hay were pleased by the way their representatives had drawn attention to the pacific interests of the United States.[15]

On that memorable Fourth of July it seemed that the conference was approaching its end. The next day the conference accepted the second commission's reports and heard White's appeal for immunity of private property at sea.[16] The first and third commissions apparently would soon report. Everyone was anxious to adjourn, for the conference had grown tiresome and the weather had become hot and humid. Unfortunately the delegates had to remain at The Hague for almost four more weeks.

3

When Descamps presented the report of the *comité d'examen* to the third commission on July 7, his eloquence won prolonged applause, but there was no discussion of the draft convention. Bourgeois announced that the commission would suspend debate for a week to enable delegates to consult their governments. N. P. Delyanni of Greece requested an additional delay of two days, claiming that communication with his government was slow. Beldiman of Rumania seconded this request, observing that the delay would make it unnecessary for Bourgeois to preside on Bastille Day. Of course Bourgeois was pleased by Beldiman's remarks, and the commission acceded to Balkan wishes, setting its next meeting for July 17.[17] It is unlikely that either respect for France or communication problems had anything

---

[14] *Ibid.*, July 6, 1899, pp. 331–332.
[15] Hay to A. D. White, July 8, 1899, A. D. White Papers.
[16] See above, pp. 133–135. [17] *Proceedings, 1899*, pp. 593–602.

to do with the Balkan requests. It is more likely that Delyanni and Beldiman had discerned objectionable features in the draft convention and wanted more time in which to prepare protests.

Delegation leaders sent the text of the draft convention to their foreign offices, and within a few days most of them received instructions. Secretary Hay was pleased, and on July 8 he wrote White:

Today the despatches give a full account of the scheme of arbitration reported to the Conference. So far as I can judge from a hurried reading of its provisions, it seems to have included all the essential features of the American plan. You and your colleagues have done many things in the course of your lives which redound to your own glory and the welfare of the world, but I do not believe that in looking back over your lives there will be anything which will give you more pleasure to consider than the part you have taken in this great Congress of Peace.[18]

The secretary of state erred in believing that the convention contained the essential features of the American plan, yet his approval was gratifying to the American delegates.

Other foreign ministers were not pleased with the documents they received. Rumania, Serbia, and Greece were exceedingly unhappy. All three states opposed the provisions for international commissions of inquest, and Rumania and Serbia also opposed Article 27 (Article D'Estournelles) and articles regulating good offices and mediation. Turkey, too, opposed these articles, but her delegates took little part in debate. Still, other nations were aware that in these matters the three Balkan kingdoms were acting in concert with the Turks. The principalities of Bulgaria and Montenegro were the only Balkan states which did not condemn the work of the *comité d'examen;* of course, Russia was casting Montenegro's vote, and Bulgaria while technically a Turkish vassal had a pro-Russian government.

So loud were the Balkan protests that Bourgeois called a special meeting of the *comité d'examen* on July 15, and it re-

[18] Hay to White, July 8, 1899, A. D. White Papers.

quired three more special sessions of the *comité* and five sessions of the full third commission before Balkan objections and other difficulties could be disposed of and the arbitration convention presented to the conference. Frequently Balkan representatives and other interested diplomats attended the special meetings of the *comité*.

Tempers of the delegates were warm during debate in the *comité d'examen* and the third commission in late July. Voislave Veljkovitch of Serbia observed that since the offer of good offices was not an unfriendly act it should likewise be stated that the refusal of those offers was not unfriendly.[19] Despite Veljko- vitch's remarks, the Balkan delegates made little issue of the good- office and mediation articles. Their leader, Beldiman, concen- trated on commissions of inquiry and Article 27. He feared that those articles, even more than articles on good offices and mediation, could be used by the great powers to intervene in Balkan affairs.

To counter the Balkan attacks the delegates from the great powers drew together. Holls, who was primarily responsible for the word "recommend" in the articles on commissions of inquiry, defended use of that word. It was reported that he was considering a proposal to give the permanent court authority to suggest establishment of the commissions, but he never made the proposal in the *comité d'examen*.[20] Representatives of the major states determined to defend those parts of the draft con- vention providing for the commissions of inquiry. After all, the convention stated that commissions were to be instituted only in cases not involving honor or vital interests. The Balkan objec- tions, therefore, seemed ridiculous.

[19] *Proceedings, 1899*, p. 648.
[20] Manchester *Guardian*, July 17, 1899. Holls circulated copies of his proposal among members of the *comité d'examen*. In the Holls Papers is a note Pauncefote wrote Holls on July 8, 1899, hailing the new "Article Holls" and pledging support. So far as can be determined, no copies of Holls's proposal survive, and there are no documents which explain why he did not present his plan to the *comité*.

The great powers defended Article 27 more strongly than they defended commissions of inquiry. As expected, the French led in this defense, but it was surprising to find the Germans standing beside them. Zorn admitted that the expression of duty in that article did go a bit far for German tastes, but there should be "no insurmountable difficulties in the way of expressing and emphasizing this *moral* duty." Holls, forgetting his doubts, told the commission:

I desire to lay stress upon the following fact, which is the cause of my personal conviction: the absence of Article 27 would have been fatal to the Convention, which without this article would be in danger of not being utilized and of becoming a dead letter. It was necessary to express the idea of the *moral duty* of the States, not only toward themselves, but toward mankind. . . . It is in this sense that the clearcut adhesion of the American delegation, of the entire committee of examination to the proposal of the two French delegates was brought about. As for me, I rejoice that such an idea was formulated, for I consider it the necessary culmination of the task we have in hand.[21]

So strong were the counterattacks of the great powers that the Balkan nations agreed to the provisions on commissions of inquiry, good offices and mediation, and Article 27—after a few unimportant changes were made in the articles on commissions of inquiry. Yielding, they made declarations that nothing in those articles was to justify intervention in their affairs.[22]

Unfortunately the Balkan protests seemed to encourage other objections. Zorn and Martens were unwilling to accept certain articles in the draft convention. They made use of special sessions of the *comité* and the final meetings of the commission to repeat their objections.

Zorn asked the *comité* to drop the name "Permanent Court of Arbitration." He argued that the convention was not establishing a court—only a list of possible arbitrators. This demand

[21] *Proceedings, 1899*, pp. 660–662. See below, pp. 176–180.
[22] *Ibid.*, pp. 671–675, 790–794.

irritated other members of the group. Descamps warned that dropping the name would have a bad moral effect, and Asser reminded Zorn that to please Germany the *comité* had already changed the name from "tribunal" to "court." Holls pointed out that the Supreme Court of New York was, in fact, a list of judges and that only a few jurists from that list were selected to try each case referred to the court. Why should anyone question use of the word "court" for the institution about to come into existence? [23] These arguments ended the dispute, but Zorn later placed his government's objections on record before the full commission.[24]

Unlike Zorn, Martens did not renew his objections before the *comité*. He presented them to the full commission. At its meeting of July 17 he repeated earlier arguments against Holls's proposal for rehearing of arbitral cases. In a long discourse Holls again defended this provision. The American spoke nervously in English; outside the window a loud-voiced nightingale competed for attention. When Holls finished his speech, D'Estournelles translated it into French so eloquently that even Holls applauded his own address. Martens restated his objections only to have them refuted by Low in a short speech summarizing Holls's remarks. The Russian delegate had to accept defeat.[25]

The Americans, too, wanted changes in the convention. An article in the American court plan had provided that parties to an arbitration should share expenses of the tribunal. During the first phases of its work the *comité* had not discussed expenses, but Holls on July 18 asked that this matter be cleared up; accordingly it was decided that each party should pay its own expenses and share in the expenses of the court. Securing this decision was only a minor accomplishment for the American delegation, but it did mean that one more feature of their court plan would enter into the convention.[26]

[23] *Ibid.*, pp. 775–777.   [24] *Ibid.*, p. 652.
[25] *Ibid.*, pp. 618–625; Manchester *Guardian*, July 18, 1899.
[26] *Proceedings, 1899*, p. 788.

The Americans were less successful in their request for another amendment to the convention. Inspired, no doubt, by that provision in the American Constitution which forbids senators and representatives to hold federal civil offices, Low asked the conference to prohibit members of the court not acting in judicial capacities from serving as advocates or delegates before the court. Holls modified this proposal to forbid court members from serving as agents for any government other than their own. The *comité* approved an amendment very like Low's suggestion. But in the full commission so many objections arose that Holls did not ask for a vote and the amendment was lost.[27]

Debate in the *comité d'examen* and the third commission from July 15 to July 22 had thoroughly reexamined the draft convention. Despite the length, brilliance, and even vehemence of some speeches, the draft convention remained unchanged except in a few unimportant details. The debate did demonstrate that sensitive nationalists would oppose even the most modest steps toward international cooperation. The high idealism of the Grotius celebration had looked to a reign of law among nations, but debate on the arbitration convention indicated that men would long place national pride before the interests of all humanity.

[27] *Ibid.*, pp. 668, 795–797, 675–676.

XIII

Closing the Conference

WHILE the first commission was concluding debate, other subdivisions of the conference were preparing final reports. The second commission had reported on July 5, but the first commission, although it had nearly finished work on June 30, reported on July 21. De Staal in June had appointed Renault, Stengel, Martens, Raffalovich, Nigra, and Descamps to a committee to draft the final act and the official texts of the convention and other documents; later he added Low and an Austro-Hungarian delegate, Mérey von Kapos-Mére.[1] It was expected that the documents would soon be ready for signature. And signature would end the Hague Peace Conference.

I

The first commission held its last meetings on July 17 and 20. In these sessions and before the full conference on July 21, the American and British delegates again voiced objection to important decisions of the commission. Mahan went so far as to restate traditional American isolationism. On behalf of his

[1] *Proceedings, 1899*, pp. 49–50.

delegation he declared that the United States, while concurring in rejection of the Russian proposal to fix military budgets and armies and navies at the *status quo,* was expressing no opinion as to the course European states should follow. He dwelt on the small size of American armaments. He said that his declaration did not reflect indifference to a difficult problem but expressed "a determination to refrain from enunciating opinions upon matters into which, as concerning Europe alone, the United States has no claim to enter."

The commission again voted on its three declarations. The prohibition against throwing projectiles from balloons passed unanimously. Since several delegates had voted for the declaration against asphyxiating gas on condition of unanimous vote, Karnebeek appealed to Mahan to change his vote. Mahan refused and Admiral Fisher, reversing his earlier stand, joined him in opposition.[2]

The British soon had their reward for Fisher's vote on the asphyxiating gas prohibition. Before the full conference Crozier attacked the declaration against expanding bullets. He denounced that declaration as aimed only at the dumdum despite the fact that no one had proved that bullet to be excessively cruel. He proposed a new declaration outlawing all needlessly cruel bullets, particularly explosive types. Of course, Crozier's proposal would have pleased the British, for they did not consider their perforated dumdum to be unusually cruel. But few individuals cared to please the British. The conference refused Crozier's request and approved the declaration as reported from the first commission. Only the British and American delegates voted against it.[3] This example of Anglo-American cooperation brought wry comments. A delegate leaving the House in the Wood observed that "blood is thicker than water." Another laughingly responded, "Yes, the English and Americans do good business." [4]

---

[2] *Ibid.,* pp. 327–329.   [3] *Ibid.,* pp. 79–88.
[4] Manchester *Guardian,* July 22, 1899.

2

With the first commission's report and virtual conclusion of the third commission's work, the delegates discussed arrangements for signing the conventions and declarations. The drafting committee had given the arbitration treaty first rank and the name of Convention for the Pacific Settlement of International Disputes. The agreements produced by the second commission became the second and third conventions. They were called respectively the Convention with Respect to the Laws and Customs of War on Land and the Convention for the Adaptation to Maritime Warfare of the Principles of the Geneva Convention of August 22, 1864. There was talk of including the three declarations drawn up by the first commission in a fourth convention, but it was decided not to dignify those insignificant resolutions in that way.[5] They were to go before the conference as separate documents, hardly more important than the numerous recommendations attached to the final act.

Within the American delegation debate arose as to signing the agreements drawn by the conference. Of the three declarations the Americans could sign only the prohibition against throwing projectiles from balloons, for Mahan and Crozier had opposed the other declarations in the first commission. White wished to sign all three conventions but met with strong opposition.

All delegates agreed that the second convention was a meritorious document, but Crozier and Mahan feared it could conflict with existing American laws of war. It was decided to withhold signatures while recommending that the State Department refer it to proper authorities for examination. The delegates believed the United States could eventually accept this document.[6]

White, a believer in the traditional American views on private

<hr>

[5] *Proceedings, 1899*, p. 325.

[6] A. D. White, Diary excerpts, July 26 and 29, 1899, *Autobiog.*, II, 343, 346; General Report of the American Commission, July 31, 1899, in James B. Scott, *The Hague Peace Conferences*, II, 20–21.

property in maritime war, was anxious to sign the third convention. Mahan, however, determined that the Americans should not sign that document. When he received his copy of the convention he wrote his friend Sir John Fisher: "Possibly because I am a pig-headed cuss, I am not wholly satisfied with Renault's form. I say nothing of his French for I know nothing." [7] Mahan was even more dissatisfied with the contents of the convention. His colleagues in the second commission had refused consent to amendments he had proposed, and on July 20 he had withdrawn his proposition. Mahan stated that the American delegates still desired those amendments but that they were withdrawing them to facilitate agreement.[8] The captain nonetheless balked at the convention, and White, Low, Newel, and Crozier could not sign.

At first not even Mahan objected to signing the first convention, but on July 21 the Manchester *Guardian* published an editorial in which it enthusiastically maintained that had Article 27 of the arbitration convention been in effect in 1898 mediation between America and Spain would have been the duty of European powers and war would probably have been averted. Mahan had given little attention to the recent debates on Article 27, but the *Guardian* aroused his suspicion. He reread Article 27. Could it mean that in signing the convention the United States would obligate itself to interfere in foreign affairs? That European powers could use Article 27 to interfere in American affairs? Mahan concluded that Article 27 departed from the traditional American policy of avoiding entangling alliances. He informed Crozier and Newel of his apprehension. Showing Newel a copy of the *Guardian* he declared that if this construction were given to Article 27 he would never assent to the convention without reservation. Newel agreed. Soon the entire delegation knew of Mahan's objections, and White called a meeting for the morning of July 22 to consider the matter.

Much troubled, the delegates awaited the meeting. Sir Julian

[7] July 18, 1899, Mahan Papers.   [8] *Proceedings, 1899,* p. 88.

Pauncefote called to discuss arrangements for signing the final act, but the difficulties raised by Mahan were uppermost that day in the minds of the American delegates. As soon as White called the meeting to order, the captain threw in his "bomb," as White called it.[9] With conviction the naval authority declared that Article 27 endangered the traditional American policy of avoiding entangling alliances and even that the article threatened the Monroe Doctrine. Holls had praised the article extravagantly and now he opposed tampering with it, but believed that a reservation would protect American interests. He said nothing about his statement to the *comité d'examen* that the United States would have to examine the article with care to see that it would not conflict with traditional policy.[10] Mahan relentlessly demanded either amendment or reservation; to him the word *devoir* in the French text was much too strong. He reminded his colleagues of the Senate's record on treaties. Everyone remembered the fate of the Olney-Pauncefote treaty and the narrow margin by which the treaty of Paris of 1898 had received ratification. Holls maintained that the article could not have the dire effects feared by Mahan, but the captain's arguments prevailed. The long-pent-up antagonism from Mahan and Newel toward Holls burst forth. The question was raised how Holls came to be a member of the *comité d'examen* since he was not a delegate with full powers. White and Holls made explanations, yet Holls's critics were not satisfied. Even White, staunchly loyal to Holls, yielded to Mahan, and thanked the captain for timely observation.[11]

It was clear that something quickly had to be done. If the delegation were to refuse the great convention or have any members

[9] White, Diary excerpt, July 22, 1899, *Autobiog.*, II, 338.

[10] For a possible explanation of Holls's silence on this point, see pp. 194–195, n. 28.

[11] Newel recalled the American delegation's meeting of July 22 in detail in a letter to Mahan dated Dec. 18, 1900, in the Mahan Papers. The Minutes of the American Commission of July 22 and 24, 1899, contain only brief accounts of the controversial aspects of these meetings.

refuse to sign, it could be embarrassing in view of the prominence taken by Americans in framing that document. It was also embarrassing to have to request other powers to change Article 27. Consultations were held with leaders of other delegations. The French, who had proposed the article, were, White said, "as much attached to it as is a hen to her one chick." They refused to abandon it and did not wish a limiting or explanatory clause. At noon on July 24 the American delegation gave a luncheon at the Oude Doelen. De Staal, Nigra, Pauncefote, Bourgeois, Basily, D'Estournelles, De Bildt, and a number of less important personages were present. The Americans urged the French to accept modification of the clause in question. The words *autant que possible* or similar words should follow that word *devoir*, said the United States delegates. Bourgeois and D'Estournelles refused. Bourgeois made a long speech defending the article. In detail he expounded on the meaning of *devoir*. His explanation, White later declared, "showed that the Jesuits are not the only skillful casuists in the world." France would not yield, and that was definite. Ambassador White had yet another alternative. Hastily that morning he had written out in pencil the rough draft of a declaration upholding the traditional American principle of abstaining from purely European affairs. This declaration he proposed to make before the full conference. Bourgeois and D'Estournelles could see no harm in White's declaration and neither could the other luncheon guests.

Later the American delegation met to consider White's declaration, and Low suggested that the declaration be extended to include a statement that signing the convention would not require abandonment of the traditional American attitude toward American affairs. This suggestion met with approval, and White and Low revised the declaration.[12] White wired the State Department for approval and awaited the outcome of his delegation's intricate maneuvers.

The third commission was to hold a brief closing meeting on July 25 and afterward present its report to the conference.

[12] White, Diary excerpt, July 24. 1899, *Autobiog.*, II, 339–340.

The Americans would have opportunity to bring their declaration to the conference at that time. This they resolved to do, although no answer had come to White's wire to Washington. Carefully White prepared the notes of a speech defending the declaration. As the time of the meeting approached, his anxiety grew. There was little sleep for him that preceding night, and as he tossed about in his bed he thought of the objections which could be raised. All the American delegates feared the conference would not receive the declaration, although they had secured consent in advance from several prominent members of the conference.[13] As matters turned out, the declaration was handed to Raffalovich, the Russian secretary. First the final act was read. Then Raffalovich brought out the American document. Slowly he read the statement:

Nothing contained in this Convention shall be so construed as to require the United States of America to depart from its traditional policy of not intruding upon, interfering with, or entangling itself in the political questions or policy or internal administration of any foreign State; nor shall anything contained in the said Convention be construed to imply a relinquishment by the United States of America of its traditional attitude toward purely American questions.

De Staal asked the conference whether any person present had objections or observations. The dread moment had arrived.

White listened for a voice from the floor.

There was only silence.

The declaration was recorded as part of the proceedings.[14]

The American delegates went forward with their remaining tasks. On the morning of July 27 a telegram arrived approving their reservation. Yet their stand did not go unquestioned, for Pauncefote, although he had ample experience with the vagaries of the American Senate, disapproved. He told White that "it

[13] *Ibid.*, July 25, 1899, pp. 340–341.

[14] *Proceedings, 1899*, pp. 99–100; trans. corrected by reference to other versions, esp. James Brown Scott, ed., *The Hague Conventions and Declarations of 1899 and 1907* (New York, 1915), pp. 84, 87.

will be charged against you that you propose to evade your duties while using the treaty to promote your interests." White feared that the distinguished Briton would raise objections before the open conference, but perhaps because he desired no disputes with his American friends Pauncefote did not do so. To ease the Englishman's mind White promised a public statement. Revising the speech he had ready for the conference—and which he had not needed—he called in William Lavino, the correspondent for the London *Times*, and Lavino put the speech into form of a telegram and wired it to his newspaper. When Lavino's account of the interview appeared in *The Times* it received favorable comment. Pauncefote told Holls of his personal approval.[15]

3

With disposal of the reservation problem it appeared that the closing days of the conference would be serene, and yet one more controversy arose. Catholic delegates, particularly some members of the Austrian and Belgian delegations, demanded that the pope be granted the privilege of signing the conventions. Among these delegates the great international lawyer, Descamps, a professor at the University of Louvain, demanded this privilege for Leo XIII. The Italian delegates, mindful of any step which could be interpreted as recognition for the temporal powers of the Holy See, rejected the idea. Great Britain opposed this move, not that she cared whether the pope could sign but because she disliked a precedent which would enable powers not participating in the conference to give their adherence without consent of all signatory powers. The Transvaal Republic, with which a state of war threatened, might avail herself of the privileges of the conventions.

The American delegation opposed entry of Leo XIII into the benefits of the conference. Holls and White both cherished deep antipapal feelings, and the rest of the delegation agreed that contracting parties should assent before a new power could sign.

[15] White, Diary excerpt, July 25, 1899, *Autobiog.*, II, 341–342.

Seth Low clearly stated this opinion before the drafting committee. The committee drafting the final act agreed to leave to ordinary diplomacy the question of admission of powers not participating in the conference. This meant that no representative of the Holy See could sign.[16]

At ten o'clock on the morning of July 29 the conference assembled in the House in the Wood for its next to last meeting. Documents were laid out on the long table in the palace dining room. The Dutch Foreign Office made arrangements according to strictest protocol. Wax seals had been prepared for each of the delegates. Proudly Andrew White had turned over to the foreign office a seal ring made from an ancient Roman carnelian intaglio which Goldwin Smith had given him. Often in his eventful life he had seals made from it to apply to documents, but never before had he used it in so important a ceremony. When the time for the American signatures came, the ambassador signed first, as befitted his rank. He signed the arbitration convention and the first of the declarations, but with regret he left the other documents unsigned. Following him the other members of the delegation, except Holls, who did not have the powers of a plenipotentiary, took turns at the table. Signing the conference documents took all the forenoon. There followed luncheon, which was a gay affair. The delegates extravagantly expressed sentiments for the future happiness of one another and drank countless toasts.[17]

Following the luncheon the conference assembled in the great hall for a final session. Press representatives and distinguished guests crowded the gallery. Staff members of each delegation stood about the room. Queen Wilhelmina was represented by Prime Minister Pierson. At three o'clock Baron de Staal opened this last session, presiding with far more self-possession than he had shown on the opening day of the conference. Jonkheer van

[16] *Ibid.*, July 26, 1899.
[17] *Ibid.*, July 29, 1899, pp. 345–346; Frederick W. Holls, *The Peace Conference at The Hague*, pp. 335–336.

Karnebeek reported that all powers represented had signed the final act, but that only seventeen of the powers had signed all conventions and declarations. Of the great powers Russia and France had signed all documents. Delegates of Great Britain, Italy, Germany, and Austria-Hungary chose to sign no conventions and declarations, preferring to leave to their governments all decision concerning those documents. The United States signed the first convention and the first declaration.

Following Karnebeek's report De Staal announced that the Dutch government had asked him to read a letter which Queen Wilhelmina had sent to the pope on May 7, together with His Holiness' reply. Doubtless the Dutch officials had asked to have these letters read to mollify their nation's Catholics, who held the political balance of power in the Netherlands. While the conference listened, Leo XIII through his letter placed his opinions on the record. Queen Wilhelmina had requested papal sympathy for the endeavors of The Hague. The pope had replied courteously to the queen, and grandly declared:

We consider that it comes especially within our province not only to lend our moral support to such enterprises, but to cooperate actively in them, for the object in question is supremely noble in its nature and intimately bound up with our august ministry, which, through the divine founder of the Church, and in virtue of traditions of many secular instances, has been invested with the highest possible mission, that of being a mediator of peace. In fact, the authority of the supreme pontiff goes beyond the boundaries of nations; it embraces all peoples, to the end of federating them in the true peace of the gospel. His action to promote the general good of humanity rises above the special interest which the chiefs of the various States have in view, and, better than any one else, his authority knows how to incline toward concord peoples of diverse nature and character. . . . Even unto us, notwithstanding the abnormal condition to which we are at present reduced, it has been given to put an end to grave differences between great nations such as Germany and Spain, and this very day we hope to be able soon to establish concord between two nations of South America which have submitted their controversy to our arbitration.[18]

The pontiff had his say after all. He maintained his age-old claim as arbiter of Christendom, and he had given Italy a thinly-veiled rebuke for mistreatment of the Holy See. It was too late for anyone to raise an objection.

The final session of the conference could only go on to its conclusion. De Staal made a speech, which White termed excellent. Affecting satisfaction with the conference, the baron minimized its failure to limit arms—the greatest object the czar had in proposing the meeting in the first place. He said that if the first commission had not reached many "material results, it is because the Commission met with technical difficulties and a series of allied considerations which it did not deem itself competent to examine." He referred to the work of the Brussels Conference, called twenty-five years before upon the initiative of the Czar Alexander II to consider laws of war; he professed pleasure in the Hague Conference's elaboration of measures begun in the Belgian capital so long ago. The presiding officer declared his elation over the arbitration convention. In closing he said:

Well, gentlemen, the first step has been taken. Let us unite our goodwill and profit by experience. The good seed is sown. Let the harvest come. As for me, who have reached the end of my career and the decline of life, I consider it a supreme consolation to see new prospects opening up for the good of humanity and to be able to peer into the brightness of the future.[19]

It fell to Count Münster to reply—a difficult task for the German representative. The count from the first had scorned the conference and he did not like De Staal.[20] Yet as senior delegate he had to make a laudatory address, and summoning all the

---

[18] *Proceedings, 1899*, pp. 222–223.   [19] *Ibid.*, pp. 224–225.
[20] White. Diary excerpt, July 29, 1899, *Autobiog.*, II, 346.

forbearance learned in his years as a diplomat he did his duty. Speaking extemporaneously, he made a graceful reply in French. He praised De Staal but avoided giving that gentleman his due by offering Karnebeek greater praise. The chief Dutch delegate had been the "prime mover of the Conference" and had "worked more than any of us." There was little praise for the accomplishments of the conference. In closing, Münster asked the conference to rise in honor of De Staal—and Karnebeek.

D'Estournelles followed the German statesman. Making a speech praising the conference delighted the peace leader. Said he: "Let us unite in the hope, gentlemen, that our countries, in calling other conferences such as this, may continue to assist in advancing the cause of civilization and of peace."

De Beaufort rose to express similar sentiments and to assure his colleagues of the pleasure of the Dutch government in acting as host for the conference.

After De Beaufort sat down, De Staal again declared satisfaction with the conference. With these pleasant sentiments he declared the conference adjourned sine die.[21]

As soon as the conference ended, Ambassador White went to Scheveningen for the night. Dreading the task of writing reports, he returned to The Hague the following morning. Although it was Sunday, for the first time in his life the old diplomat worked on that day. This course could not be avoided. The other delegates were anxious to leave the Dutch capital as soon as possible. As he wrote, the ambassador found himself hampered by necessity of wording his report in such a way that Captain Mahan would approve of it. At 5:00 P.M. the delegation met, and to White's amazement even Mahan had no serious objection. Seth Low suggested some changes, the value of which White recognized. White turned his draft over to Low, who worked on it that evening. At eleven the next morning Low presented his draft, omitting several passages which White would have liked to have retained. One was an appeal in behalf of arbitration, but

[21] *Proceedings, 1899*, pp. 225–227.

the ambassador was anxious for unanimity and did not object. Late in the afternoon the delegation gave its reports final consideration. Crozier and Mahan each had made special reports. Low, Holls, and White had prepared a report on the third commission. These documents in addition to the general report were signed, and the delegation adjourned for the last time.[22]

The final days of the conference had been strenuous. All delegates were glad to be free of their duties, but for many of them much work in connection with the late conference remained. What interpretation would they give of its deliberations? How would they advise their governments of its decisions? Many delegates, among them the Americans, were thinking of answers to these questions as they left The Hague.

[22] White, Diary excerpts, July 29 and 30, 1899, *Autobiog.*, II, 347–348.

XIV

Ratification

UPON adjournment of the conference the State Department sent the American commissioners a congratulatory dispatch, and President McKinley sent word that their work met with his approval.[1] Happy in knowledge that their efforts were appreciated in Washington, the commissioners separated. Newel, Crozier, and Mahan had misgivings about the decisions of the conference, but Holls, White, and Low left the Netherlands convinced they had helped further world peace. Low expressed this feeling in conversation with the British pacifist Francis William Fox:

The main point of a whole thing is that Arbitration has been made easy; it was only possible before. There is a great deal of public opinion in the air in favour of Arbitration, and so is there of electricity; and that electricity is useless until there is a motor. The Peace Conference has furnished the standing parts of the machinery, which will admit of the practical working of Arbitration; it has furnished the motor.[2]

[1] Low to McKinley, Aug. 5, 1899, McKinley Papers.
[2] Francis W. Fox, *Some Historical Incidents*, p. 19.

I

Crozier, Holls, and Mahan returned to America; Newel resumed his legation duties, and White returned to Berlin. Low went to Lucerne for a vacation and to begin an account of the conference. Shortly before the conference convened, the *North American Review* had offered him $500 for an article and he was eager to begin writing.[3] He had preserved copies of the more important documents, but since they were in French he found his initial task that of a translator. Having little confidence in his linguistic ability, he was unaware even of the correct English titles of the conventions. When he arrived in New York in September, the article was almost finished, but desiring to check the accuracy of his translations he delayed publication until November.[4]

Captain Mahan may have been concerned less than Low about accuracy of translation of the Hague proceedings, for he was the first of the American delegates to publish an account of the conference. In October the *North American Review* published his article, "The Peace Conference and the Moral Aspect of War." The captain said that the strong feeling in favor of arbitration was "a subject for congratulation almost unalloyed," but he warned that "such sentiments, from their very universality and evident laudableness, need correctives, for they bear in themselves a great danger of excess or of precipitancy." He displayed no concern about making the Hague decisions effective. He feared that growth of arbitration sentiment could cause mankind to be reluctant to use war in defense of liberty and national aspiration.[5] Privately he had greater doubts about arbitration and he would have welcomed safeguarding amendments to the

[3] *North American Review* to Low, May 9, 1899, Low Papers.
[4] Low to Mahan, Sept. 19, 1899, Low Papers.
[5] Alfred Thayer Mahan, "The Peace Conference and the Moral Aspect of War," *North American Review*, CLXIX (1899), 445–446.

Hague conventions.[6] Mahan's article was, in fact, a thinly veiled criticism of the conference of which he so recently had been a member.

Other critics having no connection with the conference were not at all restrained in analyses of the Hague proceedings. T. E. Holland, professor of international law at Oxford, said that the negative results of the conference were more important than its achievements. He thought the prediction that it would give the czar's proposals for limiting armaments a first-class burial had been fully justified. Further he said that the "substantive provisions contained in the Arbitration Convention amount really to nothing, since everything in them which savoured of an obligatory character was omitted, in deference to the arguments of which the German delegation was the mouthpiece." [7]

Goldwin Smith also criticized the conference. Andrew White's close friendship with Smith did not deter the internationally famous professor from making scathing remarks about the conference and the American role in its deliberations. Writing in the Toronto *Sun*, he said that the

only tangible fruit, apparently, will be a permanent board of arbitration, which, we are told, is a priceless boon to mankind. Curiously enough, its merits appear to be most eloquently proclaimed by the ambassador of the United States, a power which, in forcing war upon Spain when she had tendered arbitration in the case of the *Maine*, has most flagrantly trampled on the principle, and, being bent on grasping its prey, would not have been deterred by the existence of an international board.[8]

In the United States one of the most bitter condemnations of the conference appeared in the same issue of the *North American Review* which contained Mahan's article. "In the Clutch of the

[6] In a letter dated Sept. 28, 1899, Low rebuked Mahan for his private views (Low Papers).

[7] T. E. Holland, "Some Lessons of the Peace Conference," *Fortnightly Review*, N.S., LXVI (1899), 957.

[8] Quoted in *Literary Digest*, XIX (Aug. 26, 1899), 261.

Harpy Powers" was the title which R. M. Johnston gave his article in the *Review*. He insisted that the American delegates had abandoned the principles of American foreign policy and entangled their country in European intrigues. Johnston professed sympathy for Ambassador White and his colleagues. They had been surrounded, he said, by "Young Turks, old Armenians, emancipated and enthusiastic women, ancient revolutionists of the forties," who had "buzzed about The Hague like bees." In this atmosphere he thought it understandable that the American representatives had been so carried away that they had participated in framing the arbitration convention. He added: "Let but the Senate decline to ratify the Convention, and we shall forget all else but the humane and elevated sentiments that inspired their action." [9]

Johnston's attitude was like that of other Americans who feared for the safety of their traditional principles of foreign policy, and it was not dissimilar to that which Mahan had voiced at The Hague. Some individuals were otherwise critical of the American role at The Hague. Some peace advocates were displeased because they thought that not enough had been attained for arbitration and armament limitation. Others were unhappy because the recent behavior of the United States in foreign affairs was inconsistent with ideas advanced at The Hague by American spokesmen. *The Nation* said that cynical persons should not be blamed for pointing out that neither Britain nor the United States, while talking so eloquently about arbitration, was willing to arbitrate the only serious controversies which each had on hand.[10] And there were grounds for *The Nation*'s criticism. Settlement of the Canadian-Alaskan boundary still seemed far in the future, and the McKinley administration refused to resort to arbitration. Britain's quarrel with the Transvaal, acute throughout the year, erupted in war with that republic and with

[9] R. M. Johnston, "In the Clutch of the Harpy Powers," *North American Review*, CLXIX (1899), 453.

[10] LXIX (Aug. 3, 1899), 82.

the Orange Free State in October 1899. To suggestions that she arbitrate her difficulties with the Boers, Britain replied that Queen Victoria was suzerain of the South African republics and that arbitration of a dispute with a subject state was unthinkable. Cynical persons regarded the Boer War as proof that the Hague Conference had achieved nothing. Peace advocates hoped that the arbitration convention, when ratified, could end the conflict. American delegates to the conference often found it necessary to explain that the convention could not apply in this instance; their understanding of the matter was identical with that of the British government.[11]

But most peace leaders differed with critics of the conference. Dr. Darby of the London Peace Society was exultant as he surveyed conference achievements. He said that the conventions made the conference "possibly one of the greatest of human agents that have ever existed for the advancement of civilization." [12] Articles in the *Advocate of Peace* expressed the satisfaction of the American Peace Society. The Universal Peace Union was much more enthusiastic than the older society, and an editorial in *The Peacemaker* proclaimed:

It has turned the stone that the advocates of peace have been trying in vain to move. It has established a Tribunal and a Bureau. The governments and representatives of peace have now to follow up this work on the ground plan laid out, and war and its barbarisms will soon become abhorrent to the mass of mankind. It is well worth all the talk, money and effort that peace people have exerted.[13]

As for persons high in American public life, they were rarely either critical or enthusiastic about the conference. Neither President McKinley nor Secretary Hay appears to have given much thought to documents the delegates turned over to them. In

[11] Low to Tunis G. Bergen, Oct. 23, 1899, Low Papers; Holls to J. J. Rochussen, Jan. 17, 1900, Holls Papers; Sir Edmund Monson to Salisbury, Oct. 24, 1899, *British Documents*, I, 232.

[12] Quoted in Fox, p. 19.

[13] XVIII (1899), 48.

the State Department only Assistant Secretary Hill had strong interest in the results of the conference. Nor did the close of the conference cause concern in the Senate, the body which would determine whether the United States would accept the Hague conventions and declarations. Among advocates of naval and military preparedness the conference decisions aroused neither approbation nor opposition. New York's Governor Roosevelt told his friend, Maria Storer, that he earnestly desired peace but that "peace often comes only as the result of labor and strife." The governor believed that something had been done for peace at The Hague but that "our influence was due to the fact that we came in as a strong man and not as a weakling." [14]

Opinions of the American delegates concerning the Hague decisions were of course welcome in influential quarters. Mahan, through his article and his contacts in political and naval circles, spread doubts about arbitration and the limitation of armaments. It is probable that Crozier communicated to his army friends views similar to Mahan's, but he was not widely known and he published nothing about the conference. Low, publishing his article "The International Conference of Peace," sent copies to McKinley and other powerful people.[15] The Columbia president lauded the conference, but made no extravagant claims for the arbitration convention. "No one supposes that this Convention, even if universally signed, will prevent all war," he wrote, "but it will compel the nations, in a new way, to justify war to the public opinion of mankind." [16]

Holls had much more to say about the conference than did Mahan, Low, and Crozier. His prediction that the conference would prove a good thing to talk about was fully realized. He

---

[14] Roosevelt to Maria Storer, Oct. 28, 1889, in Elting E. Morison, John M. Blum, and John J. Buckley, eds., *The Letters of Theodore Roosevelt* (Cambridge, Mass., 1951–1954), II, 1089.

[15] Low to McKinley, Oct. 14, 1899, McKinley Papers.

[16] Seth Low, *North American Review*, CLXIX (1899), 638.

was to devote much time and energy to writing and lecturing about the conference and America's obligation to carry forward the work begun there. For several weeks after return to America he had to turn his mind to other matters, for his legal practice and political interests required attention, and he also had an attack of lumbago. He was anxious to report to President McKinley and Secretary Hay about his services as a diplomat, but his first visit to Washington after return from The Hague was to smooth out difficulties concerning appointment of a friend to a German consulate.[17] Certain State Department officials were not glad to see him. "Such beings as Holls drive me frantic by their overweening egotismus," said Assistant Secretary Alvey A. Adee.[18] When Newel, on leave, paid a visit to the State Department early in the winter, he thought it his duty to tell everyone what he considered the truth about Holls. Talking with Hay and Hill, the disgruntled diplomat was unrestrained. He told them that only Mahan had saved the commission from a terrible blunder "thro' Holls' inefficiency in the place he improperly occupied on the Comité d'Examen." [19]

Even so, no criticism from Newel could shake Hill's confidence in his friend. Holls, while slow to report to Hay, had visited with Hill at the assistant secretary's summer cottage in September. There the two spent a pleasant Sunday discussing the conference, "including many things which it was interesting to know," so said Hill, "but which can never appear in official reports." After hearing his visitor's impressions, the assistant secretary declared that he could never cease to be grateful that White's "wisdom and experience" had been yoked with Holls's "fresh, dashing energy." [20]

[17] Holls to Hill, Oct. 26, 1899, Hill Papers.

[18] Adee to Hay, Sept. 16, 1899, Hay Papers. In a note in his *International Arbitration from Athens to Locarno* (Palo Alto, Calif., 1929), p. 256, Jackson H. Ralston recalled that Hay in 1903 had bitterly denounced Holls. The secretary of state said that for whatever White, Low, or he himself had proposed at The Hague, Holls claimed credit.

[19] Newel to Mahan, Dec. 18, 1900, Mahan Papers.

[20] Hill to A. D. White, Sept. 25, 1899, A. D. White Papers.

As soon as his affairs were in order, Holls began devoting a major part of his time to informing his fellow citizens about the conference. Invitations to lecture came from Harvard and Johns Hopkins, from Wellesley, and from Boston's Century Club. He accepted, and instructed his sponsors not to refer to him, when announcing his lecture, as "delegate and secretary" but simply to call him a "Member of the Conference from the United States of America." He told Hill that he had made this change in his title for reasons of accuracy.[21] At the State Department this new title caused some embarrassment, and Whitelaw Reid's inquisitive Washington representative, M. G. Seckendorff, called at the department to learn the truth about Holls's status at the conference; Assistant Secretary Adee flatly said that only by a stretch of his imagination could Holls consider himself a member of the delegation. Hill said that his friend had not been, strictly speaking, a delegate, but he highly praised his work.[22]

Unaware of the impression he was making in Washington, Holls undertook his lecture engagements with enthusiasm, and learned groups and peace leaders listened to him with respect. He won favor with pacifists. When talking with them, he told how helpful their support had been to the delegation. In detail he described his experiences at the conference; his mission to Berlin provided his most dramatic subject, and he never tired of telling about that journey. Long after his death peace leaders were to remember him as one of the great adventurers in the war against war.[23]

Holls was not content to lecture; he wanted to write; and while at The Hague, and encouraged by Pauncefote, he had begun planning a book about the conference.[24] He told his friends that the work would be the only book in the English language by a member of the conference and he was undertaking the task "only upon the urgent solicitation of both the American

[21] Holls to Hill, Jan. 31, 1900, Hill Papers.
[22] Seckendorff to Reid, Nov. 23, 1900, Reid Papers.
[23] Edward Everett Hale to Choate, June 19, 1907, Choate Papers.
[24] Holls to Leopold J. Maxse, Oct. 11, 1900, Holls Papers.

and English delegations." [25] As secretary of the American delegation he had secured documents published during the conference; these he sent to Washington. Shortly after return to New York he asked to use them, but the papers had been mislaid, and after they were discovered there was delay before they could be rendered into English and sent him. Inconsiderately the State Department's translator chose to take an October vacation. There was delay before Holls could obtain the final report of the conference. For months that document lay unprinted in the Dutch government's printing office.[26]

Holls finally secured the necessary documents and began work, and until the book was published in the autumn of 1900 it required much time—although he never neglected his other interests. He did not intend to produce a popular work, for he was writing for scholars and hoped that his book, while it would not enjoy large sale, would be in most libraries. He did try to create some interest in the forthcoming work. He took care that his friends and the acquaintances he had made at The Hague were fully informed. He wrote Nicholas II requesting the Russian monarch to accept the dedication of the book. The emperor granted his petition, and Holls communicated this interesting fact to his friends, warning them to keep it secret until the book appeared. He hoped Congress would accord him recognition by authorizing publication at government expense. Soon after the close of the conference Senator William Boyd Allison of Iowa had hinted that this course could be possible.[27] To all suggestions that he ask Congress for appropriation Secretary Hay, however, had no definite answer. Finally the Macmillan Company published *The Peace Conference at The Hague and Its Bearings on International Law and Policy*.[28]

[25] Holls to Theodore Lange, June 25, 1900, Holls Papers.
[26] Holls to Hill, Dec. 7, 1899, Hill Papers.
[27] *Ibid.*, Sept. 23, 1899.
[28] On pages 269–270 of his book Holls claimed that the Monroe Doctrine declaration originated with his reservation in the *comité d'examen*. Mahan sharply challenged this claim, and his charges became

Before his book appeared, Holls acquainted the American reading public with his impressions of the conference through an article in the *American Monthly Review of Reviews* for November 1899, "The Results of the Peace Conference in Their Relation to the Monroe Doctrine." In the following month he published in *The Independent* a similar article, "America at the Peace Conference." Appearance of these essays was timely, for there were rumors that the Hague conventions would meet with opposition in the Senate. Holls presented able pleas for the conference agreements. He refuted R. M. Johnston's charge that the American delegates had compromised their country's foreign policy in signing the arbitration convention. In both articles he quoted the declaration which the American commission had made at the conference on July 25. He maintained that it not merely upheld the Monroe Doctrine, but that the representatives of other powers, by immediately and unanimously consenting to this act of the Americans, had given the Monroe Doctrine its first official international recognition.[29] In his article for *The Independent* he dwelt lovingly on "La Proposition Holls," yet in both articles his concern was to inform the public of the merits of the court to be set up by the arbitration convention. Admitting that the work of the conference could not lead to aboli-

___

even stronger when Newel reported a rumor that Holls had had his reservation inserted in the minutes after adjournment of the conference. Holls admitted that he had requested this amendment, but insisted that desire for accuracy had motivated him. He secured letters from other members of the *comité* in which they recalled that he had made such a reservation. In a letter which he wrote Holls on March 12, 1902, Mahan withdrew his charges. Holls accepted this withdrawal in a letter written two days later. While Holls did clear himself of those charges, he failed to establish a connection between his reservation and the declaration. Holls's letter and a copy of Mahan's are in the Mahan Papers. Very many long letters in the papers of both Mahan and Holls are concerned with this controversy.

[29] Frederick W. Holls, "The Results of the Peace Conference in Their Relation to the Monroe Doctrine," *American Monthly Review of Reviews*, XX (1899), 563; Frederick W. Holls, "America at the Peace Conference," *The Independent*, LI (Dec. 28, 1899), 3473.

tion of war, at least for a long time, he expressed conviction that it began a new era. He claimed a good deal for the arbitration convention:

For the first time in the history of the world the ideas of justice and right have been agreed upon by a great representative Parliament of Man as the true basis of international relations. International Law, which heretofore has consisted only in suggestions of what it ought to be as contained in the books and treaties defining it, so far as the purposes of the parties were concerned, has now received its Magna Charta—its fundamental law.[30]

2

It was desirable to maintain interest in the work of the conference, for both Secretary Hay and Assistant Secretary Hill had heard that a move was on foot to defeat the treaties in the Senate. Neither the secretary of state nor the president was in a hurry to send the agreements already signed at The Hague to the Senate. They were considering the conventions and declarations which their delegates had left unsigned. Finally they concluded that it would be unwise to seek Senate approval of the declarations against asphyxiating gas and expanding bullets which Mahan and Crozier had so opposed at the conference, but they decided to have Newel sign the second and third conventions and to press for Senate approval of those treaties.

The third convention—the convention extending the Geneva principles to the sea—presented a special problem to McKinley and Hay. They disliked its tenth article. This article had provided that a neutral state should guard shipwrecked, wounded, or sick belligerent military persons who entered its ports and prevent them from returning to combat. Mahan at the conference had opposed this provision, and his objections were shared by the president and the secretary of state. With relief, Hay learned that Britain, although her representatives had voted in the conference for the measure, had informed the Dutch government in

[30] Holls, "America at the Peace Conference," p. 3473.

early November 1899 that she wished to adhere to the convention while not assenting to this particular clause. No power could make a reservation in its ratification of one of the conventions without consent of the other powers, and the Dutch communicated the British request to the governments concerned. The Washington government gave its permission and at the same time requested an identical reservation. The Dutch secured consent of all the nations at the conference to exclude the clause from the convention.[31]

While the State Department was studying the conventions, several of the country's peace spokesmen became fearful that opponents of the arbitration treaty were being given opportunity to organize. The most ardent peace leaders, of course, came at once to the support of the conference. The Universal Peace Union's Alfred Love planned a public meeting in favor of ratification. He wanted members of the American delegation to give the principal addresses and invited both Low and Mahan. Low had refused at least twenty invitations to lecture on the conference, but he did not decline this request until he learned of Mahan's decision. As for Mahan, he hesitated not a moment— he refused. At the same time he made clear the low esteem in which he held the Universal Peace Union.[32] Low rejected the invitation more courteously, but was frank with the Philadelphia pacifist. He told Alfred Love that it would be an error to hold the meeting. "If the Commissioners to The Hague identify themselves with the extreme position occupied by your Union," he wrote Love, "so far from helping the cause that you have at heart I think it would be an obstacle in its path." [33]

Other peace leaders sought to aid the cause. There were several peace spokesmen whose prestige was so great that they could not be accorded treatment of the kind given Love by Low and

[31] Hay to A. D. White, Nov. 29, 1899, A. D. White Papers; Frederick W. Holls, *The Peace Conference at The Hague*, pp. 127–130.

[32] Mahan to Alfred Love, Nov. 22, 1899, copy in Low Papers.

[33] Low to Love, Nov. 20, 1899, Low Papers.

Mahan, individuals such as Dr. Edward Everett Hale. Talking with Hill at the State Department in mid-November, the famous clergyman learned that ratification of the arbitration convention was in doubt. Hale offered to hold meetings, but both Hay and Hill dissuaded him, for they thought such meetings could arouse antagonism rather than quiet it. Hale acquiesced, although he concluded that the State Department was only halfhearted in support of the treaty.[34] He was so upset that as soon as he returned to Boston he wrote President McKinley: "We thought and boasted that America had won the greatest of victories at the Conference at The Hague;—and now we are told that the Senate will not even pick up the poor foundling of a treaty from its doorstep!" He urged the chief executive to plead for ratification in his annual message.[35]

The president's message went to Congress on December 2, but in the meantime Hale was not idle. No corporation lawyer understood the art of lobbying better than he, and he employed all his talents. He enlisted support of William E. Dodge and he told Low of the danger.[36] Low was quick to offer President McKinley his aid.[37] Hale did not limit himself to getting his friends to put pressure on the chief executive. The danger was on Capitol Hill, and it was necessary to carry the battle into the Senate. He was on quite friendly terms with the two Massachusetts senators, George F. Hoar and Henry Cabot Lodge, and from them he obtained assurance that they would support the treaty. He successfully contacted other New England senators. Using the organization of the Boston Peace Crusade and the correspondence committee of the WCTU, he pressed many Southern and Western senators.

The key to the whole problem, however, seemed to lie with the enigmatic chairman of the Senate Foreign Relations Committee, Cushman K. Davis. All peace leaders remembered the

[34] Hale to A. D. White, Jan. 16, 1900, Holls Papers.
[35] Hale to McKinley, Nov. 16, 1899, copy in Low Papers.
[36] Hale to Low, Nov. 21, 1899, Low Papers; Dodge to Hale, Dec. 14, 1899, copy in Holls Papers.
[37] Low to McKinley, Nov. 22, 1899, Low Papers.

part he had played in defeat of the Olney-Pauncefote treaty. Would Davis again hinder the advance of arbitration? Hale feared to approach the senator directly, so he asked a mutual friend to sound him. The intermediary learned that Davis knew little about the convention; indeed he was sure that the senator had not yet read it.[38] What could one expect from such a man?

McKinley's annual message of December 2, 1899, was all the arbitration convention's supporters desired. In his matter-of-fact way McKinley gave a brief account of the conference and the conventions which it had framed. He emphasized the arbitration convention and urged favorable action in the Senate. As if anticipating objection on the ground that ratification would cause the United States to depart from its traditional policies, he quoted verbatim his delegation's declaration of July 25.[39]

There followed a difficult period. Supporters of the arbitration convention were pleased; they expected McKinley to send the Senate the treaty immediately. Hale hoped ratification could be before Christmas. Days passed and there was no word of further executive action. Hale wrote Senator Davis urging immediate senatorial action. The Minnesota senator's reply was cordial; he favored ratification and declared he would be "glad to bring about so desirable a result," but the Senate, he said, could not consider the treaty until the president submitted it.[40] Davis' reply should have eased Hale's mind. Still, the Bostonian told Frederick Holls of his doubts about the senator. The chairman of the Foreign Relations Committee was to have constant pressure until ratification of the treaty. Davis and Newel were from St. Paul, Minnesota, and Holls feared that Newel's lukewarmness had already been communicated to the senator.[41] He wrote Ambassador White urging him to write Senator Davis. The ambassador promised to do all that he could and advised Holls to consult with

[38] Hale to A. D. White, Jan. 16, 1900, copy in Holls Papers.
[39] Richardson, *Messages and Papers*, IX, 6383–6385.
[40] Davis to Hale, Dec. 7, 1899, copy in Holls Papers.
[41] Holls to Hill, Dec. 7, 1899, Hill Papers.

Low, for he knew that Low's opinions were held in high regard at the White House. White told Holls that he should remember Talleyrand's dictum: *"Surtout, pas de zèle."* [42]

Actually, the president was not neglecting the arbitration treaty. The State Department was continuing its study of the convention, and at last on December 19, 1899 Secretary Hay informed the chief executive that the arbitration convention and the declaration on balloons were ready for the Senate. The following day McKinley submitted them to the Senate. [43]

While the Senate waited, Hale and Holls made sure that interested persons would have opportunity to study the treaty in detail. The State Department had not released an official text, and it was thought that the sooner an accurate translation was available the better. To fill this need Hill sent Holls a British bluebook which contained the text of the convention. The secretary of the late conference was annoyed to find errors in translation. Making corrections, he turned the document over to Hale, who published it in pamphlet form. [44] Their hope of securing a decision before Christmas was not realized; Congress adjourned and the treaty was left for consideration in the new year.

While senators relaxed during the Christmas holidays, there was little rest for the peace advocates; they prepared a petition to the Senate which demanded ratification. The petition reviewed American efforts in behalf of arbitration and cited approvingly the American commission's now famous declaration of July 25 as evidence that adherence could in no way compromise American policy. Heading the list of signers was Simeon E. Baldwin, president of the International Law Association, but the most noted names were those of former President Grover Cleveland and former Vice President Levi P. Morton. Four former secre-

---

[42] A. D. White to Holls, Jan. 27, 1900, Holls Papers.

[43] Document No. 159, 56th Congress, First Session (Washington, 1900), pp. 1–2, in *Senate Documents*, X.

[44] Holls to Hill, Dec. 14 and 18, 1899, Hill Papers.

taries of state, Richard Olney, John W. Foster, William M. Evarts, and William R. Day, signed, as did a host of other former cabinet officers and assistant secretaries. The presidents of nearly all the nation's leading universities and a large number of other prominent personages likewise signed. Sponsors of the petition asked Henry Cabot Lodge to present it to the Senate. He consented. On January 10, 1900, he rose in the Senate to request that the petition and names of its signers be printed in the *Record*. The president pro tempore was surprised; he pointed out that such a request could be granted only by unanimous consent of all present; Lodge insisted, stating that the prominence of the petitioners demanded this courtesy; he had his way.[45]

Still the Senate waited. Senators had many things to discuss that January. There were questions concerning government of Puerto Rico and the Philippines. Some senators spent hours pointing out Britain's failures in South Africa. How could one find time to debate the harmless arbitration convention? Edward Everett Hale, despite all assurance, became nervous. He, too, was observing the Boer War. Could not the treaty if ratified halt that conflict? He suggested as much to Hay, and the secretary of state informed him that the convention could not apply to Britain's dispute with rebellious subject states. Further, the secretary said the United States was bound by its representatives' declaration of July 25 not to interfere in European quarrels.[46] Hale accepted Hay's explanation, for a few days later he complained to Ambassador White about delay in ratification, saying, "You see people

[45] *Congressional Record*, XXXIII, pt. 1 (1900), p. 734.

[46] Hay to Hale, Jan. 13, 1900, Hay Papers. McKinley apparently did not fully share Hay's views. In March 1900 the Boers sent an official request for good offices and mediation to Washington. Although he had not yet proclaimed American ratification of the arbitration convention, McKinley directed Hay to send the South African message, together with a formal American offer of mediation to London. Lord Salisbury promptly declined the American offer. For a discussion of this incident, see Tyler Dennett, *John Hay: From Poetry to Politics* (New York, 1933), pp. 242–243.

will mix it all up with the Philippines and the Boers, with which it really has nothing to do." [47]

At last action came on February 5, when the Foreign Relations Committee decided that it had considered the matter long enough. Late that afternoon Senator Davis moved that the Senate enter executive session. The motion carried; the doors were locked; the fate of the treaty rested in the hands of the Senate. Twenty-five minutes later the doors unlocked and the Senate adjourned.[48] Readers of the morning papers next day learned that it had given President McKinley advice and consent for ratification of the arbitration convention and the declaration on throwing projectiles from balloons.

President McKinley on April 5, 1900, sent the other conventions to the Senate. That body proved no obstacle for the convention adapting the Geneva principles to maritime warfare, for that agreement won approval on May 4. But the Senate seemed to forget the convention on the laws and customs of war on land, delaying ratification until March 1902.[49]

The Senate's slowness to act on the convention on the laws and customs of land warfare did not detract from its action on the other conventions and the declaration. Consenting to the convention extending the Geneva principles to the sea and to the prohibition on throwing projectiles from balloons, the Senate had reaffirmed American interest in lessening the cruelty of war. Approving the arbitration convention it had made possible American participation in the Permanent Court of Arbitration. It seemed in 1900 that the Senate had removed from itself the stigma of defeat of the Olney-Pauncefote treaty.

[47] Hale to White, Jan. 16, 1900, copy in Holls Papers.

[48] *Congressional Record*, XXXIII, pt. 2 (1900), p. 1502.

[49] Department of State, *List of Treaties Submitted to the Senate, 1789–1934* (Washington, 1935), p. 34; William M. Malloy, ed., *Treaties, Conventions, International Acts, Protocols, and Agreements between the United States of America and Other Powers, 1776–1909* (Washington, 1910), II, 2035, 2042.

XV

The First American Judges

McKINLEY announced ratification of the arbitration convention on April 7, 1900, and American membership in the Hague
court became official. Thereupon arose the matter of appointing
American members to the new tribunal.

Frederick Holls became almost as interested in securing proper
appointments to the court as he had been in original appointments
to the conference. It is quite possible that he had hopes of becoming one of the American judges, though he did not reveal any
such ambitions. He advocated appointment of the nation's two
former presidents, Benjamin Harrison and Grover Cleveland,
along with former Secretary of State Richard Olney and Ambassador Andrew White. Once again the energetic New Yorker
made visits to Washington, where he attempted to impose his
will at the White House. He watched the days slip by, for according to the first Hague convention a nation was to make its
appointment within three months after ratification. Yet even
conferences with McKinley could not rush that deliberate executive. Holls requested White to press the matter upon the president, and implored the ambassador "as a friend, as a Republican,
and as a patriot not to decline," should the president confer an
appointment upon him.[1] So slow was the president in making up

[1] Holls to White, Aug. 31, 1900, Holls Papers.

his mind that David Jayne Hill concluded that appointments would be postponed until after the November elections, although the Republican platform adopted in June had come out strongly in favor of what had been done at The Hague.[2]

The president at length decided not to defer longer, and Holls learned in late August 1900 that Harrison and Cleveland had been appointed. He flattered himself that McKinley had followed his recommendation and that soon Olney and White also would receive appointments.[3]

Whether McKinley had been influenced by Holls's recommendations in offering the Hague posts to his two predecessors cannot be determined. More likely he wished to give all possible dignity to the new court. Former President Harrison in his closing speech as counsel for Venezuela before the Paris arbitration tribunal of 1899 had told that court's president, Feodor de Martens, that there had been nothing in the proceedings at The Hague which had attracted his approval so much as the Permanent Court of Arbitration. "It seems to me," he then declared, "that if this process of settling international differences is to commend itself to the nations, it can only hope to set up for the trial of such questions an absolutely impartial judicial tribunal." [4] Although Harrison in these words had approved the work at The Hague, his private opinion differed widely. Frequently the Paris tribunal had to suspend hearings for days while Martens was at The Hague lending prestige to the conference called at the invitation of the czar. Paris had been unmercifully hot that summer; not even the prospect of receiving a $100,000 fee from Venezuela made Harrison's sojourn pleasant. These experiences may have influenced his privately unfavorable opinion of The Hague. Harrison also had the unpleasant experience of being

[2] Hill to Holls, Oct. 6, 1900, Holls Papers. For the Republican platform's plank on the conference, see Kirk H. Porter and Donald Bruce Johnson, *National Party Platforms, 1840–1956* (Urbana, Ill., 1956), p. 124.

[3] Holls to White, Aug. 31, 1900, Holls Papers.

[4] Quoted in Edward Everett Hale, "The Hague Peace Conference," *The Forum,* XXXI (1901), 207.

defeated in the Venezuela boundary case, and he attributed the unsatisfactory rulings of the court to partisanship of British judges. He became cool to requests that he support the arbitration movement. Still, Harrison accepted his new honor. When a friend observed that he would have little to do in the new post, the former president replied, "As to the International Court—the place I have accepted is not made less, but rather more attractive by your suggestive fact that I may have nothing to do." [5] (Harrison did not have much to do; he died on March 13, 1901.)

Former President Cleveland's reaction to his appointment was negative, although not similarly tinged by cynicism. Cleveland told the president that his "disinclination to assume any duty of a public nature was so great" that he wished permission to decline. McKinley again wrote his predecessor, urging him to accept and informing him that Harrison had already accepted. Oscar Straus wrote Cleveland. Again the former president declined. Privately he explained to a friend:

I think the conclusions arrived at by the Hague Conference were lame and disappointing ones. I did not care to be one of a few men, the majority of whom would probably be quite under the lead of Mr. Harrison; and in my particular relation to the organization of my party, I thought it better not to hold a place under the appointment of the present administration. [6]

Cleveland did not, of course, make public his opinions. It was announced that failing health was the reason for his refusal. [7]

McKinley then offered an appointment to Judge George Gray of Delaware, former senator. Gray had served on the commission to negotiate peace with Spain; in that capacity he had favored arbitrating certain Spanish-American disputes. [8] Naturally Gray was glad to accept appointment to a court of arbitration.

Announcement of the other two appointments had not been

[5] Harrison to Miller, Sept. 6, 1900, Harrison Papers.
[6] Cleveland to Wilson S. Bissel, Sept. 16, 1900, in Allan Nevins, ed., *Letters of Grover Cleveland, 1850–1908* (New York, 1933), pp. 536–537.
[7] Holls to White, Aug. 31, 1900, Holls Papers.   [8] See above, p. 49.

made by election day, November 12. Holls's hope for seats on the court for Olney and White was not realized. In his message for 1900 the president announced that the other two American members of the court would be Chief Justice Melville W. Fuller and John W. Griggs of New Jersey, attorney general of the United States.[9]

If Holls expected for himself a court appointment from McKinley, he was disappointed, but then good fortune appeared from an unexpected quarter. Halfway around the world the problem of appointing judges was also a problem for another chief of state. In the dominions of His Majesty, King Chulalongkorn of Siam, there were few experts on international law. Yet Siam had an obligation to appoint experts in that field to the new court being established in a distant little country on the shores of the North Sea. Would it not be wise to select distinguished foreigners trained in international law? The Siamese delegates at the conference recalled certain prominent personalities. Holls became a judge of the international court by authority of the sovereign of the land of the Sacred White Elephant.[10]

Gratified by this recognition from a potentate of the East, Holls discussed the new court with everyone. Peace and arbitration advocates were pleased by their champion's new status, and Holls sought to make his dignity felt by securing due recognition for the court. To Martens he wrote that one of his appointment's "most flattering and agreeable features . . . is the fact that I am again permitted to think of you as a colleague." [11] But he had no intention of waiting for a call to duty at The Hague before again going to Europe. In the spring of 1901 he crossed over, determined to call upon Europe's three emperors to focus their attention upon the promises of The Hague. William II and Francis Joseph granted him interviews and received him with outwardly

[9] Richardson, *Messages and Papers*, IX, 6432.

[10] Andrew D. White, address, in *In Memoriam, Frederick William Holls*, p. 25.

[11] May 11, 1901, Holls Papers.

sympathetic interest. It was in Russia, however, that he scored his triumph. After debating the kind of dress he was to wear at court with the American ambassador in St. Petersburg, Charlemagne Tower, he at length received an interview from Nicholas II. The czar was gracious and told Holls that he knew him through his book and that Czarina Alexandra Feodorovna had read every page of that remarkable publication. The empress had been anxious to meet Holls, but Her Majesty was not well, and their little daughter, the Czarevna Olga, was very sick. Pleasantly the two chatted about Theodore Roosevelt, American politics, and The Hague. The czar appreciated Holls's efforts at bringing Germany into line.

St. Petersburg proved a satisfying experience for Holls. At the Russian court he also met Witte, Pobedonostsev, and Muraviev. And before he left St. Petersburg he gained another appointment to the Hague court—from Persia. In Teheran, Shah Muzaffar-ed-Din like Chulalongkorn of Siam had some difficulty discovering among his subjects persons qualified to sit at The Hague, but General Mirza Riza Khan, the Persian monarch's minister in St. Petersburg, who had been on all three commissions at The Hague, knew well the work of Holls at the conference. By the time of the American's visit in Russia the Persian government decided to offer Holls a Hague appointment. This offer was made during his stay in St. Petersburg. He gladly accepted.[12]

Returning to America, the New Yorker felt that his star, which had begun to rise in the Netherlands two years before, would reach new heights. The architect of so much of The Hague's accomplishment, representative of two Eastern potentates on the international court, confident of Europe's three emperors—surely his future in world affairs was great. David Jayne Hill was impressed enough to offer "humble hospitality" at his summer cottage to "an International Judge,—a colleague and a peer of ex-presidents, and the distinguished guest of His Imperial Ma-

[12] Holls to Edward M. Burghard and Holls to Kingman, both dated June 3, 1901, Holls Papers.

jesty." [13] Vice President Theodore Roosevelt appeared to place great confidence in him.

Thus ended—for Americans and Frederick Holls—the chore of appointing judges to the Hague court. By appointing influential persons to the Hague bench, McKinley had done much to promote the prestige of the Permanent Court of Arbitration. Having done so much for the court at the outset—and with Holls on the court as a Siamese and Persian representative—the United States could be expected to continue as a strong supporter of the tribunal. Appointing the first American judges was, however, all that McKinley could do, for he died at the hand of an assassin in September 1901.

As for Frederick Holls, the man who had so dedicated himself to establishment of a great tribunal of world peace, the end of the road of life soon loomed up and engulfed him as it had McKinley. Holls had long suffered from fragile health, and he died of a heart attack on July 23, 1903.[14]

[13] Hill to Holls, June 3, 1901, Holls Papers.
[14] New York *Times*, July 24, 1903.

XVI

Success or Failure?

BELIEF in progress has been characteristic of modern civilization, and it is wise to recall this belief in drawing conclusions about American participation in the First Hague Peace Conference. The conventions and declarations of the conference represented progress of a limited kind. The arbitration convention was a first step toward establishing permanent institutions for promoting international peace. Improving the laws of war offered hope that armies would refrain from excesses, while declarations against asphyxiating gas, expanding bullets, and throwing of projectiles from balloons showed that morality could outlaw some weapons.

Establishing the Permanent Court of Arbitration, the Peace Conference of 1899 made the first attempt to found a tribunal for the world. It is true that the court, despite its name, can hardly be considered a permanent judicial body, but on several occasions before the First World War and during the 1920's nations sent disputes to courts constituted from its list of jurists. The court provided a precedent for the Permanent Court of International Justice, founded by the League of Nations in 1920. The new World Court found chambers in the Court of Arbitration's Peace Palace at The Hague and from the older tribunal borrowed methods of procedure. And there was another close bond between the two courts: the World Court Statute provided that members of the Court of Arbitration, acting in their national groups, should nominate candidates for the bench of the Permanent Court of International Justice. When the United Nations in 1945 revised the Statute of the World Court and changed its official name to International Court of Justice, it retained this method of nominating its judges.

The Permanent Court of Arbitration has had a role in the twentieth century far less important than its earliest supporters envisioned. The international catastrophes of the century have long since destroyed the hopes of many individuals who believed that permanent international tribunals could prevent war. But during those fateful years after the Peace Conference of 1899—the years prior to the denouement in 1914—there were numerous occasions when peace and arbitration exponents could believe their ideas were making progress.

In the United States peace workers of that period often had special reasons for optimism. Presidents, secretaries of state, other high officials, proclaimed the Republic's desire to promote world peace. The United States sent some minor disputes to the Court of Arbitration and urged other nations to do likewise. American statesmen negotiated arbitration treaties—albeit subject to the same isolationist doctrines which inhibited the delegation in 1899. President Theodore Roosevelt was the real initiator of the Second Hague Peace Conference, which met in 1907 upon the czar's invitation. The United States tried to have limitation of armaments placed on the program of that conference, but the Russians, showing no interest in the idea which had motivated the conference of 1899, refused. The Americans did, however, win acceptance for their idea of a court of full-time judges holding regular sessions. Unfortunately the conference could not agree upon the composition of a reorganized court and decided to leave the matter for future implementation. After the Second Hague Peace Conference, American efforts for peace gained strength. Dedication in August of 1913 of the Hague Peace Palace, built with funds provided by an American citizen, Andrew Carnegie, seemed a good omen for a Third Hague Peace Conference, scheduled to meet in 1915. Few governments made greater preparation for the Peace Conference which was never to meet than did the government of the United States. It is good to recall these things—to remember that during an era when American foreign policy was often bellicose, imperialistic, and selfishly isolationist the Republic urged international agreements and institutions to prevent war.

The American tradition of supporting movements to maintain peace through judicial methods survived even the First World War and the Senate's defeat of the Versailles treaty. Presidents Warren G. Harding, Calvin Coolidge, Herbert Hoover, and Franklin D. Roosevelt urged ratification of the World Court Protocol, but their efforts were thwarted by senators deeply imbued with those same isolationist traditions which had hindered American actions in behalf of peace before the First World War and had led to the defeat of the Versailles treaty. Four distinguished Americans—John Bassett Moore, Charles Evans Hughes, Frank B. Kellogg, and Manley O. Hudson—did, however, serve in succession upon the World Court from 1922 to 1945, in this way stimulating interest in the court among many influential Americans.

Ratification of the United Nations Charter in 1945 was more than a reversal of the decision in regard to the League of Nations: it was a return to the policy of supporting movements for judicial settlement of international disputes. The Charter includes the World Court Statute, and the United States automatically became a member of the court. The Senate in a resolution of August 2, 1946, chose to go farther than the Statute required any nation to go by accepting the court's compulsory jurisdiction in international legal disputes. The Statute provided that nations could accept the court's compulsory jurisdiction in certain kinds of legal decisions. But the Senate limited its declaration with the famous Connally Amendment, which was in spirit like the recent American support of the veto principle in the United Nations—and like the Monroe Doctrine declaration at The Hague forty-seven years before. The amendment excluded from the court's jurisdiction "disputes with regard to matters which are essentially within the domestic jurisdiction of the United States of America as determined by the United States of America." [1]

While one can trace international judicial developments from the First Hague Peace Conference to the present International Court of Justice and believe that the conference of 1899 did mark the beginning of considerable progress, one must conclude that the conference was essentially a failure. The avowed purpose of the conference was to promote peace, yet it is doubtful if any of its conventions other than those on the laws of war have ever benefited many people. The declarations on weapons did nothing to check the armaments race. There is no evidence that the convention for the Peaceful Adjustment of International Disputes and subsequent arbitration agreements halted the larger processes of world politics that brought the first of the grand calamities of our time—the World War of 1914–1918.

It is obvious that the attitudes of the great powers determined the failure of the Peace Conference of 1899. No great power—and few secondary powers—really desired limitation of armaments. Cherishing national and imperial ambitions, fearful of their enemies, and distrustful of their friends, nations sent representatives to The Hague not to promote peace but to prevent success for the principal Russian proposals—proposals in which the Russians themselves had no faith. It is true that some statesmen did wish limitation of armaments and did want a strong international court, but they believed that only very limited objectives could be attained. And with limited attainment they contented themselves, hoping for greater achievements by future

[1] Department of State, *Treaties and Other International Acts, Series 1598* (Washington, 1947), p. 1.

statesmen. Bitter international rivalries and hatreds proved stumbling blocks to the First Hague Peace Conference, as they were to be for almost all international conferences of the twentieth century. Had the statesmen of 1899 been willing to discuss frankly the serious questions disturbing peace and had peace leaders given as much attention to quieting international tensions as they did to providing new methods for settling disputes, the agreements of The Hague might indeed have checked those forces driving mankind toward disaster. The wonder is that, not daring to discuss serious international problems and made up of representatives of suspicious and fearful governments, the First Hague Peace Conference produced even a few innocuous documents which gave appearance of progress.

It is a pity that things went this way. If statesmen in 1899 had foreseen the rapid development of military technology, the consequences of world war, they might have sought solutions to larger problems of world politics, especially limitation of armaments, and founded a permanent court of genuine strength.

One can sadly conclude that the First Hague Peace Conference achieved little in the way of progress for humanity. The conference was backward-looking. Dreams of empire prevailed over international law and a permanent court, and the conventions and declarations at The Hague in 1899 and later agreements based upon those documents were paper achievements—masks concealing failure.

Bibliographical Note

THE published works and documentary sources available for study of the First Hague Peace Conference and other topics in the diplomatic history of the 1890's and early twentieth century are so vast that I make no attempt to include all of them in this bibliographical note; I confine my attention to those sources which are cited in this essay or have been especially valuable as background reading. My sources, while scattered and often of a particular nature, have proved extremely enlightening—especially the manuscript collections of archival and personal records which I have sought to analyze.

1. Bibliographical Aids

The best guide for American diplomacy in the 1890's and the early twentieth century is Samuel Flagg Bemis and Grace Gardner Griffin, *Guide to the Diplomatic History of the United States, 1775–1921* (Washington, 1935). Oscar Handlin *et al.*, *Harvard Guide to American History* (Cambridge, Mass., 1954), is useful. The chapter bibliographies in William L. Langer, *The Diplomacy of Imperialism, 1890–1902* (2 vols., New York, 1935; 1-vol. ed., New York, 1951), are of particular value.

2. General Studies

William L. Langer, *The Diplomacy of Imperialism*, is the best general history of international relations in the 1890's, but largely ignores American diplomacy. G. Lowes Dickinson, *The Interna-*

tional Anarchy, 1904–1914 (New York, 1926), despite the limits of
its title, also contains a good summary of international relations
from 1870 to 1900. Luigi Albertini, *The Origins of the War of 1914,*
trans. and ed. by Isabella M. Massey (3 vols.; London, 1952), is of
especial value for the Hague Conference of 1899. E. J. Dillon, *The
Eclipse of Russia* (New York, 1918), is a work by a roving British
journalist well acquainted with high czarist officials. The book is
important for the origins of the peace rescript.

Charles S. Campbell, Jr., *Anglo-American Understanding, 1898–
1903* (Baltimore, 1957), is an excellent study of American relations
with Britain at the turn of the century. Julius W. Pratt, *Expansion-
ists of 1898: The Acquisition of Hawaii and the Spanish Islands*
(Baltimore, 1936), contains one of the best studies of American
imperialism. French Ensor Chadwick, *The Relations of the United
States and Spain: The Spanish-American War* (2 vols.; New York,
1911), has a classic military account which does not neglect diplomacy. Dexter Perkins, *The Monroe Doctrine, 1867–1907* (Baltimore, 1937), is the authoritative work on the doctrine for the
period. Henry M. Wriston, *Executive Agents in American Foreign
Relations* (Baltimore, 1929), concerns an important aspect of Amer-
ican diplomacy. W. Stull Holt, *Treaties Defeated by the Senate: A
Study of the Struggle between President and Senate over the Con-
duct of Foreign Relations* (Baltimore, 1933), is an able discussion.
The best account of its special topic is Nelson M. Blake, "The
Olney-Pauncefote Treaty of 1897," *American Historical Review,*
L (1945), based on research in the Richard Olney and Grover
Cleveland papers. Clifton J. Child, "The Venezuela-British Guiana
Boundary Arbitration of 1899," *American Journal of International
Law,* XLIV (1950), deals with controversial aspects of that arbitra-
tion.

Jackson H. Ralston, *International Arbitration from Athens to
Locarno* (Palo Alto, Calif., 1929), is a general history of arbitration, devoting most attention to arbitration in modern times. A
good short history of arbitration appears in John Bassett Moore,
"International Arbitration: Historical Notes and Projects," in *The
Collected Papers of John Bassett Moore* (7 vols.; New Haven,
1944), II, reprinted from *The American Conference on International Arbitration, Held in Washington, D.C., April 22 and 23, 1896*

(New York, 1896). Moore's *History and Digest of the International Arbitrations to Which the United States Has Been a Party* (6 vols.; Washington, 1898), is a ponderous study, much of which is a collection of documents. One may find an able study of a complex subject in Helen May Cory, *Compulsory Arbitration of International Disputes* (New York, 1932).

A. C. F. Beales, *The History of Peace: A Short Account of the Organized Movements for International Peace* (London, 1931), makes an attempt to write a general history of modern peace movements in Europe and America. Merle Curti, *Peace or War: The American Struggle 1636–1936* (New York, 1936), is a good survey of the long history of American organizations to promote peace. Devere Allen, *The Fight for Peace* (New York, 1930), is based on considerable research but is a long peace tract rather than serious history. A careful, scholarly treatment of the pre–Civil War peace movement may be found in Merle Curti, *The American Peace Crusade, 1815–1860* (Durham, N.C., 1929). Christina Phelps, *The Anglo-American Peace Movement in the Mid-nineteenth Century* (New York, 1930), covers much the same ground. Edson L. Whitney, *The American Peace Society: A Centennial History* (Washington, 1928), deals with that society, based largely on its journal, *The Advocate of Peace*. Hayne Davis, ed., *Among the World's Peacemakers: An Epitome of the Interparliamentary Union* (New York, 1907), contains articles on the peace movement and sketches of its leaders, most of which are reprints of articles from *The Independent*.

The following are helpful books on military history: C. Joseph Bernardo and Eugene H. Bacon, *American Military Policy: Its Development since 1775* (Harrisburg, Pa., 1955); George T. Davis, *A Navy Second to None: The Development of Modern American Naval Policy* (New York, 1940); and Harold and Margaret Sprout, *The Rise of American Naval Power, 1776–1918* (Princeton, 1939). Archibald Black, *The Story of Flying* (New York, 1940), and Charles H. Gibbs-Smith, *The Aeroplane: An Historical Survey of Its Origins and Development* (London, 1960), tell of military interest in the first experiments with heavier-than-air flying craft.

The best general survey of American disarmament policy to the close of the 1940's is in Merze Tate, *The United States and*

Armaments (Cambridge, Mass., 1948). In *The Disarmament Illusion: The Movement for a Limitation of Armaments to 1907* (New York, 1942) Miss Tate examines in greater detail disarmament in the late nineteenth and early twentieth centuries. Based largely on published sources, this book is an important study.

3. *Special Works on the Hague Conferences*

Frederick W. Holls in *The Peace Conference at The Hague and Its Bearings on International Law and Policy* (New York, 1900) presented a eulogistic account of the conference while drawing but little on his personal experiences. The first volume of James Brown Scott, *The Hague Peace Conferences of 1899 and 1907* (2 vols.; Baltimore, 1909), has a general account by an American technical delegate to the conference of 1907. Like Holls, Scott revealed little about his personal experiences. Joseph H. Choate, *The Two Hague Conferences* (Princeton, 1913), is a series of lectures by the head of the American delegation to the second conference. The lectures are of little value. W. T. Stead, *The United States of Europe on the Eve of the Parliament of Peace* (London, 1899), was the *Review of Reviews* annual for 1899. In this book Stead advanced hopes as extravagant as its title. W. T. Stead, *La Chronique de la Conference de la Haye* (The Hague, 1901), is an account of some merit but contains nothing not found in Stead's dispatches to the Manchester *Guardian*. William I. Hull, *The Two Hague Conferences and Their Contributions to International Law* (Boston, 1908), and A. Pearce Higgins, *The Hague Peace Conferences and Other International Conferences concerning the Laws and Usages of War* (Cambridge, Eng., 1909), were among the first scholarly studies of the Peace Conferences. Walther Schücking, *The International Union of the Hague Conferences* (Oxford, 1918), and Hans Wehberg, *The Problem of an International Court of Justice* (Oxford, 1918), were first published in Munich and Leipzig, Germany, in 1912 as the first and second volumes, respectively, of a series called *Das Werk vom Haag* ("The Work of The Hague"). Translated into English by Charles G. Fenwick and published by the Carnegie Endowment for International Peace, they had an especial appeal to some American students of international law during the First World

War. Schücking convincingly maintained that the Hague Conferences had created an organization of the nations, while Wehberg urged transformation of the Permanent Court of Arbitration into a court with permanent judges holding regular sessions.

Thomas K. Ford, "The Genesis of the First Hague Peace Conference," *Political Science Quarterly*, LI (1936), is based in part on documents published in 1932 in a Soviet historical journal, *Krasnyi Arkhiv*. Margaret Robinson, *Arbitration and the Hague Peace Conferences, 1899 and 1907*, is a doctoral dissertation finished and published in 1936 at the University of Pennsylvania. Based on published documents, it is a helpful work for study of the Hague conferences.

4. Autobiographies, Diaries, and Biographies

The second volume of the *Autobiography of Andrew Dickson White* (2 vols.; New York, 1907) contains excerpts from the extended diary White kept at The Hague. The diary excerpts were separately published as *The First Hague Conference* (Boston, 1912). Robert Morris Ogden, ed., *The Diaries of Andrew D. White* (Ithaca, 1959), contains a few excerpts from the "short diary" which White also maintained at the conference. They reveal nothing of consequence. *Memoirs of Bertha von Suttner: The Records of an Eventful Life* (authorized trans., 2 vols.; Boston, 1910) is a valuable source for European peace movements. In the second volume the baroness included excerpts from the diary she kept at The Hague. *The Memoirs of Count Witte*, trans. and ed. by Abraham Yarmolinsky (Garden City, N.Y., 1921) explains the origins of the peace rescript.

W. D. Puleston, *Mahan: The Life and Work of Captain Alfred Thayer Mahan, U.S.N.* (New Haven, 1939), is the best biography of the philosopher of sea power, although it leaves much to be desired. Puleston's account of Mahan at the peace conference is unsatisfactory. Frederic Whyte, *The Life of W. T. Stead* (2 vols.; London, 1925), contains much interesting material concerning Stead's activities as a promoter of arbitration and the czar's rescript. Into the second volume Whyte incorporated letters Stead wrote Nicholas II during the conference. Royal Cortissoz, *The Life of Whitelaw Reid* (2 vols.; New York, 1921), helps in connec-

tion with the conference. Wemyss Reid, *Memoirs and Correspondence of Lyon Playfair, First Lord Playfair of St. Andrews* (London, 1899), is the biography of a leading exponent of arbitration.
Allan Nevins, *Grover Cleveland: A Study in Courage* (New
York, 1932), discusses Cleveland's role in the Venezuela controversy and negotiation of the Olney-Pauncefote treaty. Useful for
the British side of those diplomatic problems is A. L. Kennedy,
Salisbury, 1830–1903 (London, 1953).

Biographies of several secretaries of state were helpful in preparation of the present study: Charles Callon Tansill, *The Foreign
Policy of Thomas F. Bayard, 1885–1897* (New York, 1940), is
valuable for Bayard's service as secretary of state and later as the
first American ambassador to Great Britain; Matilda Gresham described her husband's efforts in negotiating an Anglo-American
arbitration treaty in *Life of Walter Quintin Gresham, 1832–1895*
(2 vols.; Chicago, 1919). Tyler Dennett, *John Hay: From Poetry
to Politics* (New York, 1933), is an outstanding biography, useful for most American diplomatic affairs at the turn of the century,
but of little help for the First Hague Peace Conference.

5. Pamphlets and Miscellaneous Material

David Dudley Field, Andrew Carnegie, Dorman B. Eaton, Morris K. Jesup, and Abram S. Hewitt, *Memorial to Congress, 1888,*
called on Congress to initiate arbitration agreements. A copy of
this pamphlet is in the Swarthmore Peace Collection. Cushman K.
Davis, *Lectures on International Law before the Faculty and Students of the University of Minnesota, October, 1897* (St. Paul,
1897), contains many of Senator Davis' ideas about American foreign policy. W. T. Stead in *Always Arbitrate before You Fight:
An Appeal to All English-speaking Folk* (London, 1896) urged
conclusion of an Anglo-American arbitration agreement. James L.
Tryon, *The Interparliamentary Union and Its Work* (Boston,
1910), gives a brief history of that organization.

In Memoriam: Frederick William Holls (privately printed, 1904)
contains addresses delivered at a memorial service for Holls at his
alma mater, Columbia University. The most informative—and the
longest—of these addresses is by Andrew D. White.

Francis William Fox, *Some Historical Incidents in Connexion with Establishment of the International Tribunal of Arbitration at The Hague in 1899 and International Arbitration* (London, 1901), is a pamphlet, a copy of which is in the Swarthmore Peace Collection; it is no more than its title implies.

6. Newspapers and Periodicals

The Manchester *Guardian* contains voluminous reports from the peace conference, largely supplied by W. T. Stead. Less extensive but frequently as useful are reports in the New York *Times*. The London *Times* is less helpful for the conference.

The *Literary Digest*, *The Nation*, and the *Review of Reviews* (English) contain important comments on the peace and arbitration movements and the conference.

Of first importance for pacifist thought and activity was the *Advocate of Peace*, official organ of the American Peace Society. Almost as valuable was the Universal Peace Union's journal, *The Peacemaker*. The only complete file of this periodical is in the Swarthmore Peace Collection. Of interest is the *Peace Crusade*, published in Boston during the conference by Edward Everett Hale. So far as one can determine, the only existing copies of the *Crusade* are in the New York Library.

Periodical articles were prime sources for this study. Belva Lockwood explained pacifist objectives in "The Growth of Peace Principles; and the Methods of Propagating Them," *American Magazine of Civics*, VI (May, 1895). Whitelaw Reid told of the bearing of American ideas about arbitration on the Paris peace negotiations of 1898 in "Some Consequences of the Last Treaty of Paris: Advances in International Law and Changes in National Policy," *Anglo-Saxon Review*, I (1899). Frederick W. Holls reflected much of the political thought of his time in "The 'German Vote' and the Republican Party," *The Forum*, XX (1896). Edward Everett Hale in "Out of the Mouth of Czars," *New England Magazine*, N.S., XIX (1899), hailed the czar's peace rescript ecstatically. After the conference Hale was convinced that his hopes had been realized and told of his happiness in "The Hague Peace Conference," *The Forum*, XXXI (1901). Benjamin F. Trueblood described his experiences at the conference in "The International Peace Conference at The Hague," *New England Magazine*, N.S., XX (1899). "Our

Delegation to The Hague," an unsigned article in *American Monthly Review of Reviews*, XIX (1899), contains useful biographical information.

The *North American Review*'s volume CLXIX (1899) contains several articles about the conference. Alfred T. Mahan, "The Peace Conference and the Moral Aspect of War," and Seth Low, "The International Conference of Peace," give contrasting views of two members of the American delegation. The prominent Russian delegate, Feodor de Martens, praised the conference in "International Arbitration and the Peace Conference at the Hague." R. M. Johnston, "In the Clutch of the Harpy Powers," is a bitter attack.

Frederick W. Holls lauded the conference in "The Results of the Peace Conference in Their Relation to the Monroe Doctrine," *American Monthly Review of Reviews*, XX (1899), and "America at the Peace Conference," *The Independent*, LI (Dec. 28, 1899). T. E. Holland sharply criticized the conference in "Some Lessons of the Peace Conference," *Fortnightly Review*, N.S., LXVI (1899).

7. *Printed Sources*

James Brown Scott, ed., *The Proceedings of the Hague Peace Conferences: The Conference of 1899* (New York, 1920), translates the *procès-verbaux* of the conference. James Brown Scott, ed., *The Reports to the Hague Conferences of 1899 and 1907* (New York, 1907), contains reports from the subdivisions of the conferences and the conventions and other agreements concluded at The Hague. James Brown Scott, ed., *The Hague Conventions and Declarations of 1899 and 1907* (New York, 1915), gives authoritative translations. Much of this material also appears in the *Proceedings*. The second volume of James Brown Scott, *The Hague Peace Conferences of 1899 and 1907* (2 vols.; Baltimore, 1909), is a documentary collection which includes instructions to the American delegates and their reports. Scott also published a separate edition of the instructions and reports under the title, *Instructions to the American Delegates to the Hague Peace Conferences and Their Official Reports* (New York, 1916). Frederick W. Holls, *The Peace Conference at The Hague and Its Bearings on International Law and Policy* (New York, 1900), likewise contains American instructions and reports, together with texts of the conventions and declarations. William

M. Malloy, ed., *Treaties, Conventions, International Acts, Protocols, and Agreements between the United States of America and Other Powers, 1776–1909* (2 vols.; Washington, 1910), contains the Hague conventions and records presidential and senatorial action on them. A. van Daehne van Varick, ed., *Documents Relating to the Program of the First Hague Peace Conference Laid before the Conference by The Netherland Government* (Oxford, 1921) is a translation of that documentary collection, first published at The Hague in 1899.

Papers Relating to the Foreign Relations of the United States, 1898 (Washington, 1901) is of some value for diplomacy leading to the First Hague Peace Conference. Many important dispatches concerning the rescript and the conference are in the first volume of G. P. Gooch and Harold Temperley, eds., *British Documents on the Origins of the War, 1898–1914* (10 vols.; London, 1926–1933). The largest collection of published diplomatic papers pertaining to the conference is in the fifteenth volume of Johannes Lepsius, Albrecht Mendelssohn Bartholdy, and Friedrich Thimme, eds., *Die Grosse Politik der Europäischen Kabinette, 1871–1914* (40 vols.; Berlin, 1922–1927). Several of the more important documents from this collection can be found in translation in the third volume of E. T. S. Dugdale, ed. and trans., *German Diplomatic Documents, 1871–1914* (4 vols.; London, 1928–1931).

In *Senate Documents,* X (Washington, 1900), is Document No. 159, 56th Congress, First Session, which contains the Hague conventions and the declaration on balloons, together with recommendations for their ratification from Secretary Hay and President McKinley. A publication of the Department of State, *List of Treaties Submitted to the Senate, 1789–1934* (Washington, 1935), was useful for the formal State Department and presidential actions on the Hague conventions and declarations. Department of State, *Treaties and Other International Acts, Series 1598* (Washington, 1947), contains the declaration by which the United States accepted the compulsory jurisdiction of the International Court of Justice.

The *Congressional Record* contains a few references to arbitration treaties and to the First Hague Peace Conference. Many speeches in the *Parliamentary Debates* indicate that British legislators took such matters more seriously than did their American counterparts.

James D. Richardson, ed., *A Compilation of the Messages and Papers of the Presidents* (11 vols.; Washington, 1912), contains

official presidential statements concerning arbitration treaties and
the First Hague Peace Conference. Occasional references to these
subjects may also be found in Kirk H. Porter and Donald Bruce
Johnson, *National Party Platforms, 1840–1956* (Urbana, Ill., 1956).
James W. Gantenbein, ed., *The Evolution of Our Latin-American
Policy: A Documentary Record* (New York, 1950), contains a few
important items on arbitration in the Western Hemisphere.

The *American Conference on International Arbitration, Held in
Washington, D.C., April 22 and 23, 1896* (New York, 1896) contains
proceedings of a conference called to promote an Anglo-American
arbitration treaty.

The *Reports of the Annual Meetings of the Lake Mohonk Conferences on International Arbitration* (Lake Mohonk, 1895–1916)
are important for the views and activities of peace spokesmen.

Several published collections of personal papers were helpful.
Allan Nevins, ed., *Letters of Grover Cleveland, 1850–1908* (New
York, 1933), contains a letter pertaining to appointments to the
Permanent Court of Arbitration. Edward J. Bing, ed., *The Secret
Letters of the Last Tsar: Being the Confidential Correspondence
between Nicholas II and His Mother, Dowager Empress Maria
Feodorovna* (New York, 1938), includes letters bearing on the peace
rescript. Elting E. Morison, John M. Blum, and John J. Buckley,
eds., *The Letters of Theodore Roosevelt* (8 vols.; Cambridge, Mass.,
1951–1954), contains only one letter by Theodore Roosevelt on
the conference of 1899.

8. Manuscript Sources

A. NATIONAL ARCHIVES

The Minutes of the American Commission, preserved in the
State Department files, are a disappointing source. The secretary,
Frederick W. Holls, dutifully recorded decisions by formal meetings of the delegation, but he included little about the discussions
through which those decisions were reached. Stanford Newel's Despatch Book of 1898–1899, also in the State Department files, provides
some information about arrangements for the conference but nothing about the conference itself. In the files of the Adjutant General's

office are a few communications from Captain Crozier to the adjutant general, H. C. Corbin.

B. SWARTHMORE PEACE COLLECTION

The Swarthmore Peace Collection at Swarthmore College is a large collection of literature and documents. The American Peace Society Papers, one of the most important parts of the collection, proved valuable for the movement for arbitration treaties but were of little help in connection with the peace conference. Alfred Love's unpublished Journal was occasionally of value.

C. PERSONAL PAPERS

Samuel A'Court Ashe Papers, Duke University Library, preserve a long letter about the conference which Alfred Thayer Mahan wrote Ashe a few weeks after leaving The Hague.

Joseph H. Choate Papers, Library of Congress, contain many documents from Choate's service as ambassador to Great Britain and as chairman of the American delegation at the Second Hague Peace Conference. Several letters in this collection have bearing upon the first conference.

Benjamin Harrison Papers, Library of Congress, are a valuable source for students of late-nineteenth-century arbitrations.

John Hay Papers, Library of Congress, are an important collection for diplomatic history at the turn of the century but disappointing in connection with the conference.

David Jayne Hill Papers, University of Rochester Library, contain several of Frederick Holls's most important letters from The Hague.

Frederick W. Holls Papers, Butler Library, Columbia University, contain the largest group of letters concerning the conference.

Seth Low Papers, Low Library, Columbia University, are disappointing in connection with the conference, but contain a number of letters concerned with ratification of the arbitration convention of 1899.

William McKinley Papers, Library of Congress, are a large collection containing a number of letters pertaining to the First Hague Peace Conference but nothing written by the president about the conference.

Alfred Thayer Mahan Papers, Library of Congress, include letters which Mahan wrote before and after the conference. They are a valuable source.

Horace Porter Papers, Library of Congress, in great part consist of documents and photographs concerning removal of the body of John Paul Jones from Paris to Annapolis. But here and there among these macabre records are letters about the conference and other diplomatic subjects. General Porter was ambassador to France under Presidents McKinley and Roosevelt.

Whitelaw Reid Papers, Library of Congress, frequently reveal interesting aspects of American policy at the conference, for Reid kept a cynical eye on the proceedings at The Hague.

Theodore Roosevelt Papers, Library of Congress, contain several letters pertaining to the conference, only one of which has been published.

Andrew Dickson White Papers, Cornell University Library, are a large collection, containing White's correspondence concerning the conference and his efforts to promote the Permanent Court of Arbitration.

Henry White Papers, Library of Congress, contain only a few references to the conference, but they are of value. The famous career diplomat was first secretary at the American embassy in London during the conference of 1899.

Index

*Recent books published for the American Historical Association
from the income of the Albert J. Beveridge Memorial Fund*

AN AGRICULTURAL HISTORY OF THE GENESEE VALLEY, 1790–1860.
By Neil A. McNall.

STEAM POWER ON THE AMERICAN FARM. *By Reynold M. Wik.*

HORACE GREELEY: NINETEENTH-CENTURY CRUSADER.
By Glyndon G. Van Deusen.

ERA OF THE OATH: NORTHERN LOYALTY TESTS DURING THE
CIVIL WAR AND RECONSTRUCTION. *By Harold M. Hyman.*

HISTORY OF MARSHALL FIELD & CO. *By Robert W. Twyman.*

ROBERT MORRIS: REVOLUTIONARY FINANCIER.
By Clarence L. Ver Steeg.

A HISTORY OF THE FREEDMEN'S BUREAU. *By George R. Bentley.*

THE FIRST RAPPROCHMENT: ENGLAND AND THE
UNITED STATES, 1795–1805. *By Bradford Perkins.*

MIDDLE-CLASS DEMOCRACY AND THE REVOLUTION IN MASSACHUSETTS,
1691–1780. *By Robert E. Brown.*

THE DEVELOPMENT OF AMERICAN PETROLEUM PIPELINES:
A STUDY IN PRIVATE ENTERPRISE AND PUBLIC POLICY, 1862–1906.
By Arthur Menzies Johnson.

COLONISTS FROM SCOTLAND: EMIGRATION TO NORTH AMERICA,
1707–1783. *By Ian Charles Cargill Graham.*

PROFESSORS & PUBLIC ETHICS: STUDIES OF NORTHERN MORAL
PHILOSOPHERS BEFORE THE CIVIL WAR. *By Wilson Smith.*

THE AXIS ALLIANCE AND JAPANESE-AMERICAN RELATIONS, 1941.
By Paul W. Schroeder.

A FRONTIER STATE AT WAR: KANSAS, 1861–1865.
By Albert Castel.

BRITISH INVESTMENTS AND THE AMERICAN MINING FRONTIER,
1860–1901. *By Clark C. Spence.*